Cities, Citadels, *and* Sights *of the* Near East

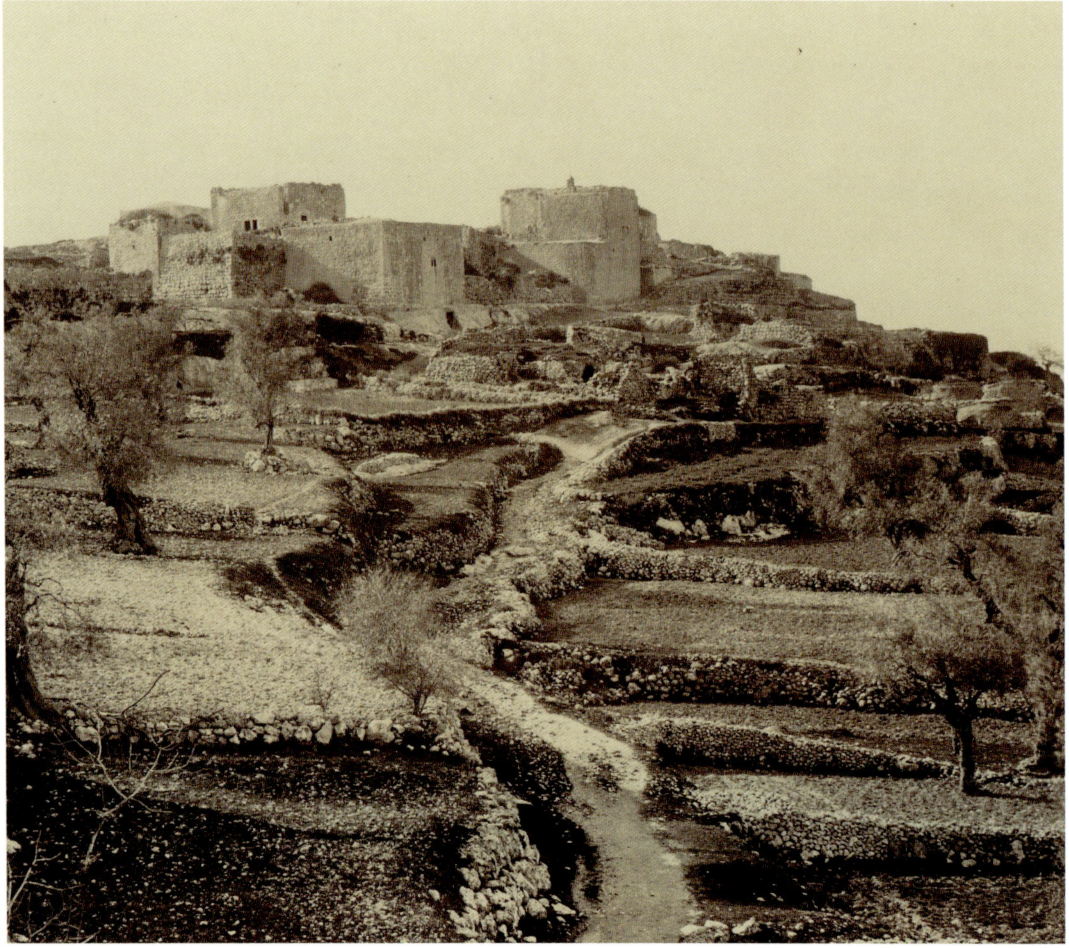

Cities, Citadels, *and* Sights *of the* Near East

Francis Bedford's Nineteenth-Century Photographs of Egypt, the Levant, and Constantinople

Text by Sophie Gordon
and Badr El Hage

The American University in Cairo Press
Cairo New York

Page ii: Gibeon, 31 March 1862

The American University in Cairo Press
113 Sharia Kasr el Aini, Cairo, Egypt
420 Fifth Avenue, New York, NY 10018
www.aucpress.com

Map by Stefan Chabluk

This edition published by arrangement with the Royal Collection Trust, York House, St James's Palace, London SW1A 1BQ

Exclusive distribution outside Egypt and North America by I.B.Tauris & Co Ltd., 6 Salem Road, London, W2 4BU

Dar el Kutub No. 2058/14
ISBN 978 977 416 670 9

Dar el Kutub Cataloging-in-Publication Data

Gordon, Sophie
Cities, Citadels, and Sights of the Near East: Francis Bedford's Nineteenth-Century Photographs of Egypt, the Levant, and Constantinople/ Sophie Gordon, and Badr El Hage.—Cairo: The American University in Cairo Press, 2014
p. cm.
ISBN: 978 977 416 670 9
1. Egypt—Description and travel
2. Photographs—Egypt
916.2

1 2 3 4 5 18 17 16 15 14

Designed by Fatiha Bouzidi
Printed in China

Contents

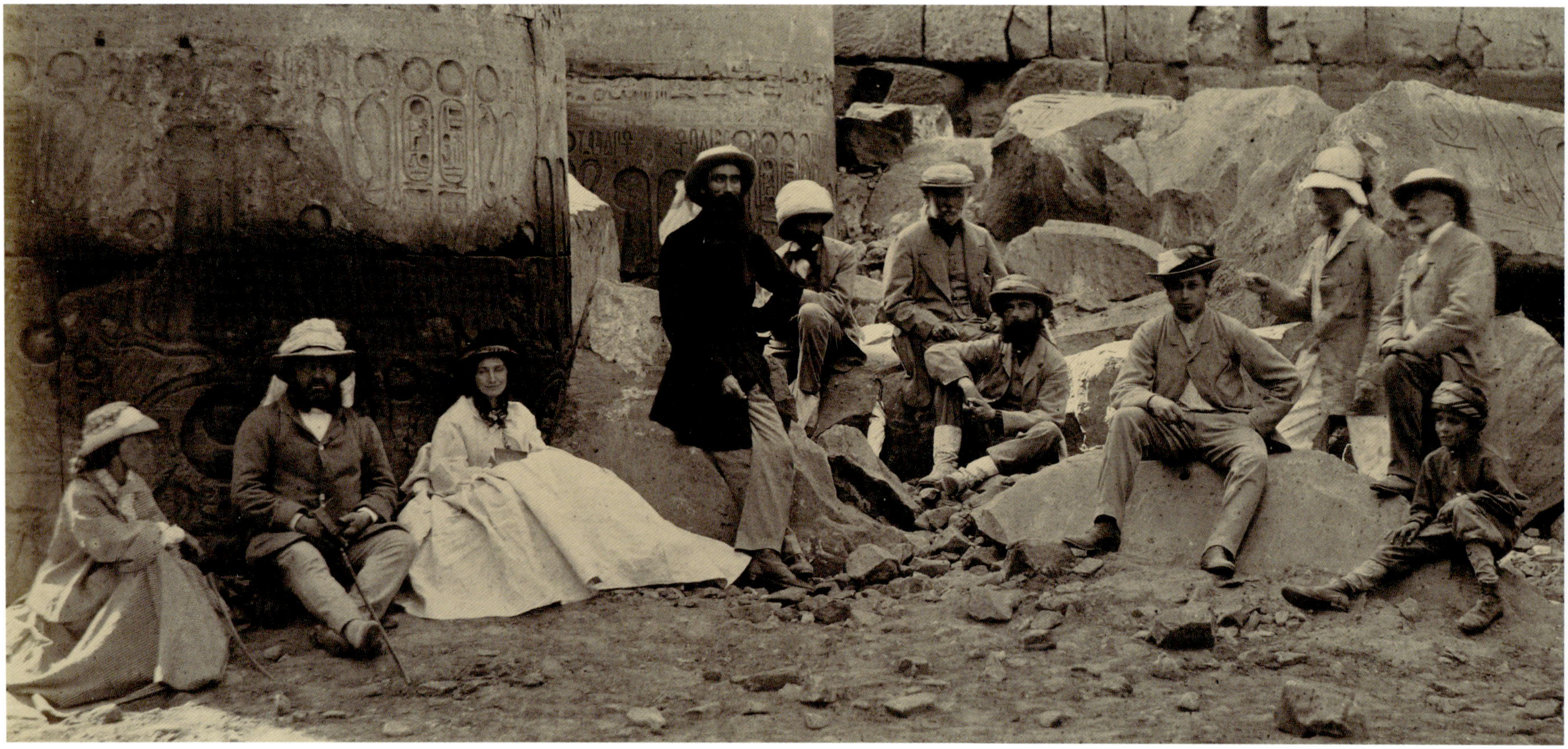

The Prince of Wales with his group in the Hypostyle Hall, Temple of Amun, Karnak, 16 March 1862

Francis Bedford: Photographer to the Prince of Wales

Sophie Gordon

Early in 1861, Queen Victoria and Prince Albert decided that their eldest son, Albert Edward, Prince of Wales (later King Edward VII), would benefit from an extended tour of Egypt and the Middle East. The prince (1841–1910) was the second of nine children born to Victoria and Albert; by 1861, his elder sister Victoria was already married and living in Prussia and the prince was finishing his education at Cambridge while his parents were busy seeking his future bride. Before the arrangements were finally made for his marriage (which took place in March 1863 to Princess Alexandra of Denmark), it was thought that a lengthy educational tour of the Middle East would provide the prince with the opportunity to learn about ancient cultures, history, and religions. The tour would also offer him the chance to meet many of the current rulers and diplomats in the region, an experience that was regarded as an essential part of his training as heir to the throne.

The Ottoman sultan Abdülaziz, based in Constantinople, nominally ruled the lands through which the prince would travel, but the reality was somewhat different, with a complex web of shifting alliances and power struggles existing across the region. The European countries of Britain, France, and Russia vied for influence and control while the Ottoman Empire appeared to be weakening and the viceroy of Egypt became increasingly independent. The recent Crimean War of 1854–55 had crystallized these alliances in British minds, while also resulting in greater public interest in the contemporary political situation in the Middle East. This interest was sustained by a series of photographs taken during the war by the British photographer Roger Fenton, which provided the British public for the first time with unmediated, first-hand evidence of the experience of the troops involved in the conflict. The photographs were exhibited in London in 1855–56, and the Prince of Wales visited the exhibition twice.[1]

Major General the Hon. Robert Bruce was to be the controlling figure for the Eastern Tour, and he was responsible for advising the queen and Prince Albert who should be asked to accompany the royal party in 1862. Opinions on the prospective tour were gathered from experts in the region: Lord Dufferin, who had been a commissioner representing Britain during negotiations in Syria in 1860, recommended the Hon. Robert Meade as an appropriate person to guide the prince in the region—Meade had assisted Dufferin in Syria.[2] Alongside Bruce and Meade would be Major Christopher Teesdale, the prince's equerry since 1858; Lt Col. Frederick Keppel, another equerry to the prince; and Dr. John Moolenburgh Minter, a Royal Navy doctor who had previously served on the Royal Yacht *Victoria and Albert*.

However, towards the end of 1861 Prince Albert fell ill and on 14 December of that year he died. The queen was devastated but was still determined to continue with the plans that her beloved husband had initiated. The tour was originally supposed to commence in late December, but Prince Albert's death meant that the start was postponed to early February the following year. In January 1862, General Bruce was at Osborne House with the queen to discuss who else to add to the party. Following an initial proposal made by Prince Albert, they chose the Revd. Dr. Arthur Stanley, Regius Professor of Ecclesiastical History at Oxford University.[3] Stanley had been in the Holy Land in 1852–53 and had published an account on his return.[4] He would meet the royal party at

Alexandria, act as a guide on the tour, and would also conduct a religious service every Sunday.

Also joining the royal party was the photographer Francis Bedford, then aged 46. His appointment had been first announced in the Court Circular on 5 February 1862: "Mr Francis Bedford has been appointed to accompany his Royal Highness the Prince of Wales in his tour through the East, for the purpose of taking photographic views of the landscapes, figures, and architecture of the various remarkable places that may be visited." This was subsequently followed by reports in the press and photographic journals.[5]

On 6 February, the Prince of Wales said goodbye to his mother, both of them still suffering from the loss of Prince Albert. The queen wrote in her journal, "Talking with Bertie, who seems nervous at the thought of leaving for this long journey. He came up later again, to take leave & was low & upset, poor Boy. So was I."[6] Nevertheless, the tour began that day with the prince and his small party joined by several assistants and servants. The entourage took an evening train from Waterloo to Dover, from where they crossed the English Channel to Calais and then proceeded by train to Mainz, the first leg of their journey toward Egypt.[7]

Photography and the Royal Family

Photography had been introduced to the public in 1839 and the British royal family took an early interest, following the lead of Prince Albert who, in February 1842, was the first member of the family to be photographed. However, relatively few acquisitions and commissions were made during the 1840s and it was Prince Albert's librarian, Dr. Ernst Becker, a keen photographer and a founder member of the Photographic Society, who was to be the bridge between the royal couple and the new photographic community. Through Becker, Queen Victoria and Prince Albert were introduced in the 1850s to the Photographic Society and to leading photographers. They began commissioning portraits of themselves and their family, and they also started to collect photographs from galleries and dealers, compiling albums and exploring the potential of the new medium.

Francis Bedford may have come to the attention of the queen for the first time in 1854 when she and Prince Albert visited the Photographic Society's exhibition on 3 January.[8] Bedford was responsible for nineteen exhibits; several of these were photographs of works of art that had been purchased from the Great Exhibition of 1851 for the Government School of Design and were then placed on view in the museum of the Department of Practical Art at Marlborough House. A number of other pieces had been placed on loan to the museum by Queen Victoria and were also photographed by Bedford. Subsequently the queen received a set of Bedford's photographs, entitled "Specimens from Marlborough House."[9]

The queen and Prince Albert continued to acquire photographs from exhibitions and through art dealers until the prince's death in 1861. They selected works by leading photographers including Roger Fenton, Oscar Rejlander, Gustave Le Gray, and Camille Silvy. Such enthusiastic royal patronage was undoubtedly a great boost to the rapidly growing photographic community and it was also to transform the career of Francis Bedford.

Francis Bedford's Early Life and Career

Francis Bedford was born on 13 August 1815 at his parents' home in Rochester Road, Camden, north London.[10] His father, Francis Octavius Bedford, was an architect, who exhibited architectural drawings at the Royal Academy from 1814 and designed a number of still extant structures, particularly churches in the Greek Revival style in London.[11]

In 1814, Francis Octavius married Sophia Curtis, from Camberwell, south London.[12] Their eldest child, Francis, was born in 1815, the first of six children.[13] Francis probably received some early professional training from his father and by the age of 18 he was exhibiting work at the Royal Academy where he was described as an "architect" in the list of exhibitors. His earliest contribution, from 1833, was an architectural work titled "New Church at Tunstall," a building designed by his father in Staffordshire.[14] He continued to contribute to the Royal Academy throughout the 1840s and at some point also spent some significant time in York drawing the city's churches and other historic buildings. This resulted in a number of early lithographic publications, including one which was based on Bedford's own drawings, *Sketches in York*, probably published in 1841.[15]

By 1843 Bedford was living at 40 Ely Place, in Holborn, London. On 1 November that year, he married Mary Graham, the daughter of William Graham, an upholsterer.[16] They were to have two sons: Arthur Francis, born in 1845, and William, born in 1846.[17] In the Register of Marriages, Bedford gave his profession as "lithographer artist." During the 1840s he continued to work as a lithographer, both copying the work of others and reproducing his own original work.

In the mid-1840s Bedford created at least three ingenious works intended to function as guides to church architecture. They appear to be small volumes, but when they are opened, the page folds out, like a map, into a single large sheet. Titled *A Chart of Anglican Church Architecture, A Chart Illustrating the Architecture of Westminster Abbey, and The Architecture of York Cathedral*, none is particularly finely produced, but they were works aimed at middle-class tourists, a new and expanding group that could travel more thanks to the growing network of railways and increased leisure time. *The Architecture of York Cathedral* sold at 5 shillings, which would be roughly equivalent to the cost of a guidebook today. As well as providing the illustrations, Bedford wrote the accompanying text, indicating that he was comfortable describing architectural features to a non-specialist audience. More significant, however, is the fact that the publication about Westminster Abbey was printed by the firm Day & Haghe (also known as Day & Son), "lithographers to the Queen."[18]

Bedford was to form a fruitful partnership with this company, which employed him as a lithographer from around 1850.[19] He produced lithographs for several significant publications illustrating works of art rather than architecture, which had been his main subject-matter up to that point. Bedford's early work for Day & Son included collaborations with Matthew Digby Wyatt; examples of Bedford's lithographs after drawings by Wyatt were exhibited by Day & Son at the Great Exhibition in 1851.[20] After the Crystal Palace was moved from Hyde Park to Sydenham, Bedford was responsible for producing lithographs from Philip Henry Delamotte's photographs of the building and new park.[21]

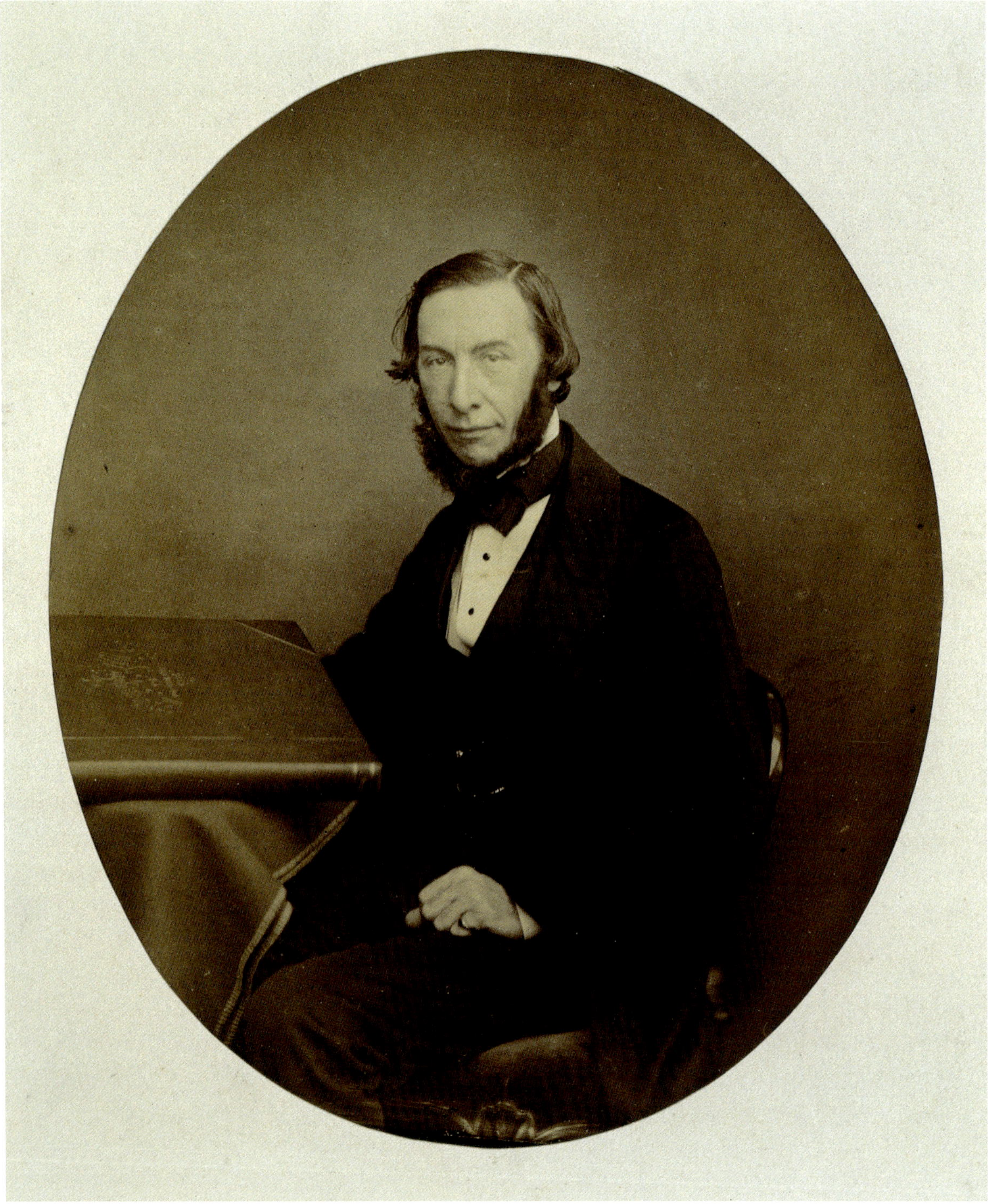

Francis Bedford, c.1856, unknown photographer, albumen print (The Wellcome Library, 24570.i)

This work for the Great Exhibition introduced Bedford to a circle of men including Henry Cole, Owen Jones, and Richard Redgrave, who wanted to improve the standard of British design through the education of artists and craftsmen. In 1853, Bedford visited Henry Cole, then general superintendent of the Department of Practical Art and as such in charge of the Government art schools and the museum at Marlborough House. Bedford met Cole with William Day, the printer by whom Bedford was employed, on 5 April 1853, and returned again on 2 May, this time alone.[22] The meetings were probably part of discussions about a publication to illustrate works in the museum. Records show that Bedford returned in August 1853 to take photographs in the museum.[23] The first publication from the Marlborough House museum following this photographic activity was *Examples of Ornament* (1855) by the printer and photographer Joseph Cundall, but Bedford contributed only lithographs after his own drawings. The photographs taken in 1853 were eventually reproduced as lithographs (also by Bedford) in *The Treasury of Ornamental Art* (*c.*1857) by John Charles Robinson.[24]

This publication, and the subsequent *Art Treasures of the United Kingdom* (1858), demonstrate the close links between Bedford's photography and lithography in the dissemination of art and design in the 1850s. Photography promised accuracy and truthfulness while lithography provided a reliable means of printing, as well as the introduction of a full color range in the image. Robinson (who was later to be appointed surveyor of the queen's pictures) wrote in *The Treasury of Ornamental Art*, "[T]he employment of Photography in aid of the greatly improved processes of Colour-printing, has been relied on for the production of transcripts of objects which, it is believed, will be found to be of hitherto unequalled accuracy."[25] These were probably the first professional photographs that Bedford took with the intention of using them as a guide for his lithographic work.[26] Bedford's contact with both Delamotte at the time of the Great Exhibition, and with Cundall through his work for the Marlborough House museum, makes it possible that either of these men could have introduced Bedford to photography.

Bedford was evidently highly adept at copying and reproducing images as chromolithographs. His work shows great attention to detail, accuracy, and evidence of patience. During the 1850s he contributed to several major illustrated publications, ensuring that, through his skilled lithographic work, the books received high praise. At the time of the Great Exhibition of 1851, Digby Wyatt wrote *Industrial Arts of the Nineteenth Century* with plates illustrating 160 objects from the exhibition considered by Wyatt to be the best examples of their type. Chromolithography was selected as the most appropriate process, and Bedford supplied 109 plates out of the 160, with some after his own drawings.[27] A few years later, *The Grammar of Ornament* (1856) was produced by Owen Jones, who had been involved in developing the curriculum at the school and museum at Marlborough House. Color played an important part in Jones's theories on architecture and design. In his previous publications, Jones had completed the printing himself because he regarded it as so central to his concerns. On this occasion, however, the task was entrusted to Bedford. The volume was to become one of the most influential books on design produced during the nineteenth century.[28]

Bedford's Early Photographic Work

Although Bedford had taken up photography by 1853, he still continued his professional work as an artist and lithographer. Initially, at least, his photography remained on an amateur level. In 1854, he exhibited photographs at the Photographic Society annual exhibition, not just the studies of works of art previously mentioned (which were subsequently acquired by the queen), but also landscapes and topographical scenes in Kent and copies of some of David Roberts's lithographs depicting scenes in the Holy Land and Egypt. Bedford continued to exhibit regularly at the annual Photographic Society exhibitions for most of his life, as well as at other venues, including the Art Treasures Exhibition in Manchester in 1857; the Photographic Society of Scotland exhibition in Edinburgh in 1858; the Architectural Photographic Association exhibitions in 1858 and 1861; and the international exhibitions held in London, Dublin, and Paris in 1862, 1865, and 1867 respectively.[29] He became vice-president of the Photographic Society in 1861 and also joined the Amateur Photographic Association that year.

Through his exhibition work and his considered contributions to the meetings of the Photographic Society, Bedford became a well-known and respected figure. He was also part of the smaller, more informal Photographic Society Club, which saw a group of friends from the Photographic Society gather together for meetings and outings, as well as contributing to an album of photographs that was then distributed to club members. Bedford supplied photographs for the album in both 1855 and 1857.

In 1857 Bedford exhibited photographs of Wales and Canterbury at the Art Treasures Exhibition in Manchester. This was an important occasion as photography had its own dedicated gallery, within an exhibition that was devoted solely to the fine arts. Bedford also made photographs of the installations and objects in the galleries, which he then reproduced as lithographs in *Art Treasures of the United Kingdom*.

The year 1857 saw Bedford receive an important photographic commission from Queen Victoria.[30] Bedford was asked to visit Coburg, in Germany, to photograph the places associated with Prince Albert's childhood. The queen intended to present the photographs as an album to the prince for his birthday on 26 August 1857.[31]

An album of sixty photographs was eventually produced, and presented to Prince Albert.[32] The results were evidently deemed to be successful because in June and July the following year Bedford was asked to return to Germany and photograph scenes in and around Gotha.

The photographs in both the Coburg and Gotha sets consist mainly of architectural views, interspersed with landscapes and picturesque topographical scenes. There are also a handful of portraits; the "peasants" in Coburg, for example, were photographed as a small group, having been asked to dress up in traditional costume. While Bedford was fulfilling a commission, he was also responding to the landscape he encountered, dealing with the short timeframe he had been granted, the uncertain weather, and lack of familiarity with his surroundings. The quality of the photographs is variable, but at best he managed to secure idyllic and peaceful picturesque landscapes. When Bedford exhibited a selection of the Gotha views in 1859 alongside a selection of his British landscapes, a critic began by commenting, "We feel that we cannot speak too highly of this artist's work; everything he does, he does well." He went on to state, however, "The new views which he has executed for Her Majesty we scarcely like so well as the first series. We do not now refer to the photographic manipulation, but to the views themselves; for this, however, Mr. Bedford is not responsible, inasmuch as the selection is not his, but that of Her Majesty."[33] The Coburg views, displayed at the Photographic Society exhibition in early 1858 and at the newly presented "photographic gallery" at the Crystal Palace in Sydenham, had been received more favorably: "A verdict has been so generally pronounced in their favour, and they have so well deserved all the encomiums which have been heaped upon them, that we can only say, Go, Mr. Bedford, and charm us again in the same manner."[34]

Bedford continued to play an active role in various photographic societies, and to make photographic expeditions to different parts of the country. By the early 1860s, Bedford was well on his way to becoming a full-time, professional photographer with a thriving commercial studio. His photographs were sold in several different formats: as full size, unmounted albumen prints, as stereo-views, and as cartes-de-visite (in fact, cropped stereoscopic views). These smaller formats were cheap to produce and print in large numbers; thus they were affordable by less affluent tourists who wanted a souvenir of the places they had visited or hoped to visit.

Initially Bedford began by issuing the stereo-views himself, but in around 1860 he passed the printing and distribution to the firm Catherall & Prichard, based in Chester. The firm published the views as distinct series, reissuing some of the earlier negatives from the 1850s, and creating general series titles such as "North Wales Illustrated" or "Chester Illustrated"; each individual view was given a number and a title on the front of the card.[35] Almost all the views were topographical scenes, often highly picturesque compositions conforming to the aesthetic paradigms established in the late eighteenth century by British writers and artists. Bedford also issued at least one sequence of studies titled "Welsh Costumes," significant for concentrating on people rather than landscape, depicting in this case people in national dress. He probably made over three thousand stereoscopic views between the late 1850s and *c.*1867, although most date to the period between 1857 and 1862. Catherall & Prichard continued to issue Bedford's work in a book format in the late 1860s–early 1870s with titles such as *Photographic Views of Torquay* (*c.*1865) or *Photographic Views of Chester* (*c.*1872).[36]

Other firms printed Bedford's photographs, too. Francis Frith's *Gems of Photographic Art* (1862) included works by Bedford; in the late 1860s Frith's printing company incorporated sections of Bedford's stock into the "Frith's Photo-Pictures" series. Companies such as Marion & Co., Cooke & Son, and A.W. Bennett similarly issued his prints, the latter as part of William and Mary Howitt's guides to the ruined castles of England and Wales. By the early 1860s, Bedford had managed to create a flourishing business by licensing or selling his work as widely as possible, appealing both to the knowledgeable collector through formal photographic exhibitions and to the general tourist through smaller-format, yet still highly collectable, prints sold through local firms.

The Eastern Tour, 1862

Bedford's position as an accomplished photographer who had successfully fulfilled two royal commissions made him the ideal choice to accompany the Prince of Wales in 1862. He occupied an unusual status within the royal entourage, however. It is evident from the financial records that there was a large group of assistants and servants accompanying the party at all times, but they are rarely named in the various sources.[37] Bedford was not named in the Court Circular on 6 February as part of the prince's "suite in attendance," but he is identified several times in the archival records connected with the tour. His name is first mentioned in the records of travel expenses: the luggage for the party "including Mr. Bedford's apparatus" was sent from Calais to Mainz at a cost of 5 francs 60.[38] Bedford would have had a considerable amount of equipment with him. Although he set out with Dr. Hill Norris's dry plates to use as his negative stock, Bedford found these were not successful so he had to revert to the wet collodion process.[39] This required the preparation of each plate immediately prior to use. Chemicals, plates, tripods, lenses, a portable darkroom, and, not least, the camera itself had to follow the party through the entire expedition. At various points in the future, Bedford would comment on his photographic practice in 1862, describing how he used a white sheet hung above him to keep cool, how the collodion cases could sit out in the sun all day on the Nile without spoiling, and how "excepting for distant views, he usually gave ten or twelve seconds for 10 x 12 plates."[40]

The records also indicate that Bedford had an assistant between Egypt and Constantinople. A payment of £58 5s was made to Mr. Lowndes for "assistance to Mr Bedford" on 26 May.[41] It is probable that he appears in several of Bedford's photographs, where there is an unidentified European man.

The tour itself, which is detailed in chapter two, lasted just over four months. The prince arrived back at Windsor on 14 June.

After he returned to Britain, Bedford evidently set about printing his negatives straight away. He does not appear to have shown the photographs to Queen Victoria himself, but on 19 July 1862 the queen wrote, "Bertie showed us some of the photographs taken on his tour."[42] No further comment was given. A few months afterward, Bedford was paid the sum of £394 9s from the Prince of Wales's account for "photographs on Eastern Tour."[43]

While in the Middle East, Bedford would have been well aware of the work of those artists and photographers who preceded him. The drawings of the artist David Roberts were published as lithographs in *The Holy Land, Syria, Idumea, Arabia, Egypt and Nubia* (1842–49). Roberts had arrived in Egypt in 1838 and spent several months traveling along the Nile, before heading into the Holy Land in 1839. Roberts sketched all of the important pharaonic sites in Egypt as well as those locations with biblical and classical associations in the Holy Land.[44]

Bedford, as a lithographer, would have known of these volumes at the time of their publication. He also later made photographic copies of some of the lithographs. It was perhaps Roberts's lithographs, more than any earlier works, that presented the Middle East to the British audience as a large but discrete geographical region linked by its classical and biblical associations, as well as by a contemporary vision that romanticized the people and the ruins through colorful and exaggerated imagery, while being precise in its architectural depiction. This poetic license was tempered somewhat by photographers who later visited the region. Bedford may have known of the work of Maxime Du Camp, the French calotypist who worked in Egypt between 1849 and 1851. Du Camp exhibited his work in London in the early 1850s, and published his photographs in two volumes in 1852. It is unlikely, however, that he was familiar with the work of other early photographers such as Félix Teynard or John Beasely Greene, whose work was not exhibited or published in Britain.

Two important photographers who would have been familiar to Bedford were James Robertson and Francis Frith. Robertson exhibited photographs of Constantinople (where he was based) and of Malta in various photographic exhibitions in Britain, many of them the same exhibitions in which Bedford was also represented. Frith had made three photographic expeditions to the Middle East, in 1856–57, 1857–58, and 1859–60. The results of his travels had been widely exhibited and published in Britain, and Frith also participated in the photographic societies in London, so his work was well known, and highly praised, within the photographic community. Like Bedford, Frith had photographed the landscape and architecture of England and Wales before he went overseas. In some cases, they photographed exactly the same locations within a few years of each other. They showed their work in the same exhibitions (although not apparently their Middle Eastern work at the same time), and Frith's company was later to publish a selection of Bedford's British views. Yet, in spite of the recent publications of the work of Du Camp, Robertson, and Frith, the Middle East in 1862 remained, just, sufficiently unknown and different to warrant the presence of another photographer who would record the sites through what was generally perceived as an objective and truthful medium.

There were undoubtedly many similarities in the way Bedford and Frith worked at home and abroad. In the East, Bedford must have felt to a certain extent daunted by the task of treading in Frith's footsteps. However, their work does differ, separated by a few years that saw technological changes and shifting attitudes within Victorian society.[45] While Frith's work can be seen as part of the same vision that characterizes Roberts's drawings, full of life, romance, and detail within the truthfulness of the photographic image, Bedford's photographs, although no less accomplished technically, appear more formal and are sometimes emotionally distant. His background in architecture and draftsmanship is evident in the depiction of the buildings as subjects presented to convey the maximum amount of information, sometimes achieved through a sequence of three or four photographs, such as the views of the Dolmabahçe Palace in Constantinople, or the Dome of the Rock, Jerusalem.

Bedford's response to the ruins of Egypt, to architectural structures, and to the buildings of Constantinople is generally confident and secure. His landscapes in the Holy Land are perhaps less accomplished, though, as the sacred associations within the landscape do not necessarily translate into a successfully composed image. The critical reviews at the time, however, recognized Bedford's work not only as an artistic triumph, but also as an important record of "views never before done, and not again likely to be done, except under somewhat similar circumstances; so that there is a *real* value attaching to a large number of these photographs."[46]

When the Prince of Wales made a second tour of the region in 1869, joined by his wife Alexandra, Princess of Wales, he was accompanied by the artist Oswald Brierly and the reporter William Howard Russell.[47] Although photographs were again taken on the tour, there were very few in comparison to the 1862 tour, and most of them were private, personal records of the traveling experience, very different to Bedford's more formal response. It seems that on this occasion the romance, color, and immediacy offered by a watercolorist (alongside whom the Princess of Wales painted happily) were considered preferable to the formality and precision of the professional photographer.

After the Royal Tour

The reviews of Bedford's Eastern photographs were universally enthusiastic. He returned to Britain successful, with a business that was to grow and expand over the coming years. Bedford would undertake further photographic tours with his two sons assisting him (they often appear in his British views alongside a woman assumed to be his wife Mary). In 1863, Bedford evidently wrote to the Prince of Wales to ask him for assistance in finding one of his sons a job. The prince, keen to help, passed the letter on to his comptroller with a note: "I send you some more letters, & as regards the enclosed one, the writer, Mr. Bedford, accompanied me during the whole of my late Eastern Tour, as photographer, & is an excellent man. If I can do something for his son I should be very happy. Would [you] perhaps be kind enough to make some enquiries as to his obtaining some Civil Service appointment."[48] In the end, however, both sons ended up working with their father as photographers. Arthur ran the printing business at 326 Camden Road, which was Bedford's main premises from around 1864, and William seems to have started to take landscape and architectural photographs.[49] William and his father exhibited together at the London Photographic Society in 1867: "The name of Mr. Francis Bedford, and the quality of his pictures, are so well known, that it is quite sufficient to say that he exhibited a few of his choicest productions. Mr. William Bedford's views were also of excellent quality."[50]

Bedford undertook some new projects, including in 1863–64 photographing recently acquired works of art at the British Museum. He contributed sixteen of these photographs to R. Murdoch Smith's *History of the Recent Discoveries at Cyrene*, each of which is an exquisite still-life study of a sculpture.[51] He undertook a series of photographs of Alexandra Park, published by Day & Son, and a number of photographs of both interiors and exteriors at Warwick Castle.[52] Also during the mid-1860s, he photographed works of art designed by the architect William Burges.[53]

Bedford's elder son Arthur died in December 1867. The same year, perhaps as a consequence, Bedford resigned as vice-president of the Photographic Society.[54] He seems to have stopped taking photographs at this time, at least in any substantial quantity. He did later return to the photographic societies, and eventually took up the position of vice-president again in 1878. He also published a series of lectures on the art of being a photographer. The lectures are both poetic and practical, setting out Bedford's views on the qualities required of a successful landscape photographer alongside the various problems that might be faced in the field.[55]

From the 1860s Bedford employed assistants and possibly other family members at the studio, and his surviving son William continued to work as a photographer from the Camden Road premises. An album of William's views of Chiswick House in west London, owned by the Dukes of Devonshire, was purchased by the Prince of Wales and presented to Queen Victoria as a Christmas present in 1874. That same year, William married Wilhelmina Perch, and the following year they had a son, Francis Perch Bedford.[56]

William continued the association with Catherall & Prichard established by his father.[57] The firm went on publishing work by both father and son, and after the death of both William in 1893 and Francis in 1894, the firm operated from the Camden Road studios for some years.[58] In the 1870s–80s, Bedford had continued his involvement with the photographic societies and sometimes acted as a judge at exhibitions.

Because William predeceased his father, when Francis died on 15 May 1894 his estate passed to his daughter-in-law.[59] The amount of £17,902 6s 5d was left to her, a considerable sum. The young Francis Perch was to receive an excellent education at Charterhouse school, followed by University College, London and King's College, Cambridge where he studied Natural Sciences. He traveled to the Straits Settlements (now Malaysia and Singapore), where he discovered new species that were named after him: *Aidanosagitta bedfordii* and *Pseudobiceros bedfordi*. His mother eventually left some of her substantial inheritance to her son's universities to promote the study of zoology.[60] His promising career was cut short, however, when he died on 10 October 1900, aged only 25.

While this is perhaps a somewhat melancholy end to Francis Bedford's story, he did leave behind an extraordinary photographic legacy, much of which remains to be discovered. His commercial success in the 1860s was built not just on his skill as an artist and as a photographer, but also on his experience in the 1840s and 1850s working as a commercial printer and lithographer for some of the leading London firms. Bedford took this knowledge and applied it to his photographic work, seeking partnerships with leading scholars and publishers while identifying the need to distribute his work to as wide an audience as possible. He maintained a steady presence in the photographic societies for most of his life, and contributed knowledgeably when required. His work acquired the respect of his photographic peers and he was spoken of frequently as one of the leading photographers of the day. His professional and personal status was undoubtedly enhanced by his royal patronage in 1857 and 1862, and he took every opportunity to remind others of this. Bedford's reminiscences of the Middle East tour were heard for many years afterward, and from 1862 his cartes-de-visite were always emblazoned with the stamp "Photographer to the Prince of Wales."[61]

A Tour in the East

Badr El Hage

The rediscovery of the Holy Land and its history was a central preoccupation of European policy makers and religious institutions throughout the nineteenth century. By 1800, the British had become increasingly interested in dominating the region and securing a safe passage to India. This interest became a matter of urgency after Napoleon's invasion of Egypt and Syria, in 1798 and 1799. Bonaparte's move signaled the beginning of an era of unabated competition between the major European powers (Britain, France, Austria, and Russia) to inherit the Ottoman Empire.

For the British, securing the frontiers of their empire and facilitating communication within it was a strategic goal throughout the nineteenth century. By 1917, they had succeeded in 'recovering' the Holy Land, controlling Egypt, and securing the road to India. This was a result of collective effort by politicians, strategists, and military experts, together with scientific archaeological excavations and evangelical activities, throughout the nineteenth century. Bishops and missionaries were dispatched to serve throughout this vast empire in the name of God and for the sake of the nation.

The influx of hundreds of travelers, among them artists, military men, diplomats, scientists, missionaries, cartographers, humanists, and photographers, to Egypt and the Holy Land made the Orient more accessible to the West. Ancient Greek, Egyptian, and biblical sites and scenes became known to Europeans, especially in Victorian England, well before the invention of photography. From the late eighteenth century, a series of books was published in Europe illustrated with lithographs depicting the region's sites. Important examples of such books include the monumental work known as *Description de l'Egypte* (1809–29), which emerged from Napoleon's expedition to Egypt, and David Roberts's *The Holy Land, Syria, Idumea, Arabia, Egypt and Nubia* (1842–49), as well as work by Louis-François Cassas (1799), Luigi Mayer (1801–04), and Count Léon de Laborde (1830).

After 1820, travel to the eastern Mediterranean increased, together with a huge proliferation of interest in ancient civilizations. Oriental themes also became very popular, and the translation of Arabic, Syriac, and Persian literature flourished, along with the publication of hundreds of travel books.

In 1835 the Peninsular and Oriental Steam Navigation Company began cruising the eastern Mediterranean. Gradually, carriage roads were built and new hotels opened. The Anglo-Ottoman trade convention of 1838 reduced tariffs and in 1840 the introduction of steamships to Alexandria cut journey times. In addition to traders, European tourists and pilgrims began traveling to Egypt and the Holy Land. The first British guidebook to Egypt was *A Handbook for Travellers in Egypt* (1847) by John Gardner Wilkinson, and the first guidebook for the Holy Land was *A Handbook for Travellers in Syria and Palestine* (1858), both published by John Murray.[62] In 1867 the British travel company Thomas Cook & Son started running a program of package tours to Egypt and the Holy Land.

Consequently, the second half of the nineteenth century witnessed a dramatic rise in popular demand for images of biblical sites, Egyptian and Greek ruins, Near Eastern landscapes, mosques, local costumes, and traditional and sacred localities. This drew some of the leading European photographers of the nineteenth century either to visit or to open photographic studios in Near Eastern cities such as Cairo, Jerusalem, Beirut, Damascus, and Constantinople (modern-day Istanbul).[63] Rapid advances in photographic technology, including the introduction of the wet collodion process and the use of stereographic views, helped meet mounting European demand for images of apparently timeless landscapes under the glittering sun of the East.

Francis Bedford, Royal Photographer

In mid-February 1862, the *Photographic News* included the following announcement of Bedford's commission as a royal photographer attached to the Prince of Wales's suite:

> We have much Pleasure in announcing the first public act which illustrates that the heir to England's throne takes as deep an interest in photography as his late royal father. In the Eastern tour, which he is about to take in as private a manner as possible, accompanied by a very limited suite, eight gentlemen only, Mr. Francis Bedford, photographer, forms one of that eight. A complete equipment for photographic operations will be taken so as to secure, under the best possible conditions, photographic mementoes of a journey through scenes so fraught with historic and sacred associations. Mr. Bedford has, we believe, received permission to publish the series of photographs, when after their completion, the requirements of Her Majesty are supplied.[64]

It is thought that Bedford was the first photographer to accompany a royal tour.

After leaving London, the royal party made its way across the English Channel to Calais and from there, by train, to Austria. In Vienna, Laurence Oliphant, the British writer and traveler, was invited by the prince to accompany the party on its way east as far as Corfu. Oliphant had already visited many places on the Dalmatian coast, and was therefore an appropriate guide for this part of the journey.

The prince left Vienna for Trieste on 15 February. The following day, the royal party boarded HMY *Osborne* and headed toward Venice. After two days seeing the sites in the city, the *Osborne* steamed for the Dalmatian coast, calling in at Pula, Split, Dubrovnik, Gruž, Kotor, and Durrës, before arriving in Corfu on 23 February.

The Egyptian Tour

The royal party spent two days in Corfu. On 25 February, they sailed toward Egypt, by way of Zakynthos and the Ionian Islands. On 1 March, the prince and his party arrived in Alexandria, under the ordinary salute of twenty-one guns, despite the private nature of the prince's visit. They left immediately for Cairo, where the viceroy Muhammad Sa'id Pasha was awaiting their arrival. After a short interview with the viceroy, the party was conveyed in carriages to Qasr al-Nil on the banks of the Nile, the palace set aside for the Prince of Wales.

The royal party toured Egypt for twenty-eight days. According to the prince's journal, he visited the narrow streets of Cairo and was impressed by "the Eastern mode of life & the costumes," the Citadel, Muhammad Ali's tomb in the mosque, and the Pyramids of Giza.[65] "We had a charming little encampment

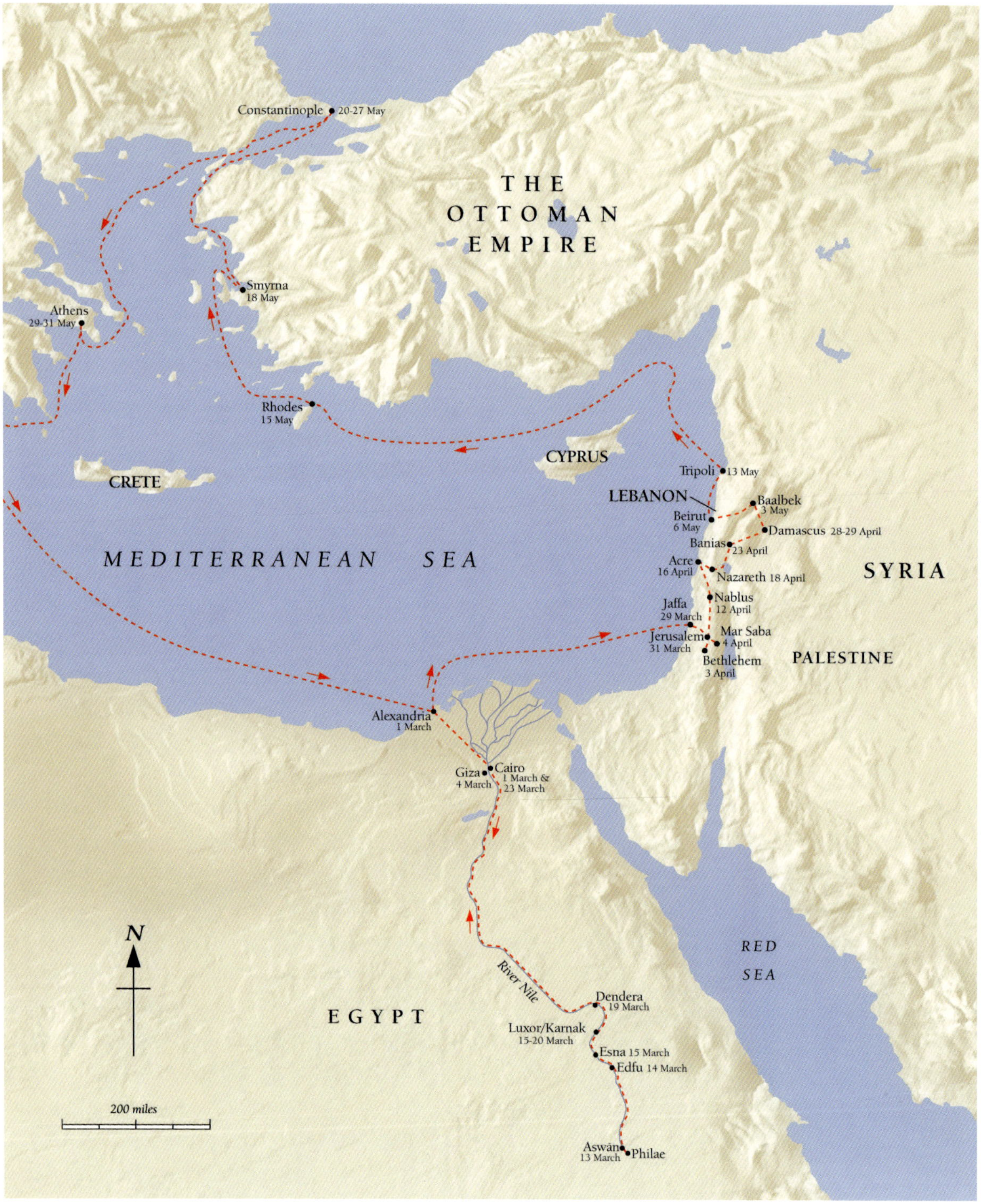

The Royal Tour of 1862: map showing countries and place names at the time

just below the Pyramids where we slept for the night."[66] On 5 March, the prince embarked on a boat lent to him by the viceroy, towed by a steamer. Another steamer carried the servants. The destination of the party was Upper Egypt. They traveled quickly up the Nile, only to turn around and then make the return journey, this time stopping en route. During the journey downstream, they halted at several major towns and ruins, the prince enjoying shooting birds and crocodiles, buying gifts, sightseeing, and swimming. They visited a great many places, including Philae, Aswan, Edfu, Esna, Thebes, and the Valley of the Kings. The party reached Cairo again on 23 March.

Between 24 and 28 March, the prince toured Cairo's bazaars and visited the Tombs of the Caliphs. On 25 March, the prince recorded an outing to Suez: "At 9.39 A.M. We went by Rail to Suez, wh[ich] we reached soon after 12. After a light luncheon, we went on board an Egyptian steamer & steamed about 14 miles on the Red Sea, then landed in a boat (belonging to Mr. West, our Consul at Suez, who accompanied us) & visited the so called Moses' Wells."[67]

While in Egypt, the prince made a few references to Bedford's photographic activities in his journal. The first mention was on 13 March at Philae: "The ruins at Philae are beautiful & most interesting & Mr. Bedford, the photographer, who came fr[om] England with me & our party, took some very good views."[68] The next day they were in Edfu, and the prince admired Bedford's work in another diary entry: "After luncheon rode to see the famous temple wh[ich] exists there; it is considered the finest in Egypt, & I admired it excessively & we went all over it. Mr. Bedford . . . took some very successful views of the temple."[69]

In an entry written in Cairo on 26 March, the prince reveals the presence of another photographer: "after luncheon were photographed, by M. Le Gray, a French photographer, who also went up the Nile with us."[70] Gustave Le Gray, who was residing in Egypt at the time of the prince's visit, was one of the most important French photographers of the nineteenth century. He had left France in May 1860 and, after stopping in Palermo and Malta, arrived in Alexandria at the end of July, having been engaged to cover the conflict in Syria. En route to Damascus, however, Le Gray fell from his horse and broke his leg, so was unable to continue with the commission. After photographing in Baalbek, he eventually returned to Egypt. He was based in Alexandria and Cairo until his death.[71]

In addition to the photographs taken by Bedford during the Egyptian tour, artists produced illustrations depicting several activities undertaken by the prince. The *Illustrated London News* published a series of images covering parts of the prince's journey. The drawings were sent from Egypt and the Holy Land by (among others) Frederick George, who was attached to the prince's party in Egypt, and the artist Frank Dillon, who although not following the prince's visit was in Egypt in 1861–62 and also sent drawings of ancient monuments for publication in the press.

The Holy Land Tour

On 29 March 1862 the royal party arrived in Jaffa. The tour of the Holy Land lasted until 13 May of that year. The most interesting aspect of the Holy Land tour was the permission granted to the prince by the Ottoman authorities to enter the two most sacred Islamic sites: the Haram al-Sharif, where the Dome of the Rock stands in Jerusalem; and the Mosque of al-Khalil at al-Khalil (Hebron) to the southwest of Jerusalem, which had never before been seen by a foreigner.[72]

Upon the arrival of the royal party in Jerusalem on 31 March, the British consul, James Finn, was already negotiating with Suraya Pasha, the governor of Jerusalem, to provide the royal party with access to the Haram al-Sharif (Temple Mount) and the Dome of the Rock. Major General Bruce was also involved in the negotiations, assisted by the interpreter to the royal party, Mr. Noel Moore, son of the British consul-general in Beirut. Negotiations were successful: the correspondent of the *Illustrated London News*, in a dispatch from Jerusalem, was jubilant: "The Prince entered the mosque and had this privilege of standing where no infidel has stood since the Crusades."[73]

Bedford was one of the first photographers to take pictures at the Dome of the Rock in Jerusalem. The mosque had become more accessible to foreigners after the Crimean War, but photography was usually not permitted at the site. For Bedford, the permission granted to the prince by the Ottoman authorities resulted in at least six pictures of the mosque's Islamic architecture.[74]

Another long round of negotiations took place with Suraya Pasha before permission was granted for the prince to visit the Mosque of al-Khalil, known as the Cave of Machpelah, the sepulcher of the family of the patriarchs. According to Stanley: "For 600 years no European, except by stealth, has ever set foot [inside the cave]."[75] After complex negotiations, Suraya Pasha sent a message promising the prince admission, on condition that only seven people accompany the prince there.[76] After the prince ended his inspection of the site, he "asked Bedford to remain behind to finish his photography with fifty soldiers guarding the photographer and his equipment from harm."[77] It is worth mentioning, however, that there are no close-up photographs of the mosque in Bedford's series. The reason was probably not technical since Bedford was able to take photographs in difficult conditions inside the mosque of Nablus, and may rather have been due to the strict prohibition then in force against the use of that medium at al-Khalil.

Dr. Georg Rosen, the Prussian consul at Jerusalem, accompanied the prince and explained to him the points of interest. Rosen was well known to travelers in Palestine because of his in-depth knowledge of sacred geography and the detailed study he had made of the topography of Hebron and its environs.[78]

A third permission was granted to the prince by the patriarch of the Greek Church to enter the Convent of Mar Saba, which the royal party visited on 3 April. Bedford was the first to photograph the town of Safed (eastern Galilee) on 22 April and the ruins of the Roman temple of Deir al-Asha'ir on the 27 April on his way to Damascus.

The prince toured the major biblical sites and ruins of the Holy Land, living in tents and accompanied by Turkish cavalrymen for protection. Every major church and mosque in Jerusalem was visited, and the itinerary of the prince's journey included the following sites and places: Jaffa, Jerusalem and its surroundings, Bethlehem, Mar Saba, the Dead Sea, the Jordan River, Beitin (biblical Bethel), Nablus, Mount Carmel, Acre, Nazareth, Mount Tabor, Tiberias, Safed, Banias, Beaufort Castle, Hasbaya, Rashaya, Deir al-Asha'ir, Damascus, Baalbek, Beirut, Nahr al-Kalb (Dog River), Sidon, Tyre, Tripoli, the Cedars of Lebanon and the island of Arwad. Most of the sites were photographed by Bedford.

The prince made references to Bedford's photographic activities while in the Holy Land in his journal. On 21 April, near the Lake of Tiberias, the prince wrote, "We lunched under a fig tree at 12 o'clock on the site of where once the city of Capernaum is said to have stood, & Mr. Bedford photographed us 'en groupe.'"[79] In another entry, written in Baalbek on Sunday 4 May, the prince wrote, "Mr. Bedford took some excellent views of it, wh[ich] will be a great addition to his collection of photographs."[80]

Photographs of the Cedars of Lebanon are absent from Bedford's collection due to a storm, which drove the royal party back to their encampment at the village of Ehden shortly after they had reached the Cedars. William M. Thompson later explained: "It is unfortunate that the royal visit to the celebrated spot was attended by a storm of wind and rain which rendered it impossible to take a photograph of the Cedars of Lebanon, although their position in a rocky, barren valley, high up the side of the mountain . . . renders this deeply interesting grove an impressive and striking subject for a picture."[81]

The second leg of the royal tour ended on 13 May when the prince and his party left the island of Arwad on the Syrian coast and sailed towards the coast of Asia Minor.

Constantinople, Athens, and Malta

The third and final leg of the journey began on 15 May. It covered Rhodes, the island of Kastro, Patmos, Smyrna (Izmir), Constantinople, Athens, Zakynthos, Cephalonia, Ithaca, Malta, and then the journey home by train through Europe.

While in Constantinople, the prince recorded in his journal on 27 May that, "At about 10.30 E. Leiningen, Moore & I went to the photographic studio of Mr. Abdullah [photographer of the sultan] & were photographed (very successfully) 'en carte de visite'. Abdullah took another photograph at the Embassy of a group of Sir H. & Lady Bulwer & all his staff, & myself & my suite."[82]

The party reached the port of Folkestone on 14 June. The prince concluded his journal by saying, "And so ended this most agreeable tour, as all the good things, must alas! in this world come to an end."[83]

Bedford's Photographic Achievements

The photographs taken by Francis Bedford during the royal tour in the spring of 1862 turned out to be the climax of his photographic career. According to the *Illustrated London News*, Bedford's pictorial achievement, "under adverse circumstances, is very extraordinary, and his results are, in almost every instance, highly successful, greatly surpassing the celebrated series of Egyptian photographs executed by M. Maximi [sic] du Camp for the French government."[84]

Bedford made at least 191 individual negatives during the tour, with a 10 x 12 inch plate camera. His work was characterized by a high degree of precision, and each plate was usually signed and dated at the corner, the date being that on which the photograph was taken and which almost always corresponds with the date on which the prince visited the site.

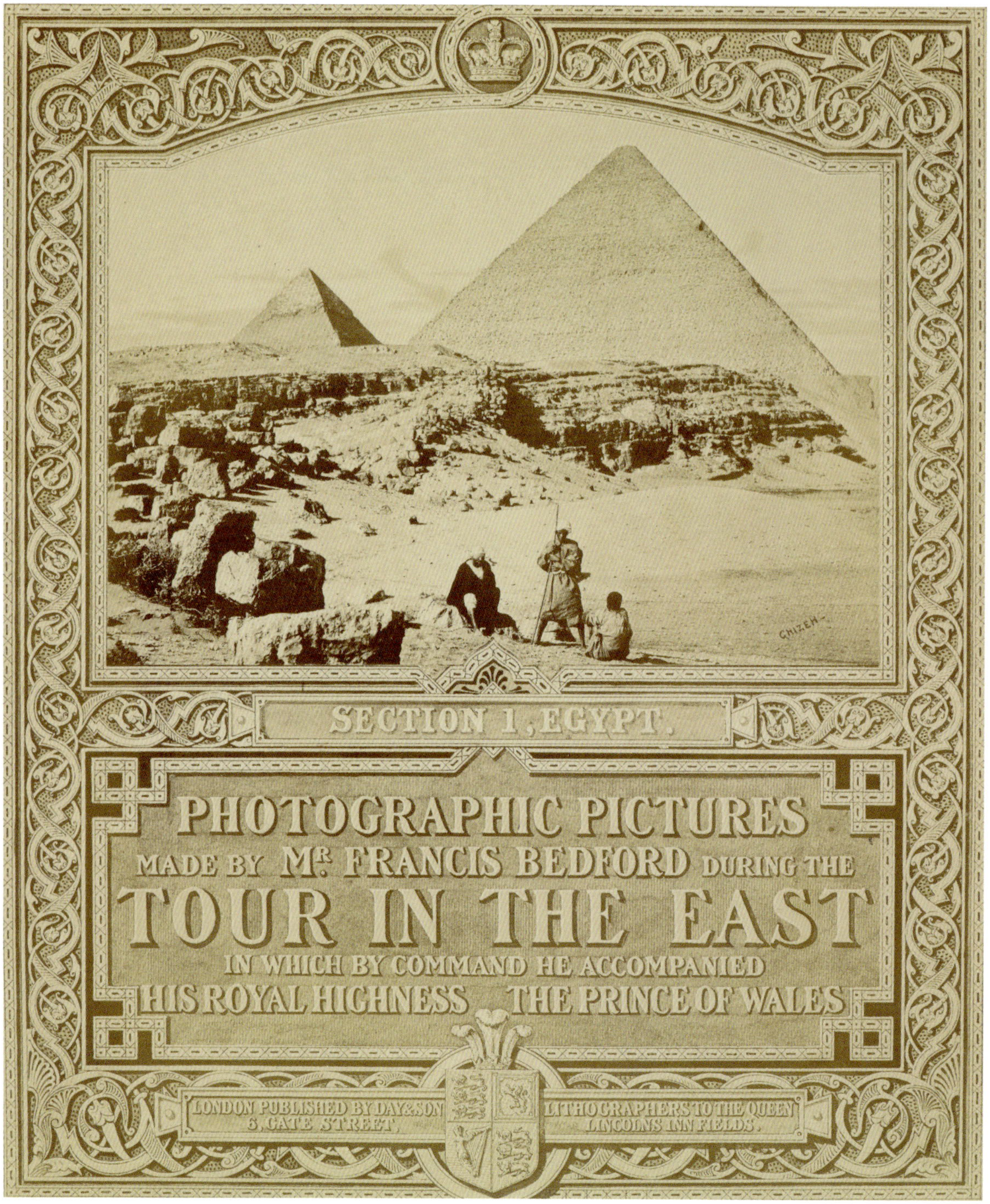

Day & Son, *Section 1—Egypt*, photographic title page incorporating a photograph by Bedford, July 1862–January 1863, albumen print, RCIN 2861516

Bedford received permission from Queen Victoria to publish a selection of the photographs, after the requirements of the queen had been met; he retained the right to use the negatives for commercial purposes. He also received permission to prepare an exhibition to be held at the German Gallery, 168 New Bond Street, London, a gallery that was owned by the publishers of the photographs, Day & Son.

Bedford initially chose 172 plates for exhibition and publication. They were published in three portfolios measuring 47 x 60 cm, comprising twenty-one parts, each containing eight or more prints. To help the public select their photographs, there was a three-page handlist, and a more substantial catalogue, with descriptive notes written by Bedford.[85] Each had an order form attached, with prices and suggestions as to the "best Architectural Subjects" or subjects "of Special Biblical interest."

The exhibition opened on 23 July 1862. The Prince of Wales visited shortly afterward, together with Meade, Teesdale, Keppel, and Stanley, all of whom had accompanied the prince on the Eastern Tour.[86] The newspapers and journals praised Bedford's achievements. The *Illustrated London News* later commented:

> The great beauty of the specimens brought home, and the general success of Mr. Bedford when working in the East, in the face of obstacles of various kinds which would have discouraged a less persevering artist, prove that the choice was well made. Mr. Bedford describes some of his trials and adversities in the pursuit of art with great humour, especially the difficulties he had to contend with when photographing the mosque of Omar at Jerusalem.[87]

In another article in the same paper, the critic wrote:

> As a mere manipulator Mr. Bedford has been eminently successful. If these photographs had been taken at home with none of the excitement and unforeseen difficulties of travel in the known conditions of our own climate, Mr. Bedford could hardly have been more successful than in the large majority of these photographs. He, has, by judicious 'exposure' and perfect control of 'developing' processes and chemicals employed, overcome the difficulty of giving the middle tint better than we have hitherto seen in photographs from Eastern subjects, in which the contrasts of light and shade are usually so violent.[88]

There were also comments on Bedford's work in the *British Journal of Photography*, that publication describing the exhibition as "perhaps the most important photographic exhibition that has hitherto been placed before the public, whether we regard it as an aid to history or as a collection in which unity of design has been a ruling principle in the artist's mind."[89]

The Times, in an article entitled "Bedford's photographs in the East," gave guidance to those who might not be able to inspect the photographs before ordering. It published various comments on Bedford's works:

> The place of honour for perfection in all that relates to out-door photography in its widest and highest sense belongs to Francis Bedford. He stands alone in being the only one who can equal all, no matter how long they may

> have practised, or how peculiarly their own they may have made any single department of landscape photography. We feel that there is a truly poetic rendering of the ruins of past ages . . . . The whole collection is remarkable for the clearness and the brilliancy of the views. They are incomparably the finest that have been produced illustrative of the historical scenes of the East.[90]

In 1865, a set of twelve photographs from the 1862 series, in a reduced format, was used to illustrate Augusta Mott's book *The Stones of Palestine*. Later in 1866, a selection of forty-eight smaller prints was published in a book entitled *The Holy Land, Egypt, Constantinople, Athens* . . . , with an introduction by William M. Thompson. This volume, issued by Bedford's publishers Day & Son, was intended to be a more affordable selection of the photographs. Over subsequent years, Bedford continued to issue mounted prints, including a number not originally part of the 172 sold to the public.

According to William Thompson, while in the Middle East the Prince of Wales had been very supportive of the photographer and

> frequently interrupted the progress of the company to allow Mr. Bedford an opportunity of making a photograph of any particular spot which Dr. Stanley's familiar acquaintance with the region, or the eye of the artist himself, might suggest as worthy of selection; while His Royal Highness, besides thus providing every facility and rendering all possible assistance to Mr. Bedford in the prosecution of his work, not seldom himself proposed subjects for pictures.[91]

The *Photographic News* also confirmed that, during the tour, the prince "manifested a deep interest, we understand, in Mr. Bedford's success, making daily enquiry as to the result of operations, and making an occasional attempt at some of the manipulations."[92]

Bedford's photographic depictions of the East demonstrated his artistic skills as a master of landscape photography as well as being important visual documents of an area that has since witnessed dramatic changes. Landscapes and architectural studies are dominant within his work from the tour. He captured the old houses of Cairo that were fast disappearing, the beautiful interiors, architecture, and decoration of the mosques and fountains in Cairo, Jerusalem, Damascus and Constantinople, the minutest hieroglyphic details of the great Egyptian temples, colonnades, statues, gateways, and the magnificent vast blocks of richly carved granite at the temples of Baalbek. In addition, his views of the destruction caused by the civil disturbances of 1860 in Damascus offer a rare visual record of the results of that tragedy. The only two portraits Bedford made on the tour were both of 'Abd al-Qadir al-Jaza'iri, who played an important role in protecting the Christians during this conflict.

The photographic press was fulsome in its praise of Bedford. In 1867 he was awarded a silver medal at the Exposition Universelle in Paris, where he displayed a few of the Middle Eastern views. One critic wrote:

> A photographic amateur remarked, while I was looking at them, that Mr. Bedford had no need to exhibit any but gems, he has such a comprehensive collection to choose

from. Out of the large number of pictures he took in the East, when he accompanied the Prince of Wales, he only shows four; and only one view in the Holy Land out of the large series he published of that ever interesting land. Yes, such veterans can make, we had almost said, a matchless display by choosing one or two pictures from each season's work. Some old photographers, however, who were once famous, can neither honour themselves by what they now produce nor by falling back on former spoils. Mr. Bedford's pictures are all well printed and show no signs of fading, which, as we proceed, will be found almost exceptional.[93]

Although the photographs taken by Bedford were considered a great achievement, one of the most important consequences of the royal visit to the Holy Land was the refocusing of British attention toward Palestine and its biblical associations. A few years after the tour, on 22 June 1865, the Palestine Exploration Fund was established for the purposes of investigating the archaeology, geography, manners and customs, geology, and natural history of the area. The Revd. Arthur Stanley was one of the fund's founders and an instrumental figure within it. Queen Victoria also contributed to the fund and became its patron.

Aside from the scientific and academic interest that lay in discovering the Holy Land, the other significant factor in the life of the Palestine Exploration Fund was Britain's strategic concerns in the eastern Mediterranean. Public figures, academics and military personnel as well as photographers were all involved in the fund's activities. In 1917, the British forces entered Jerusalem, and a new era of the history of the Holy Land began.

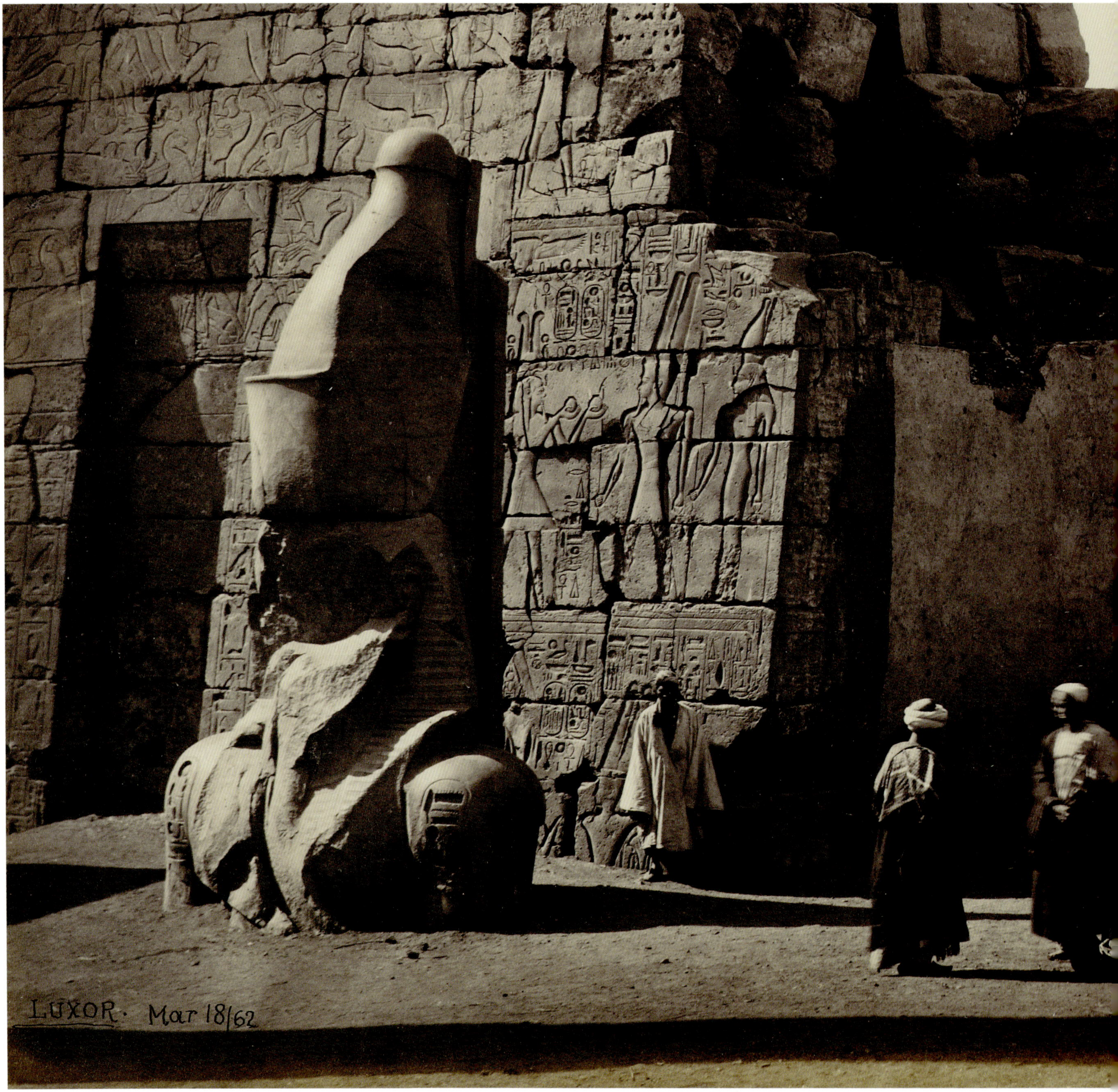
LUXOR. Mar 18/62

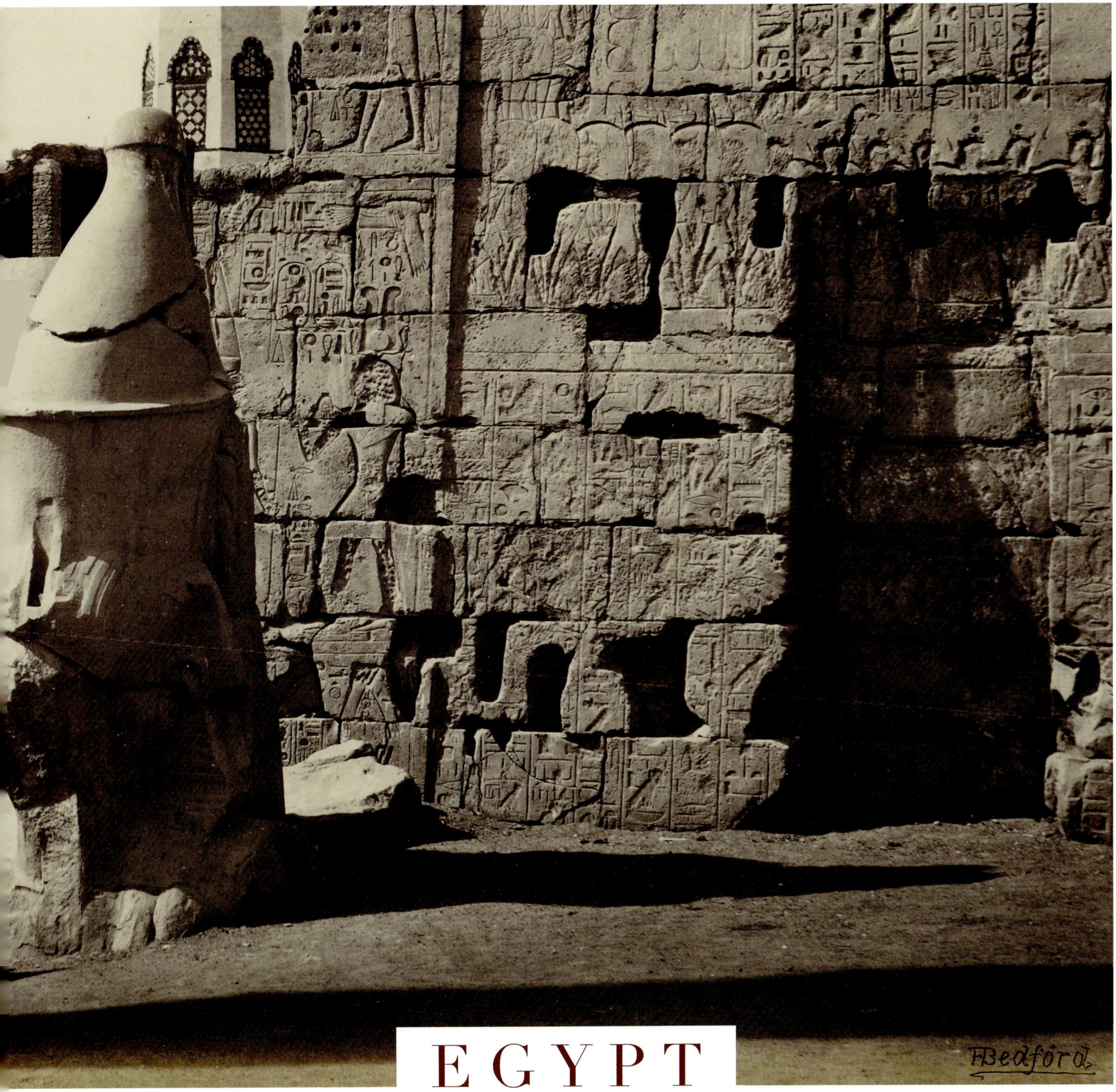

EGYPT

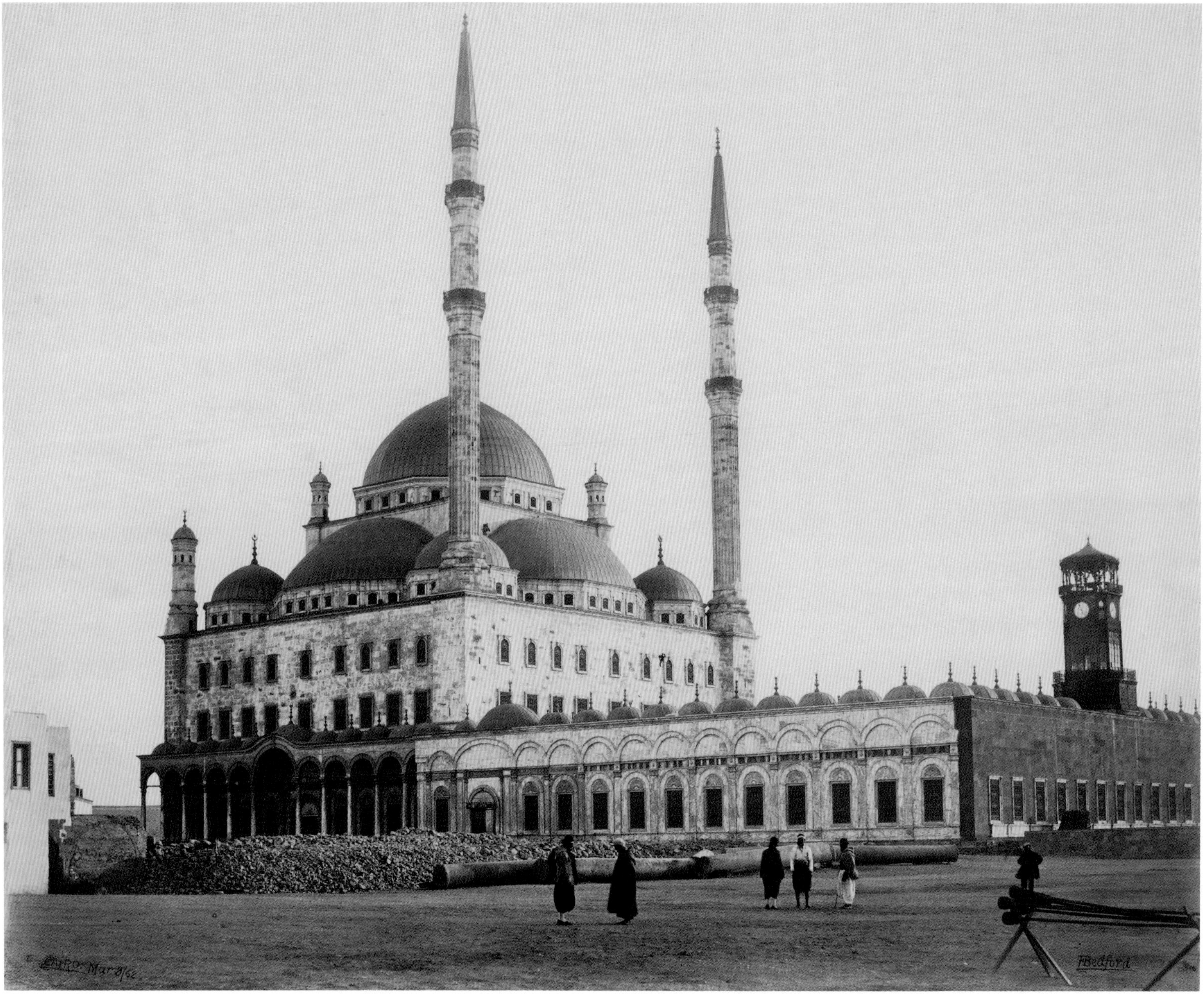

The Mosque of Muhammad Ali, Cairo, 3 March 1862

"We went to the Citadel where we saw the principal Mosque. It is a very fine building in alabaster & we had a splendid view of the town & country & the Pyramids in the distance fr[om] the roof."
Prince of Wales's Journal, 3 March 1862

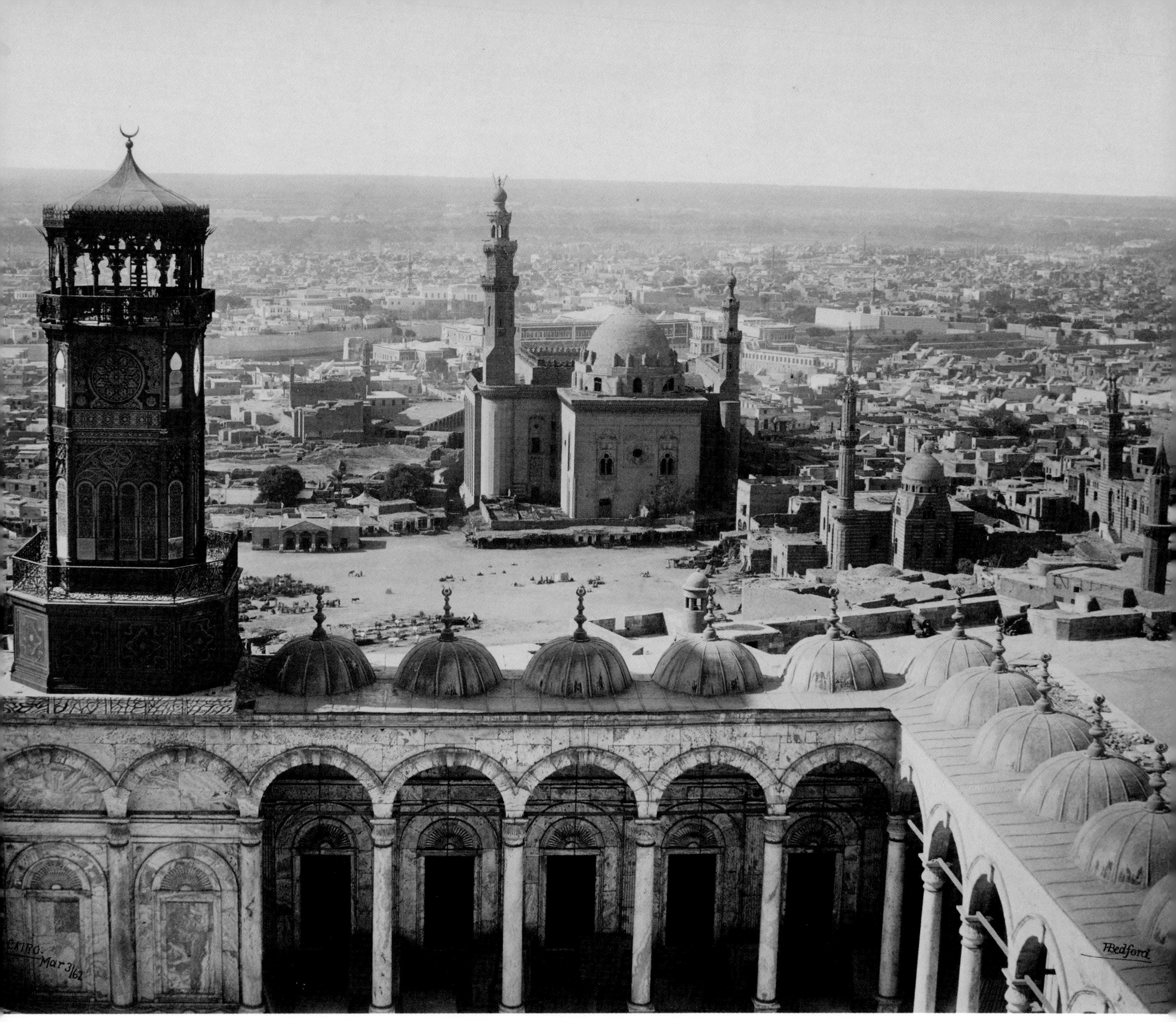

The Mosque of Muhammad Ali and the Mosque of Sultan Hassan, Cairo, 3 March 1862

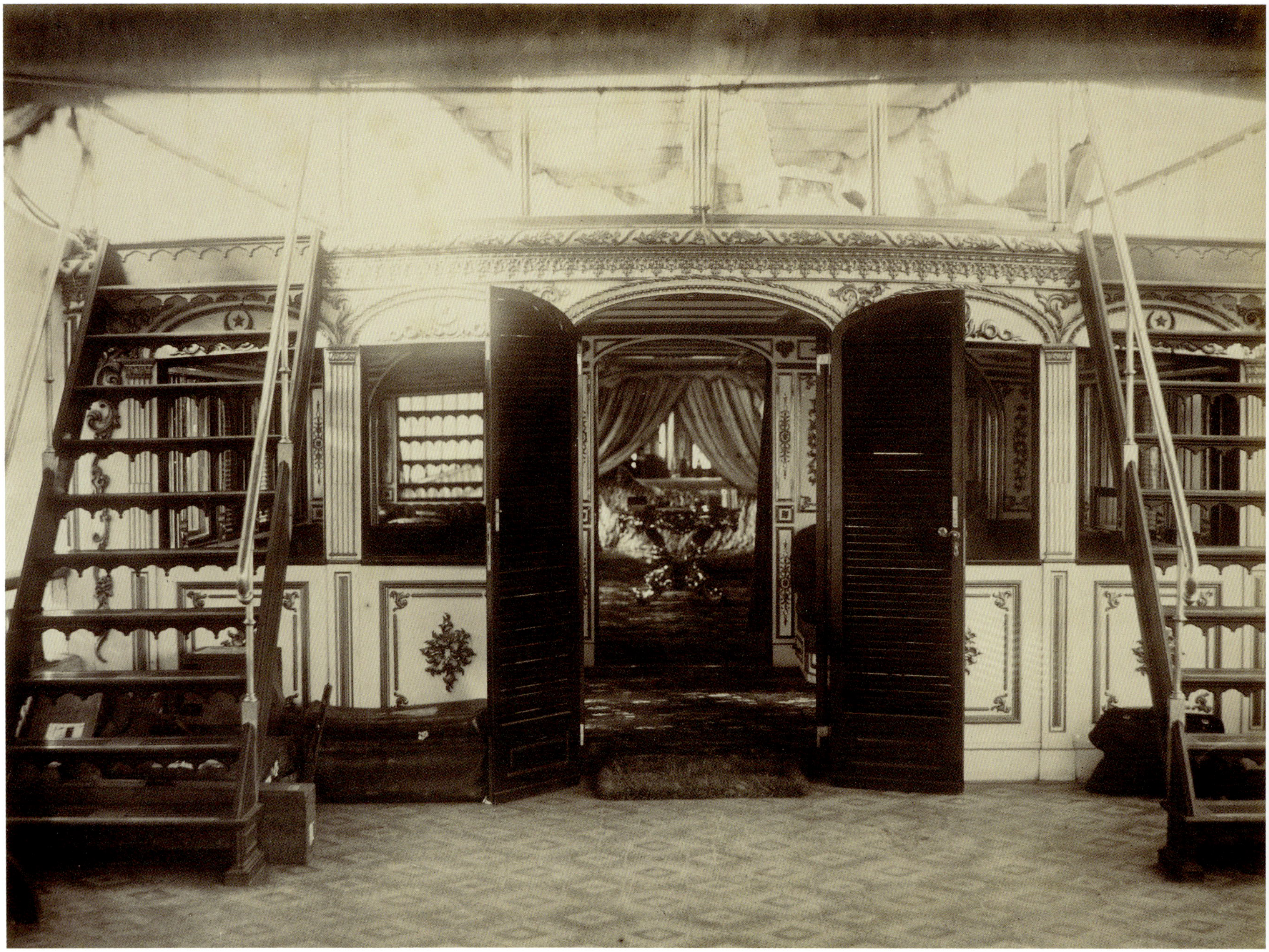

Muhammad Sa'id Pasha's *dahabiya*, 4 March 1862

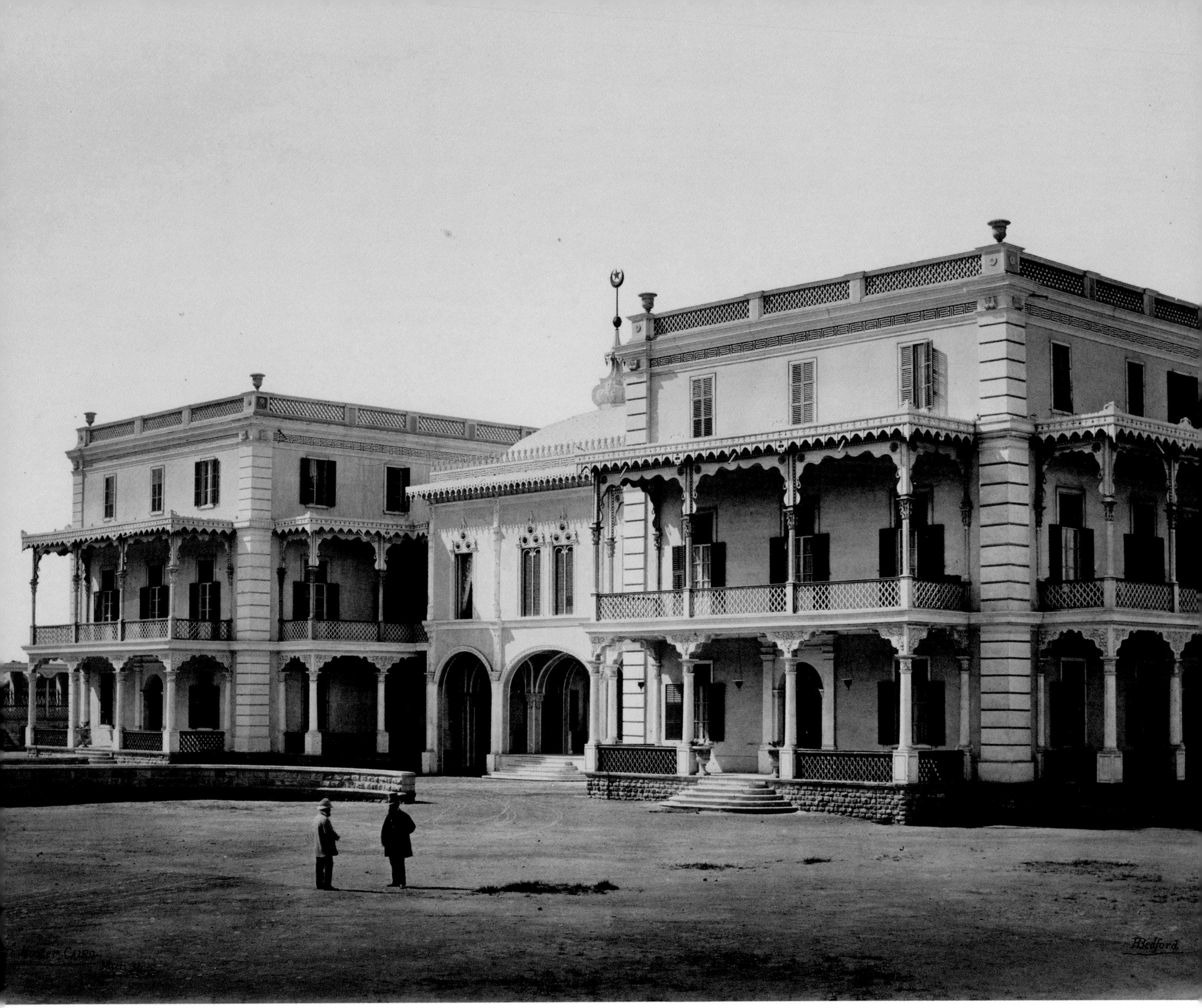

Qasr Nuzha, Shubra Road, Cairo, 3 March 1862

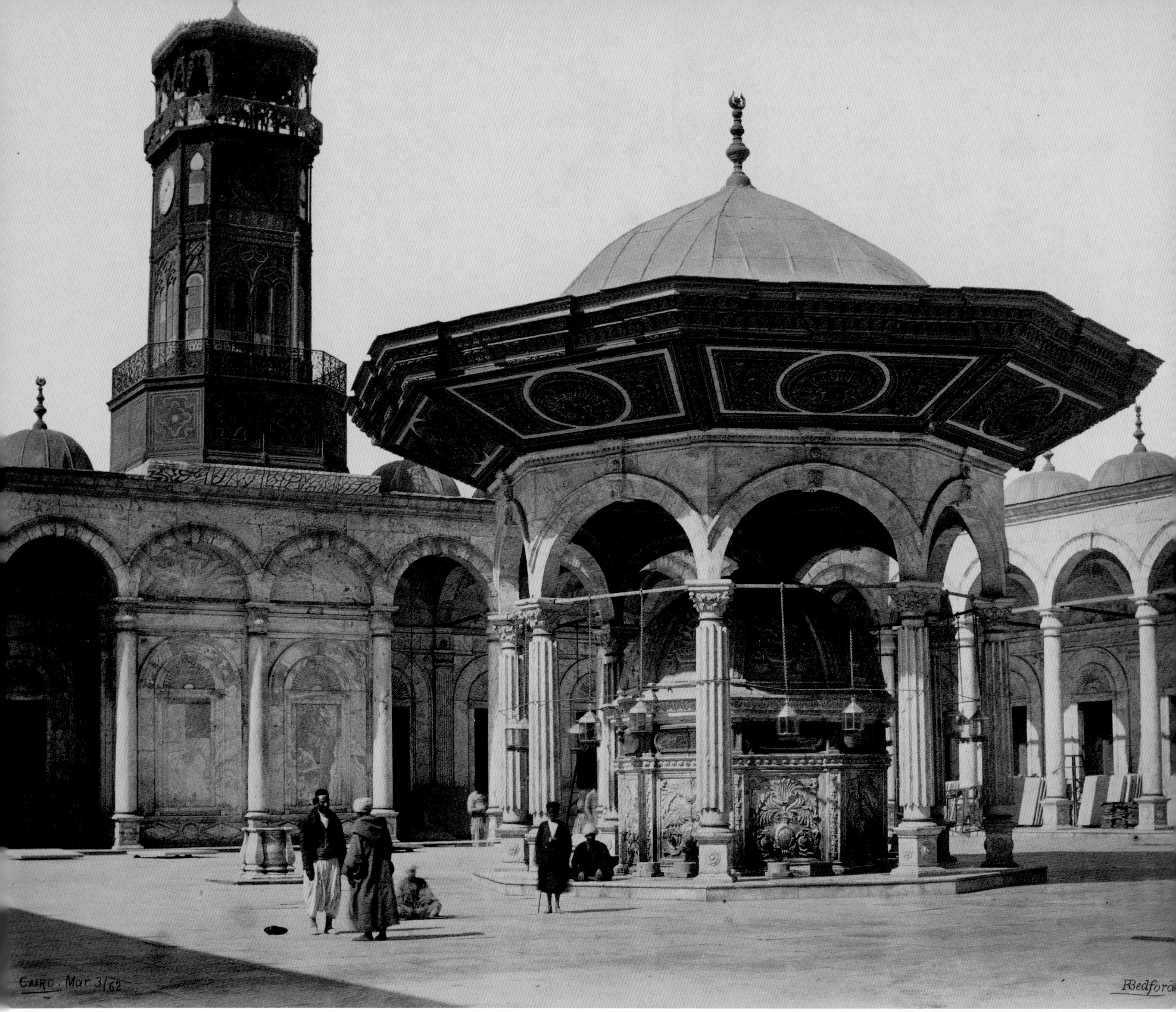

The Mosque of Muhammad Ali, Cairo, 3 March 1862

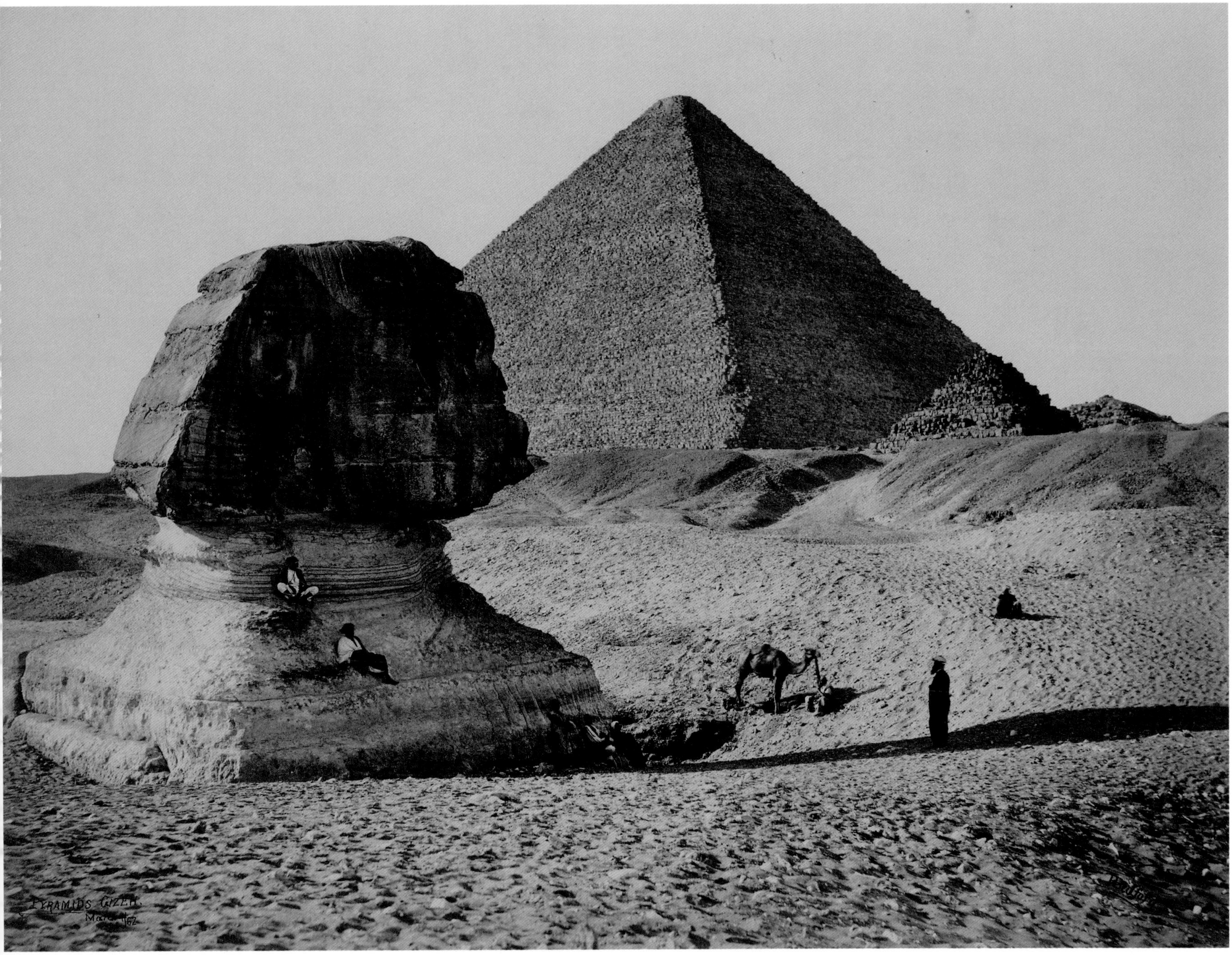

The Sphinx and the Great Pyramid, Giza, 4 March 1862

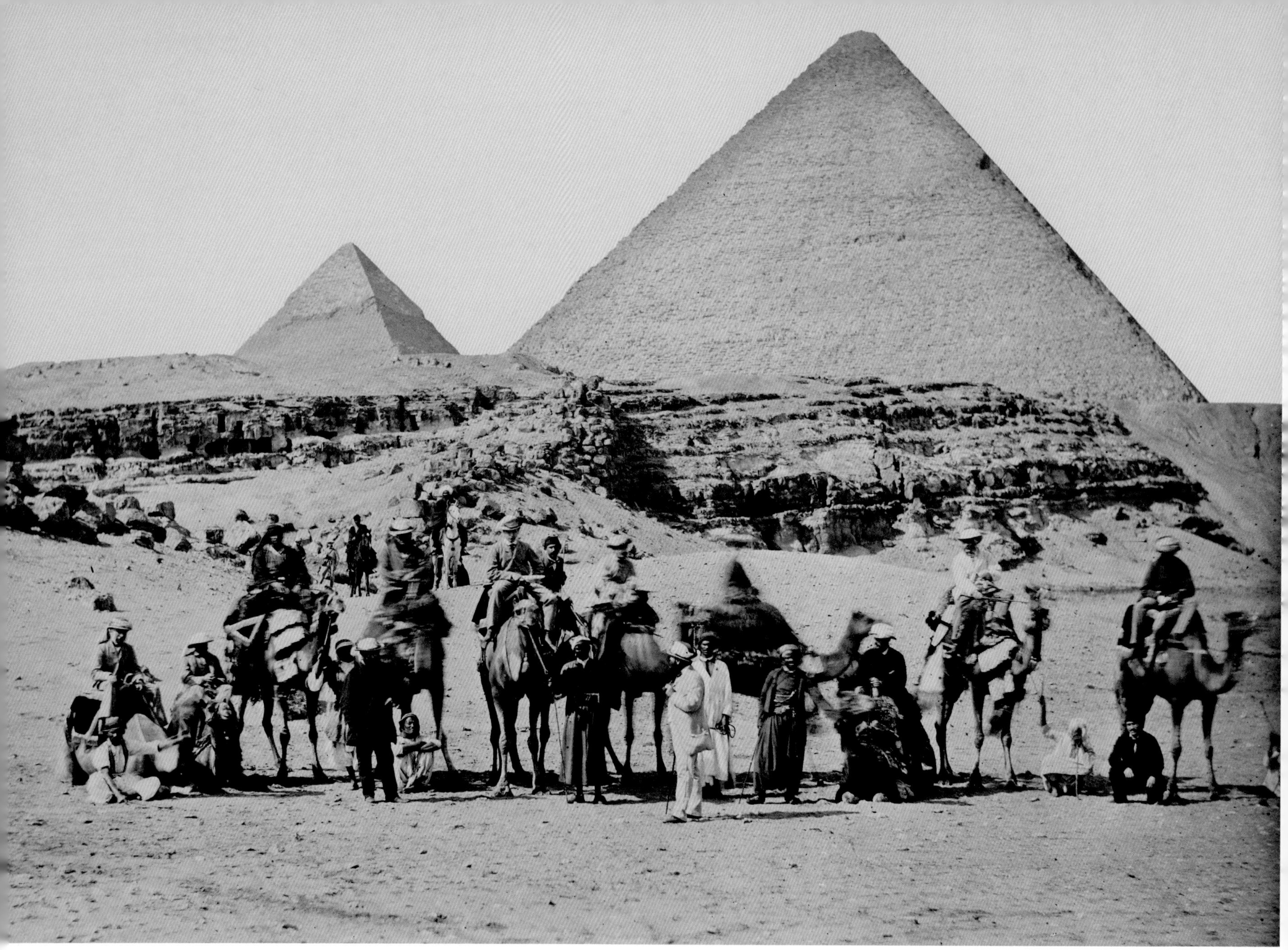

The Prince of Wales (center) and group at the Pyramids, Giza, 5 March 1862

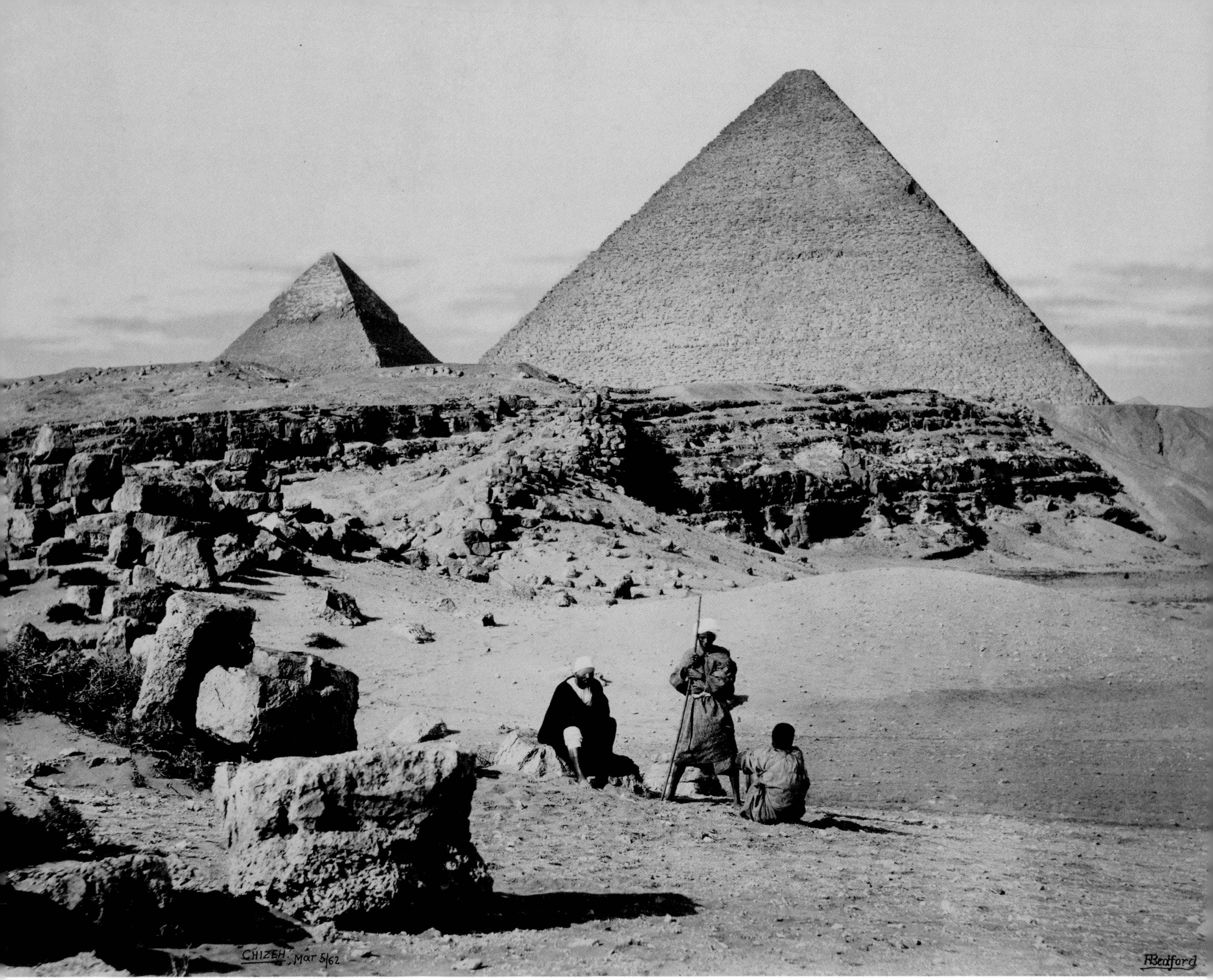

The Pyramids, Giza, 5 March 1862

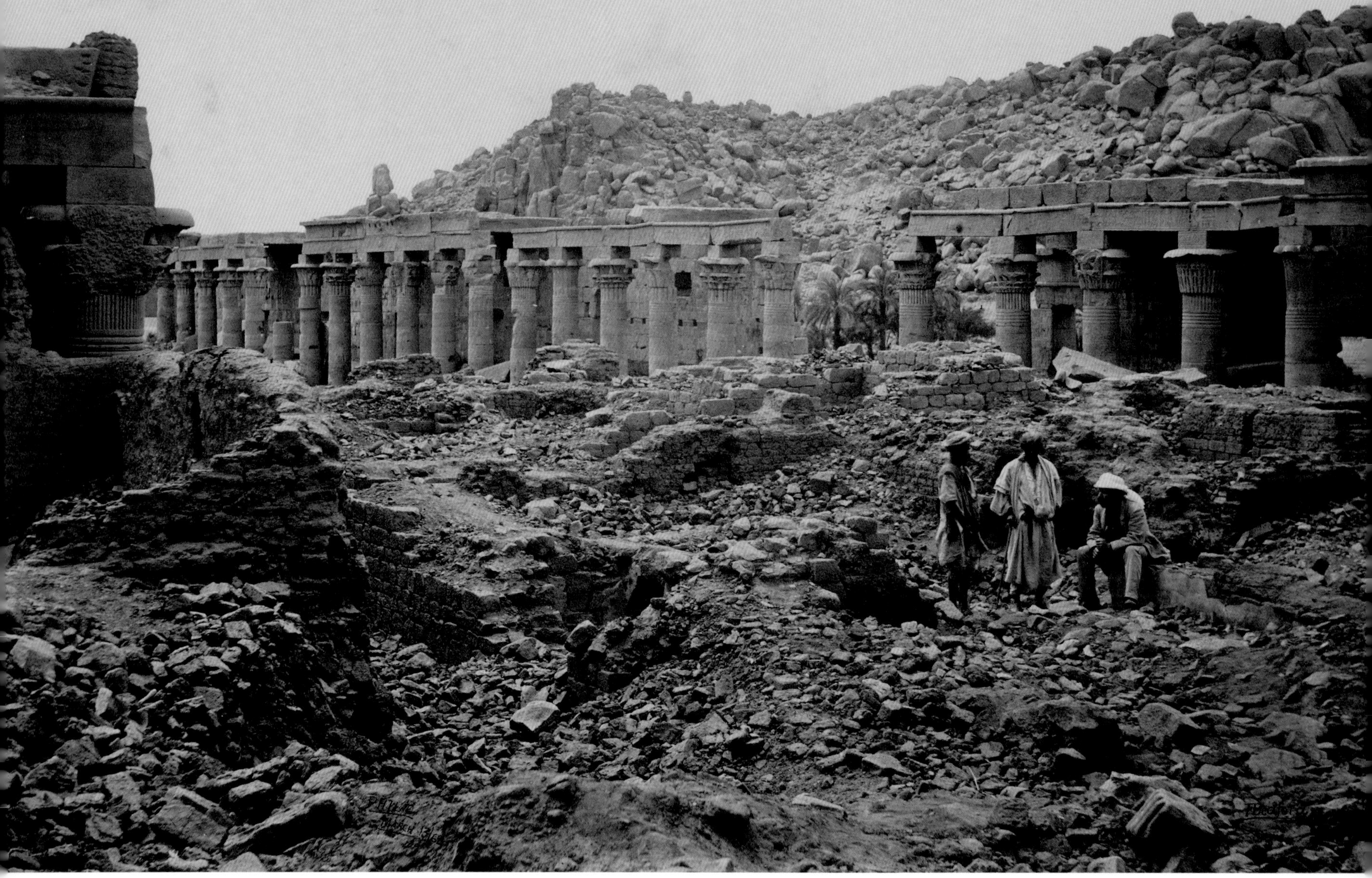

Outer court of the Temple of Isis, Philae, 13 March 1862

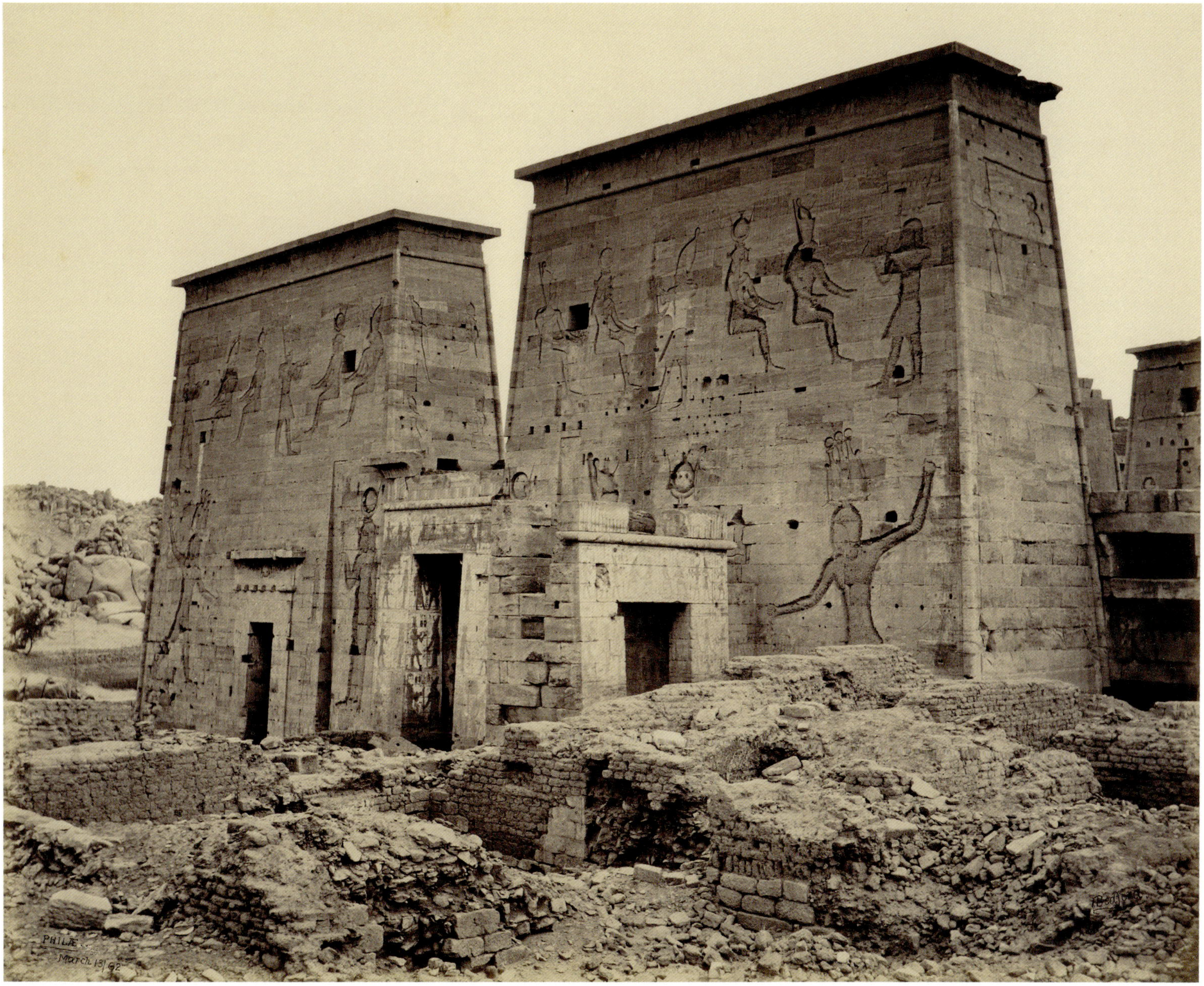

The first pylon of the Temple of Isis, Philae, 13 March 1862

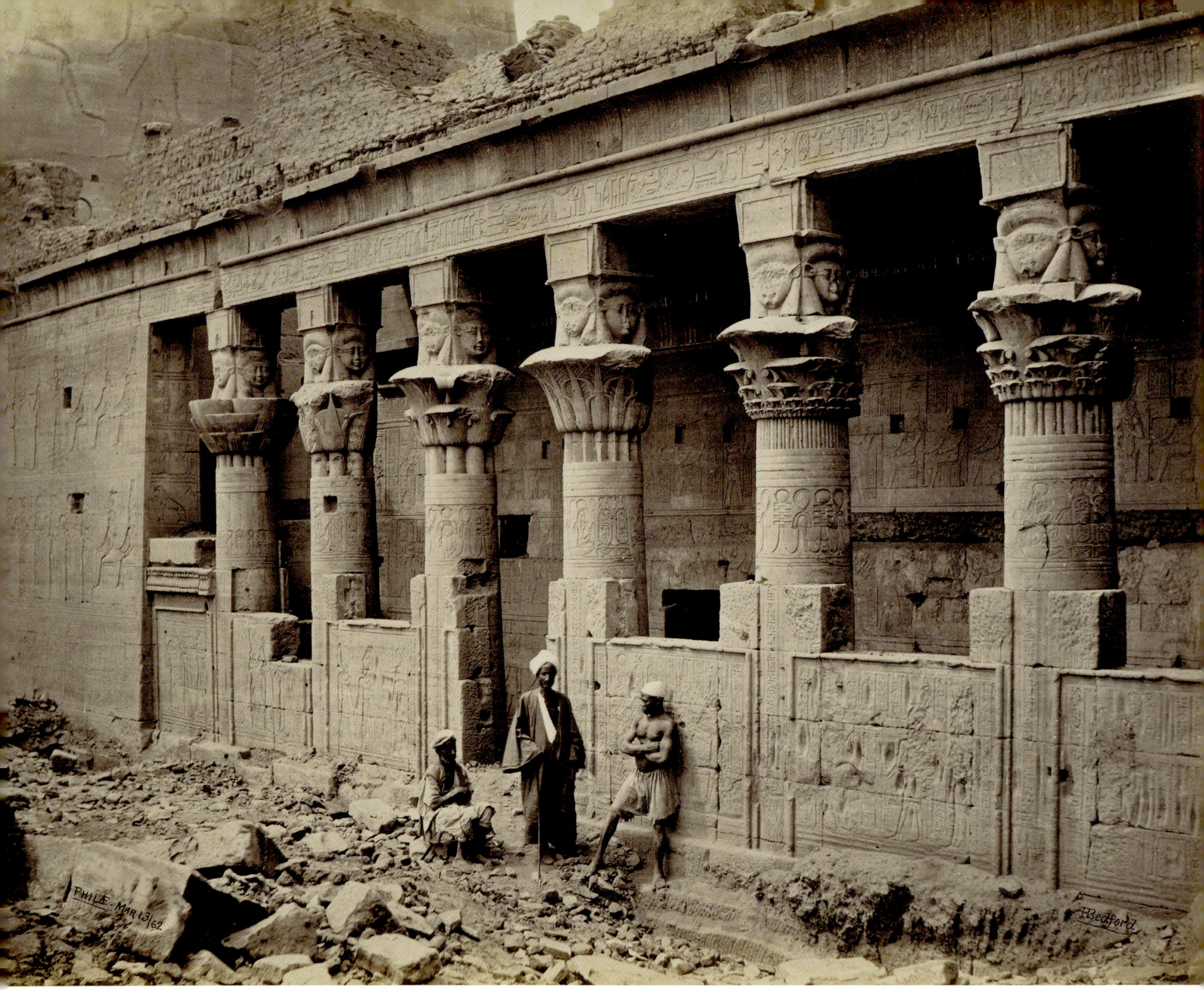

The Great Court of the Temple of Isis, Philae, 13 March 1862

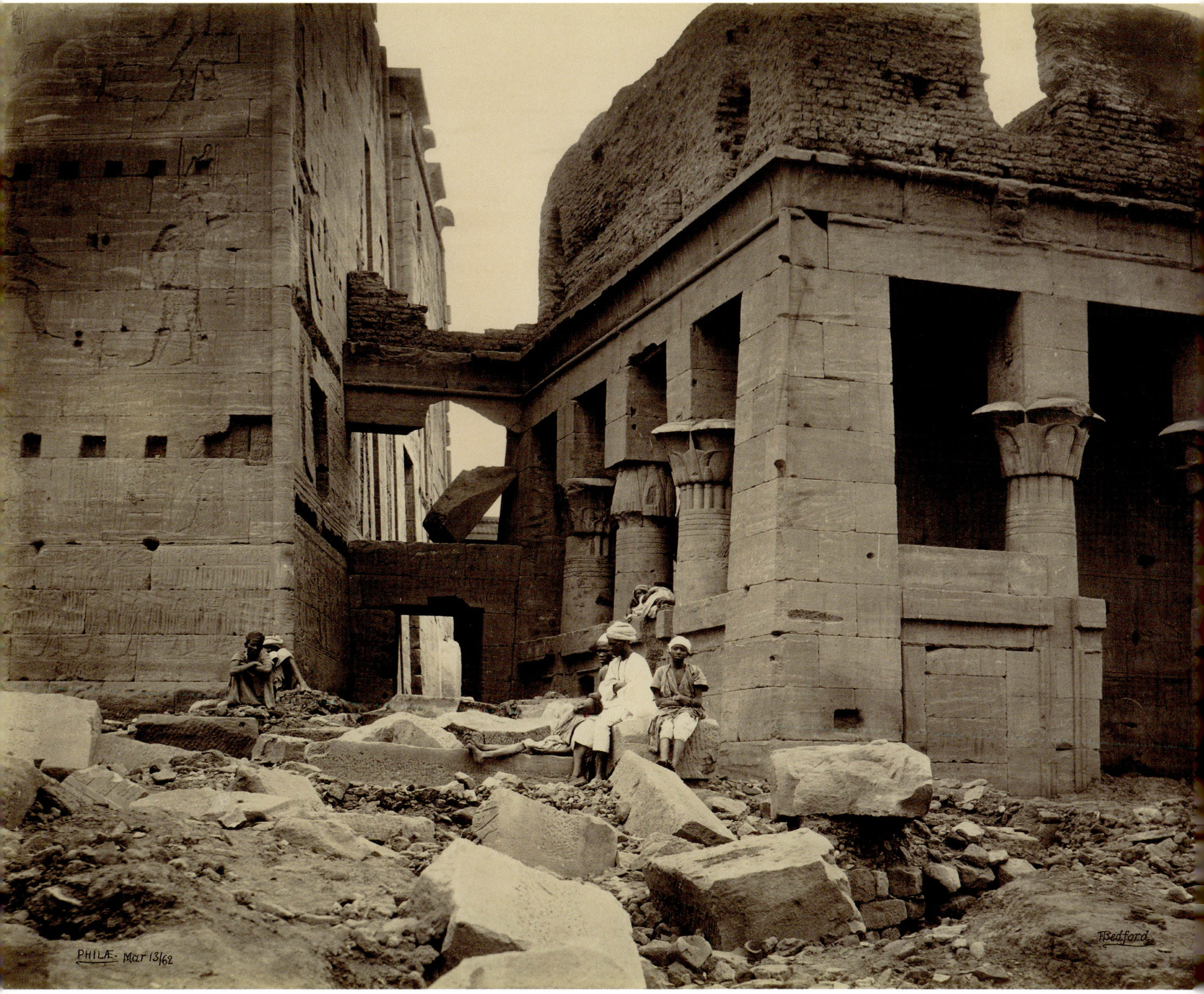

The Chapel of Horus, Temple of Isis, Philae, 13 March 1862

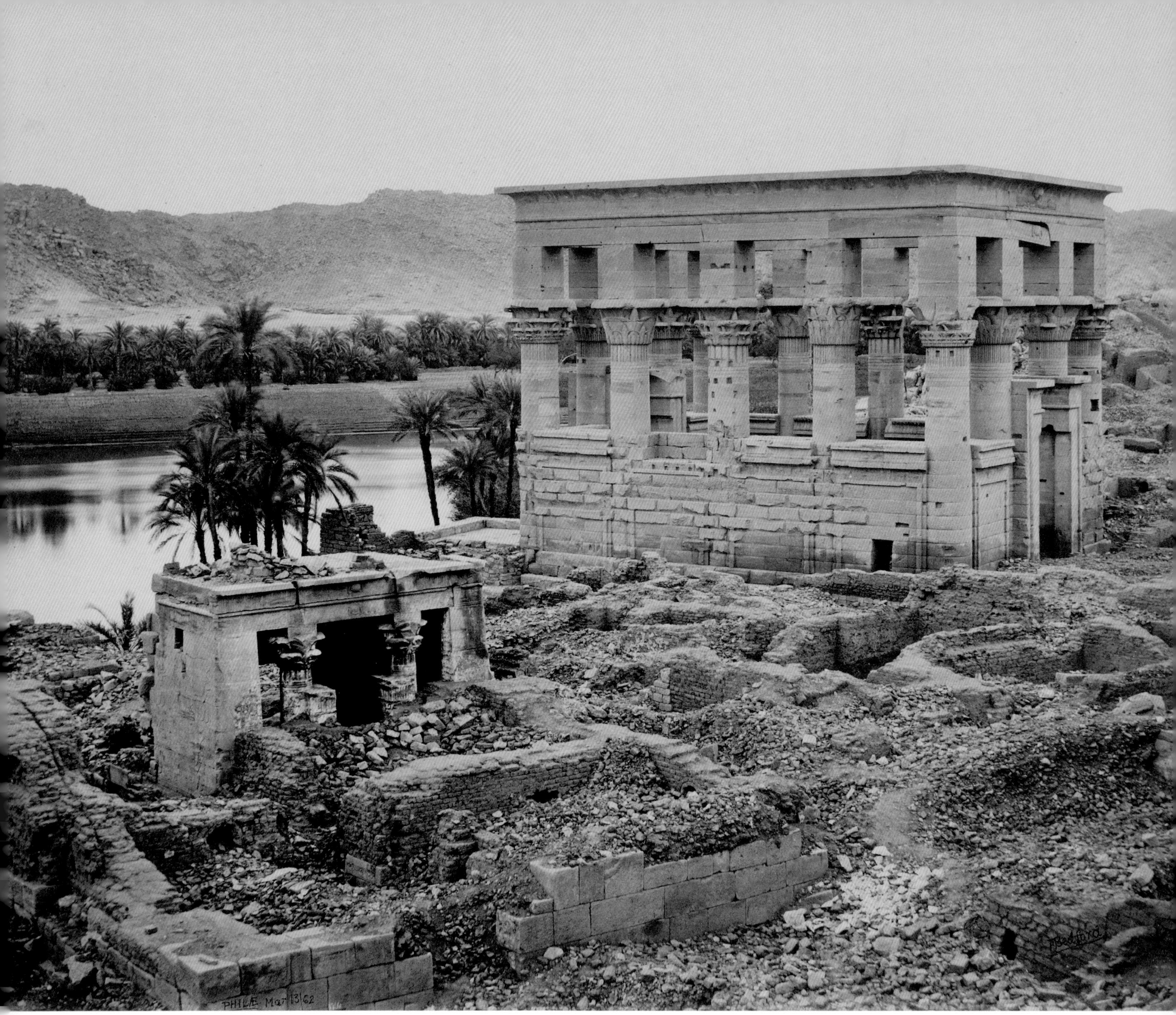

The Kiosk of Trajan, Philae, 13 March 1862

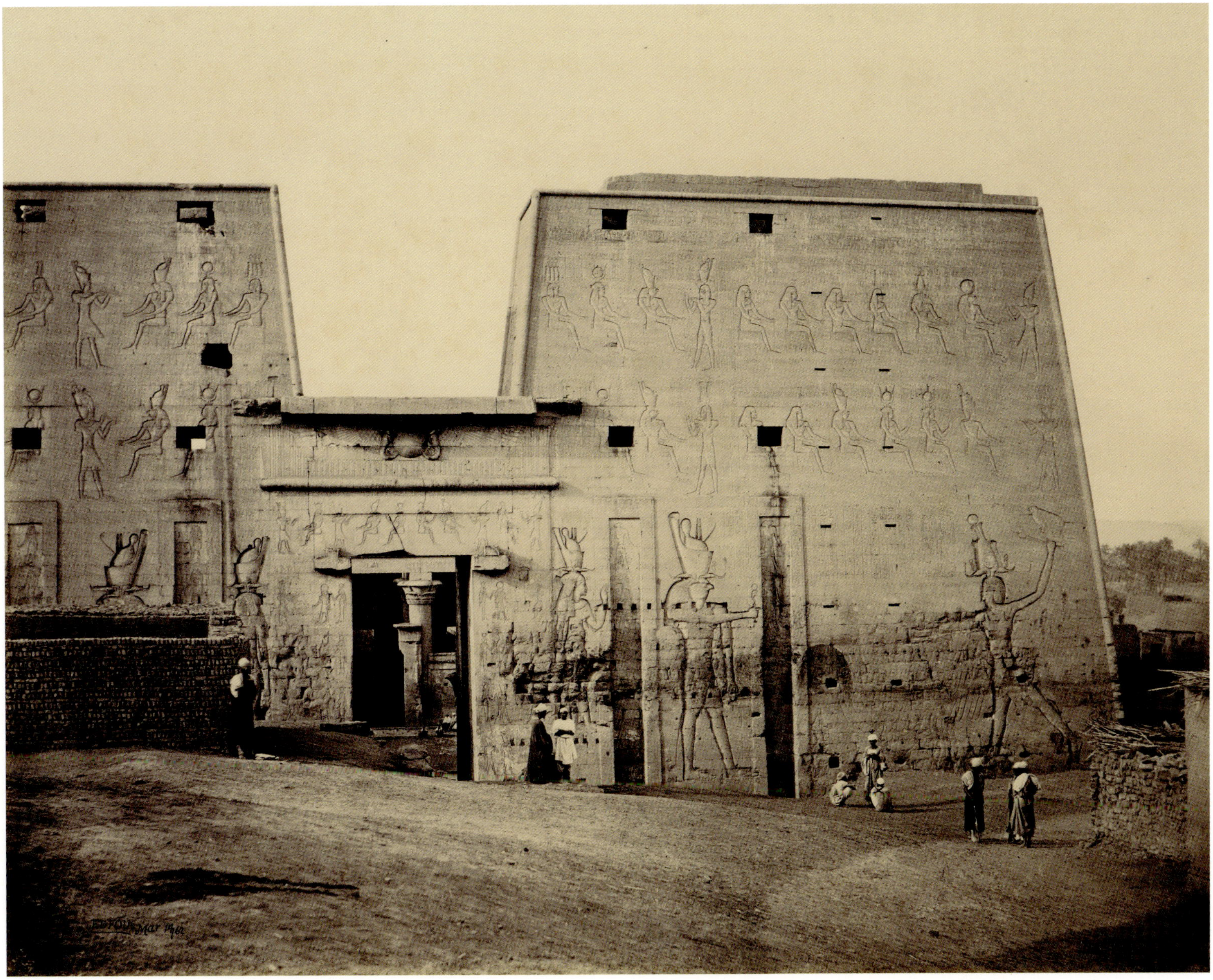

The pylon of the Temple of Horus, Edfu, 14 March 1862

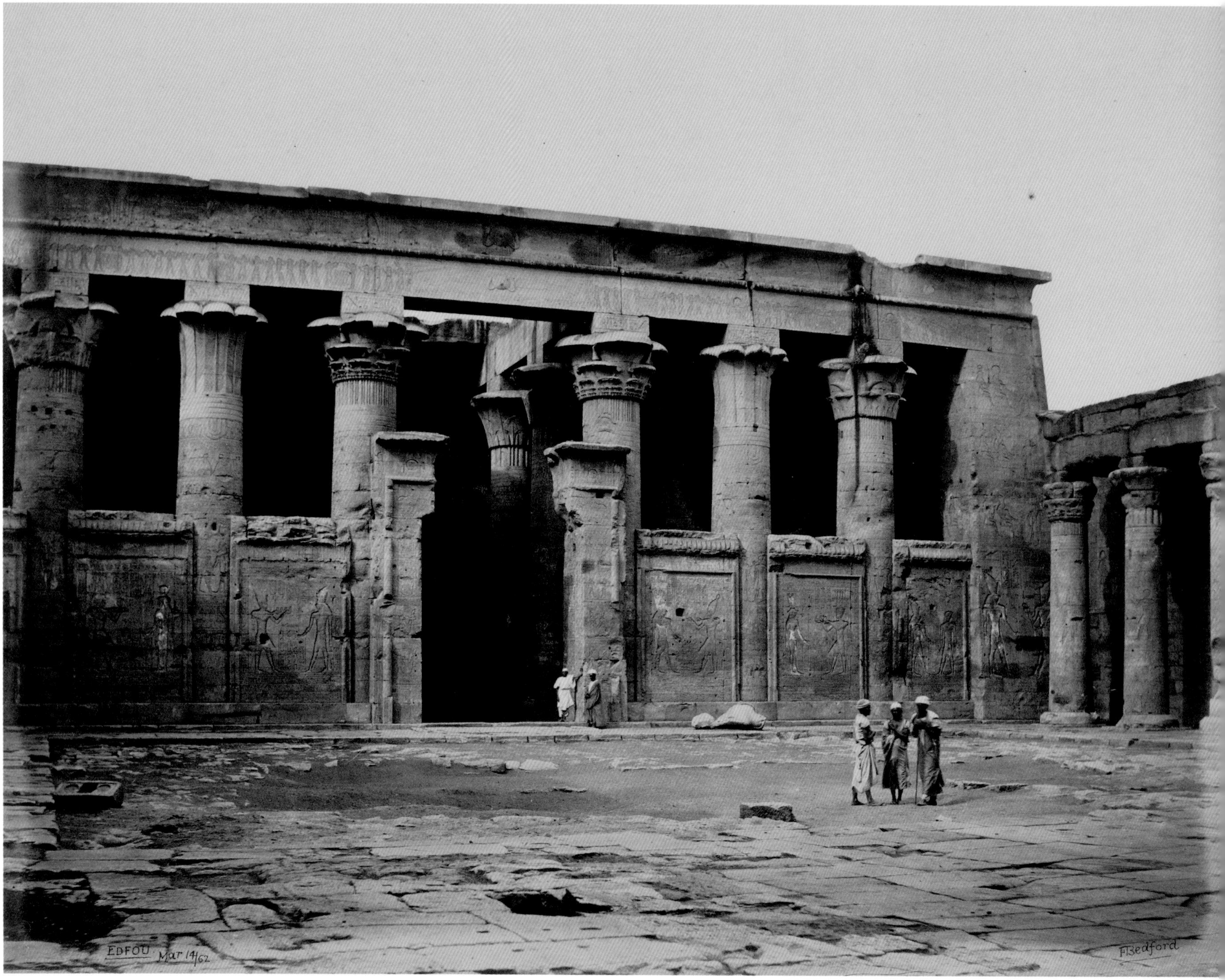

The Temple of Horus, Edfu, 14 March 1862

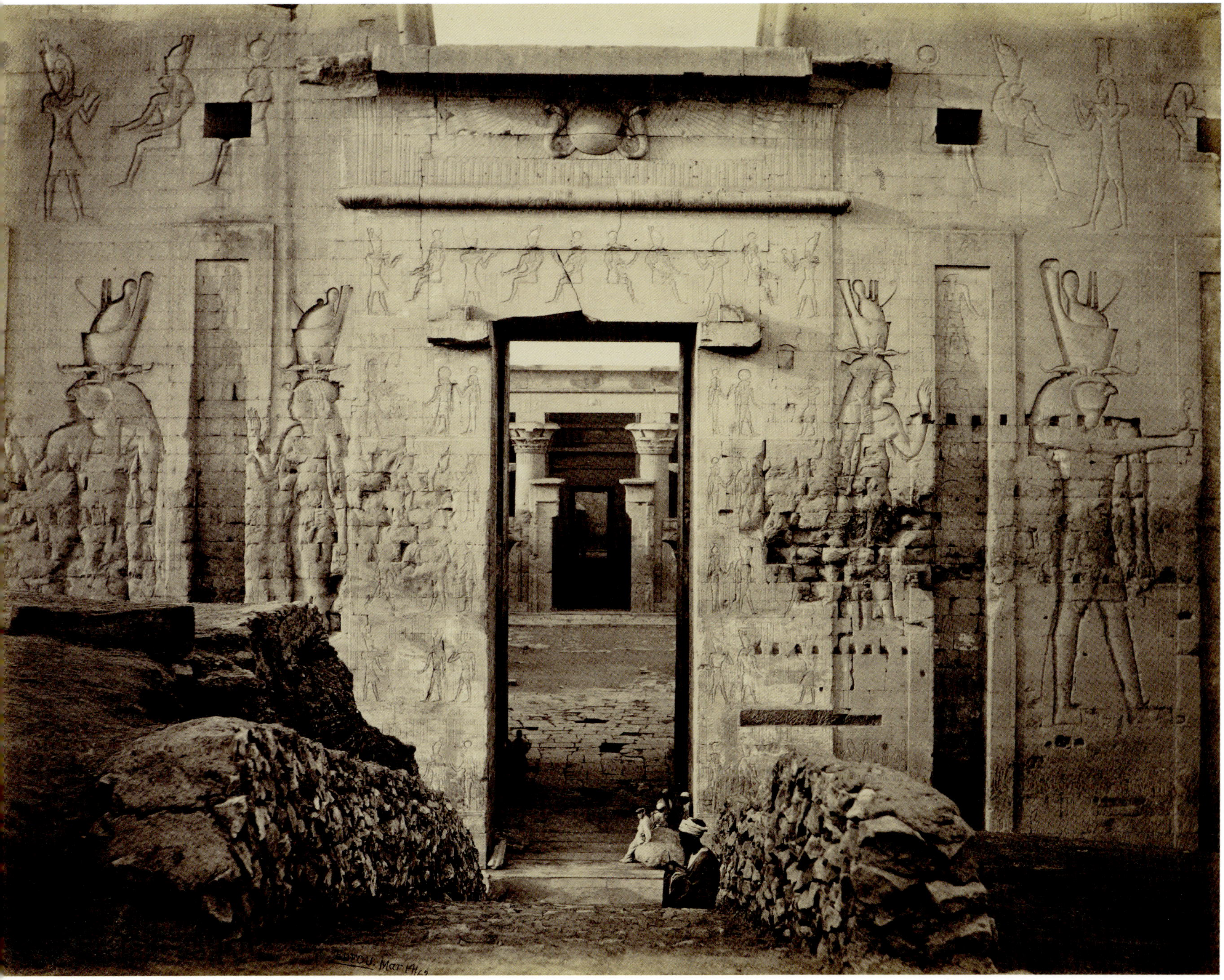

The Temple of Horus, Edfu, 14 March 1862

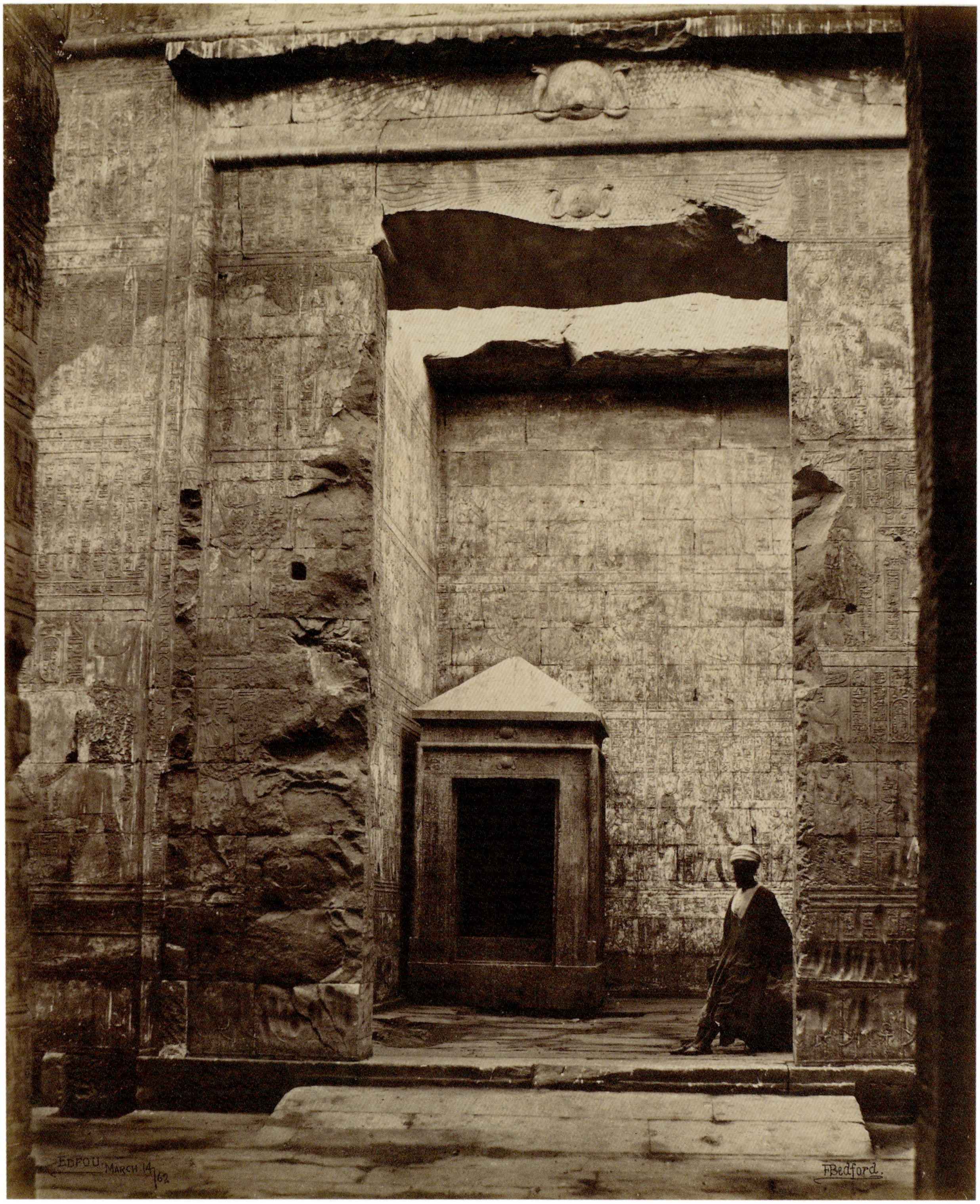

The shrine in the Temple of Horus, Edfu, 14 March 1862

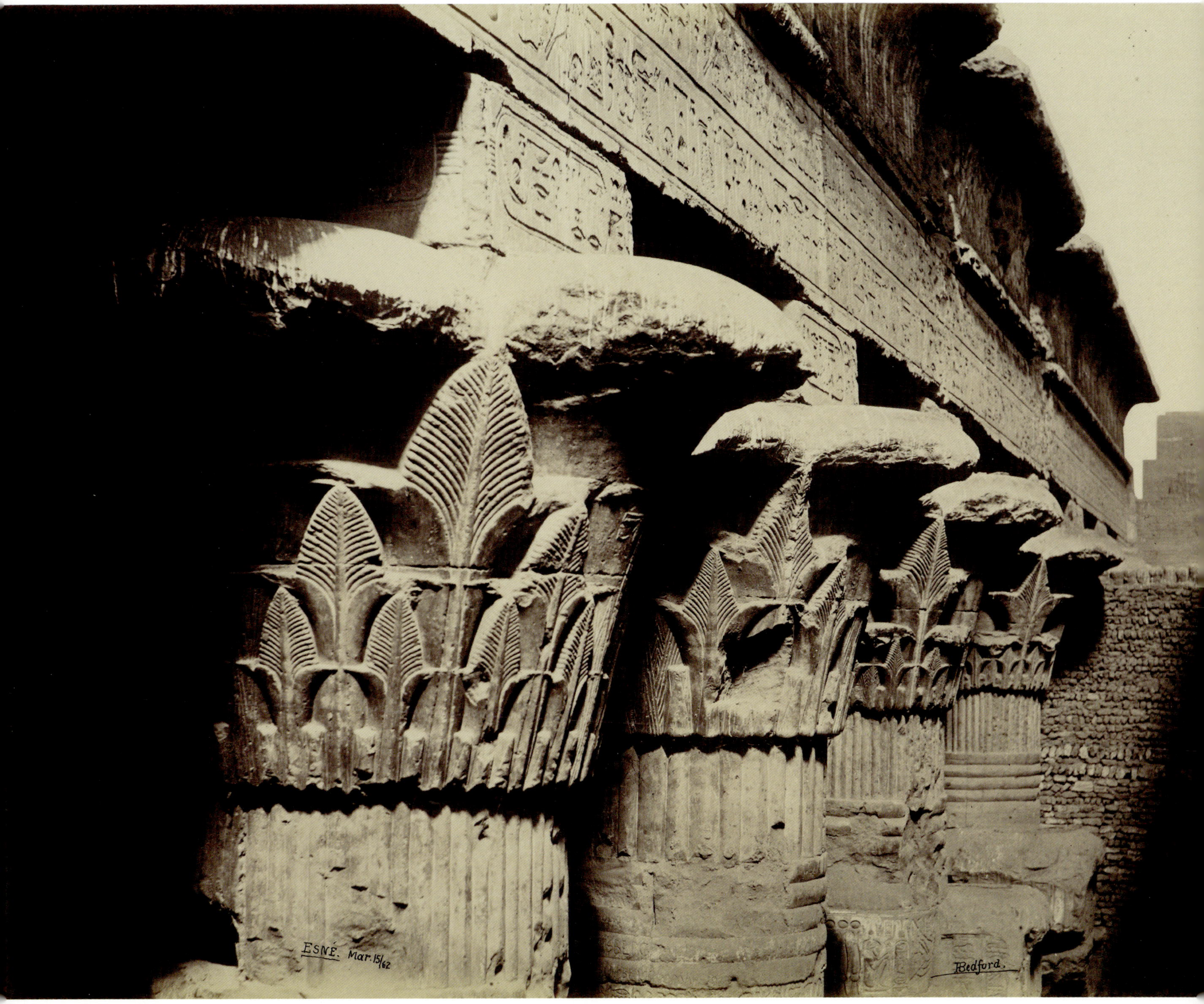

The Temple of Khnum, Esna, 15 March 1862

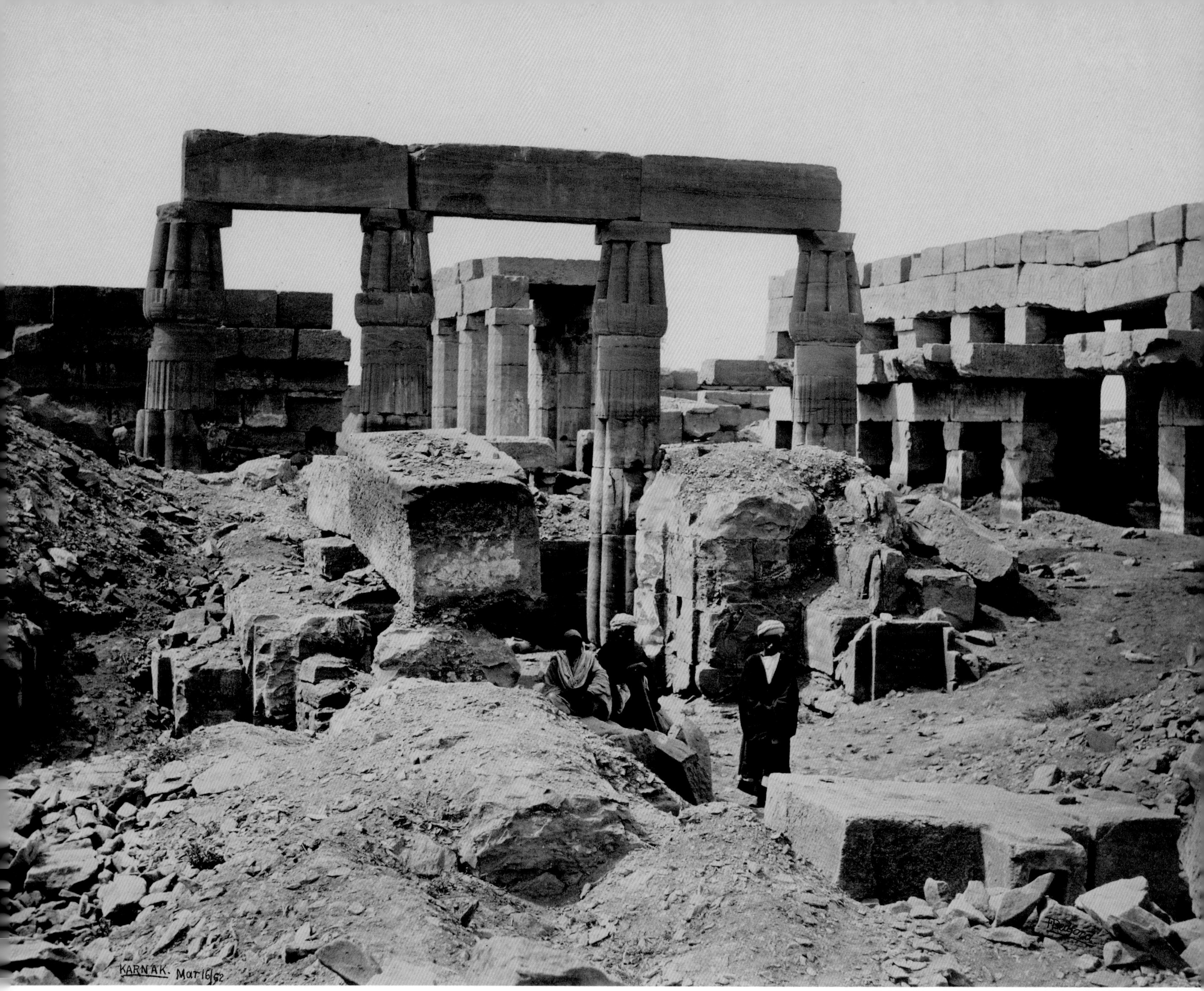

The Temple of Amun, Karnak, 16 March 1862

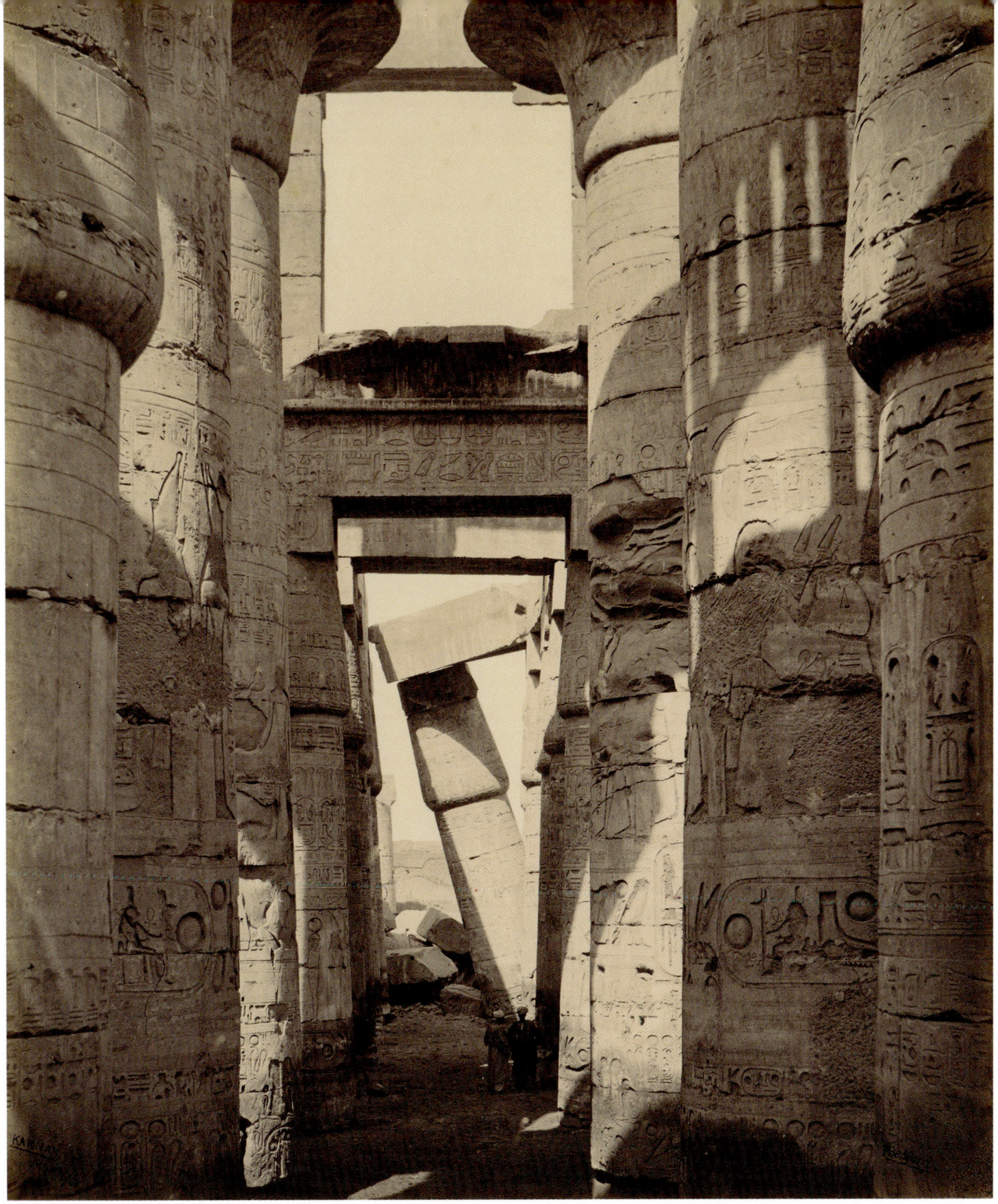

The Hypostyle Hall, Temple of Amun, Karnak, 16 March 1862

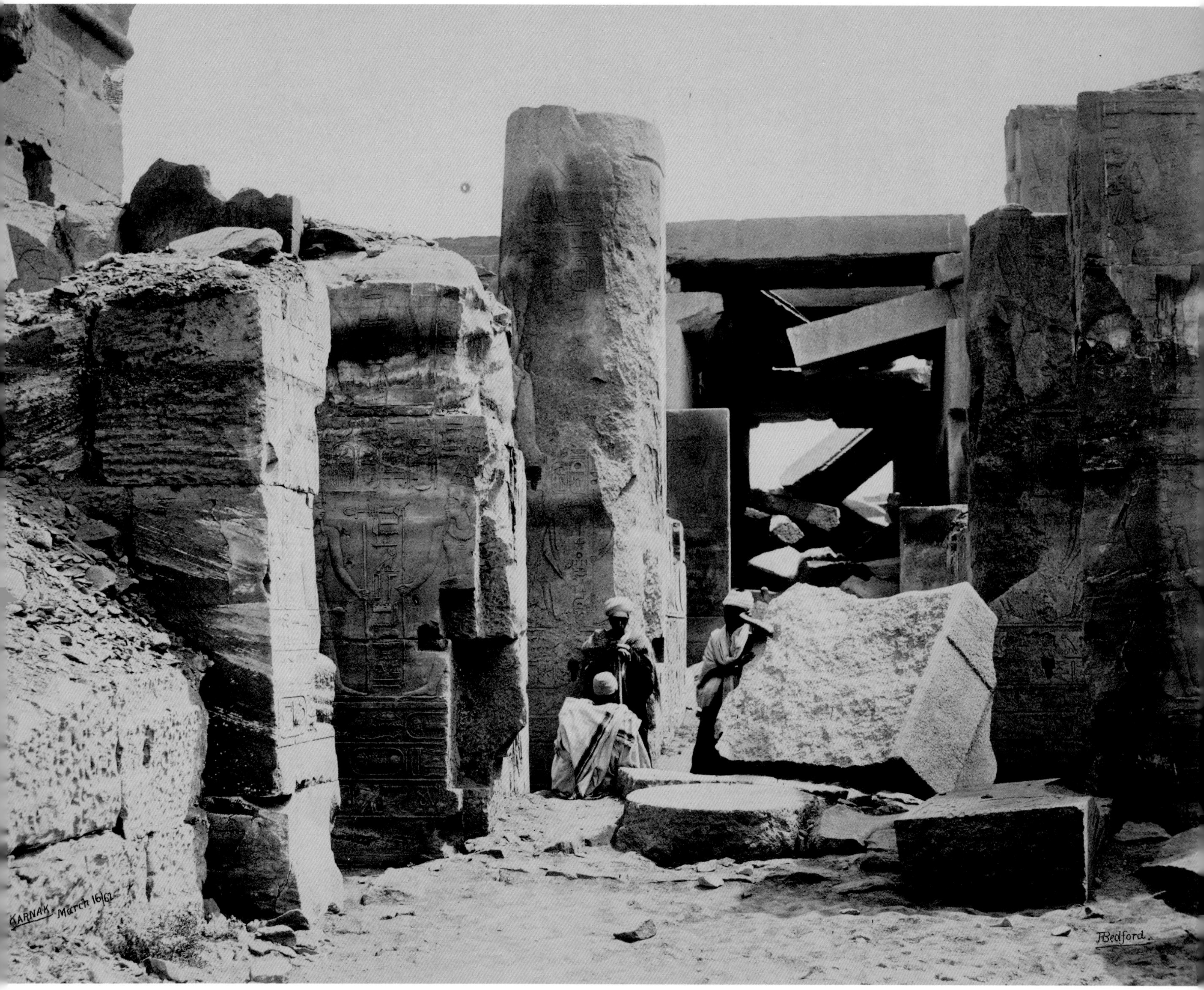

The Temple of Amun, Karnak, 16 March 1862

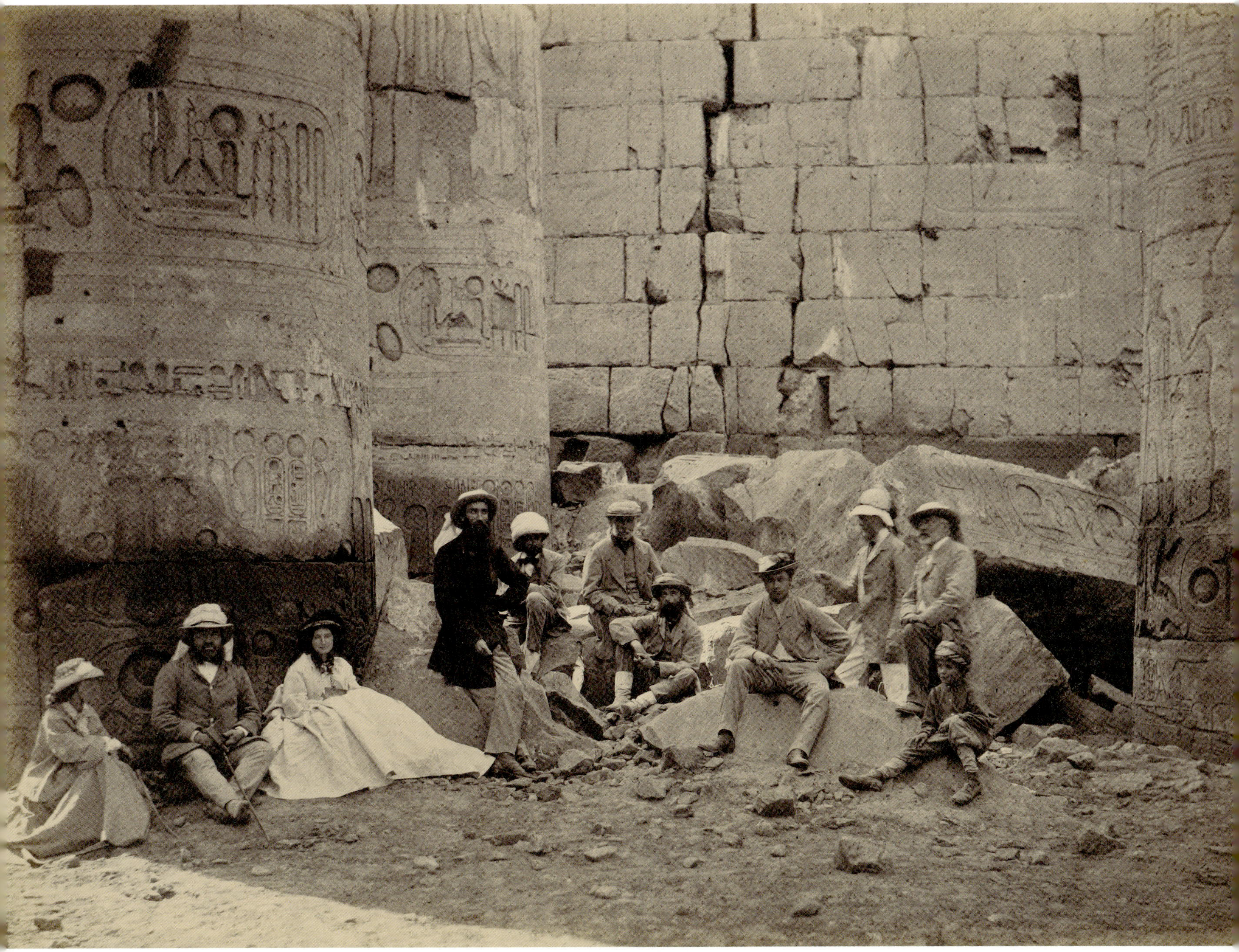

The Prince of Wales with his group in the Hypostyle Hall, Temple of Amun, Karnak, 16 March 1862

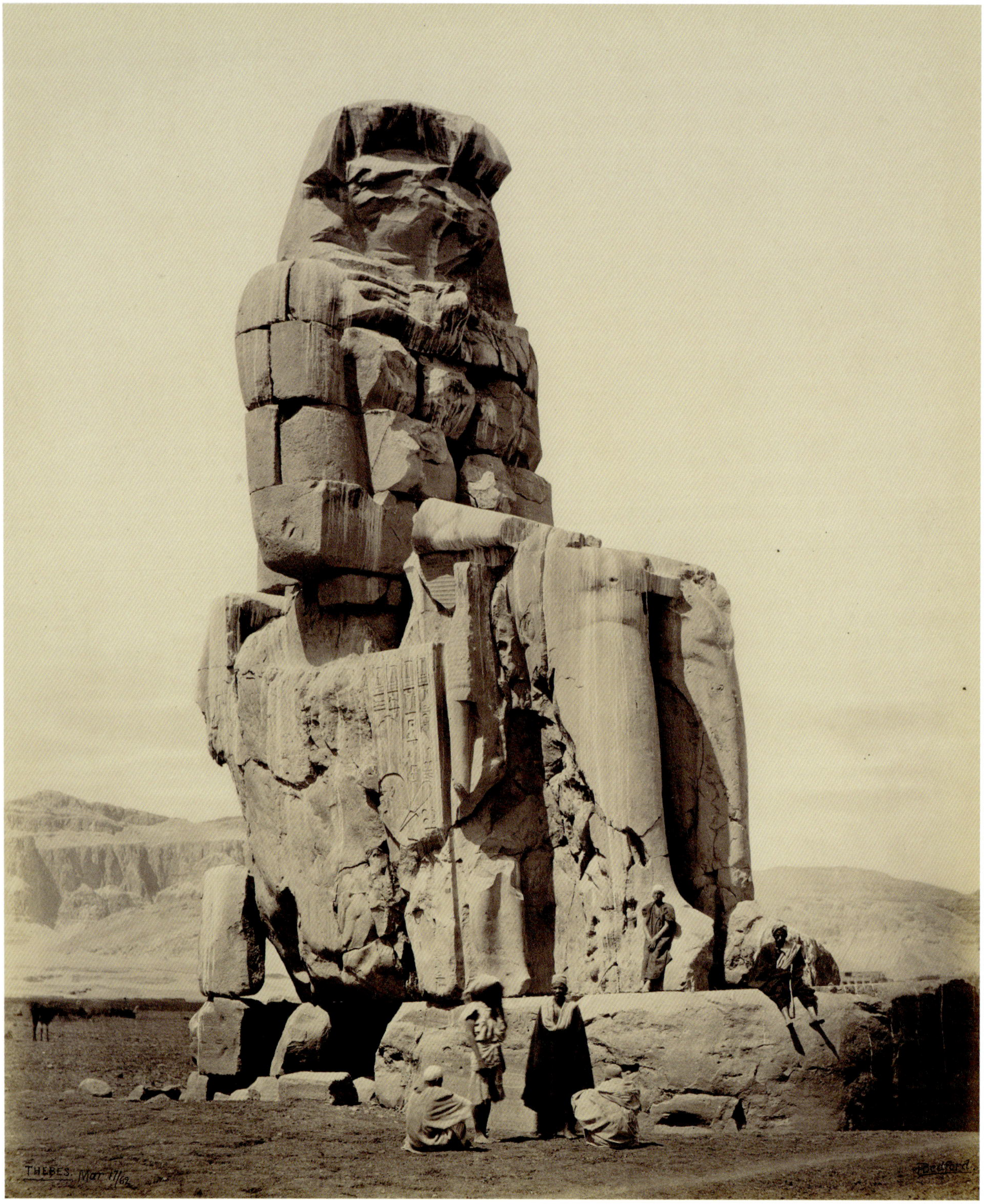

The northern Colossus of Memnon, Luxor West Bank, 17 March 1862

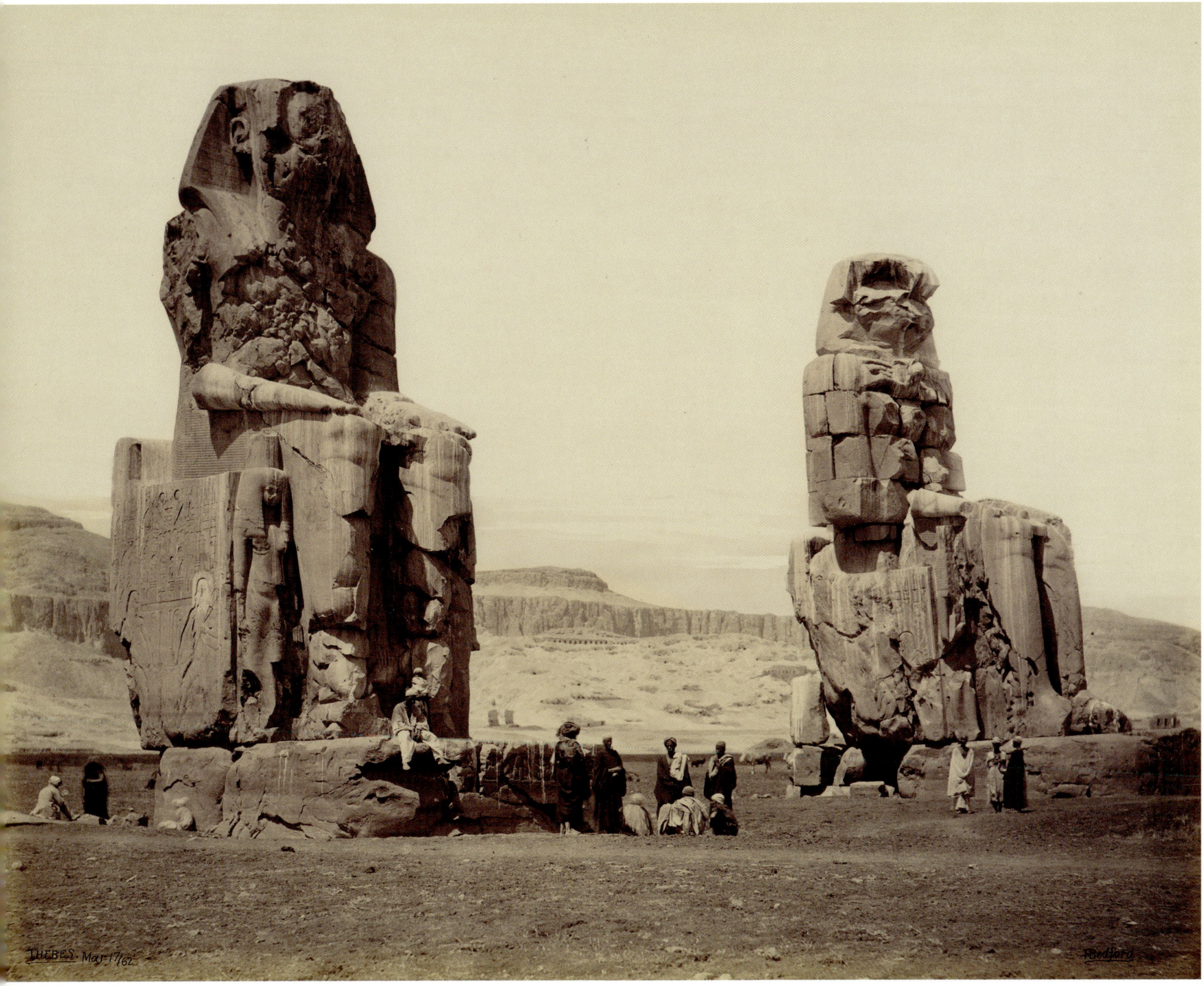

The Colossi of Memnon, Luxor West Bank, 17 March 1862

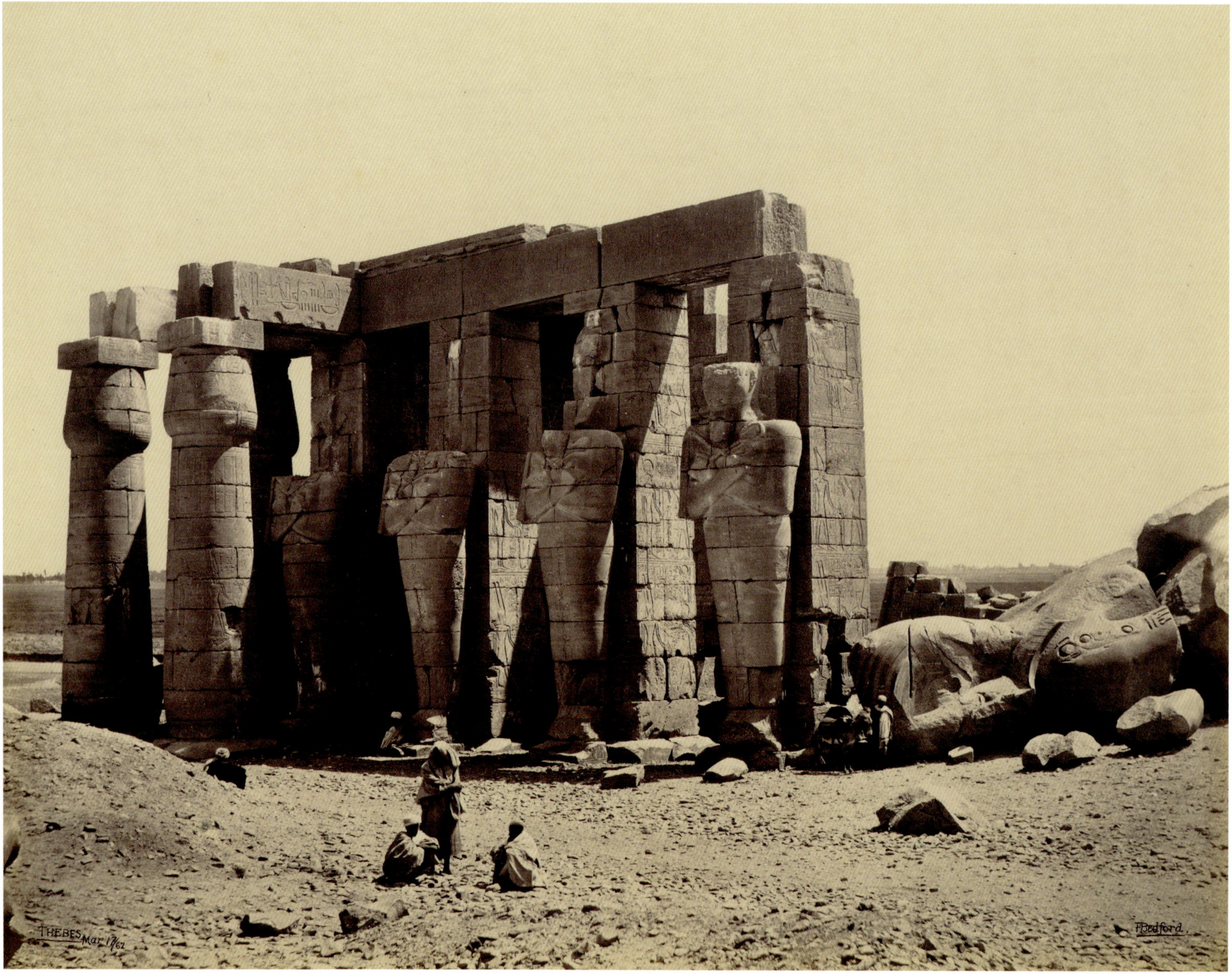

The head of the fallen colossus of Ramesses II, the Ramesseum, Luxor West Bank, 17 March 1862

"We rode over first to see the temple of Rameses II . . . it is the finest, I think I have seen & is very extensive. We remained there some time & lunched there."
Prince of Wales's Journal, 17 March 1862

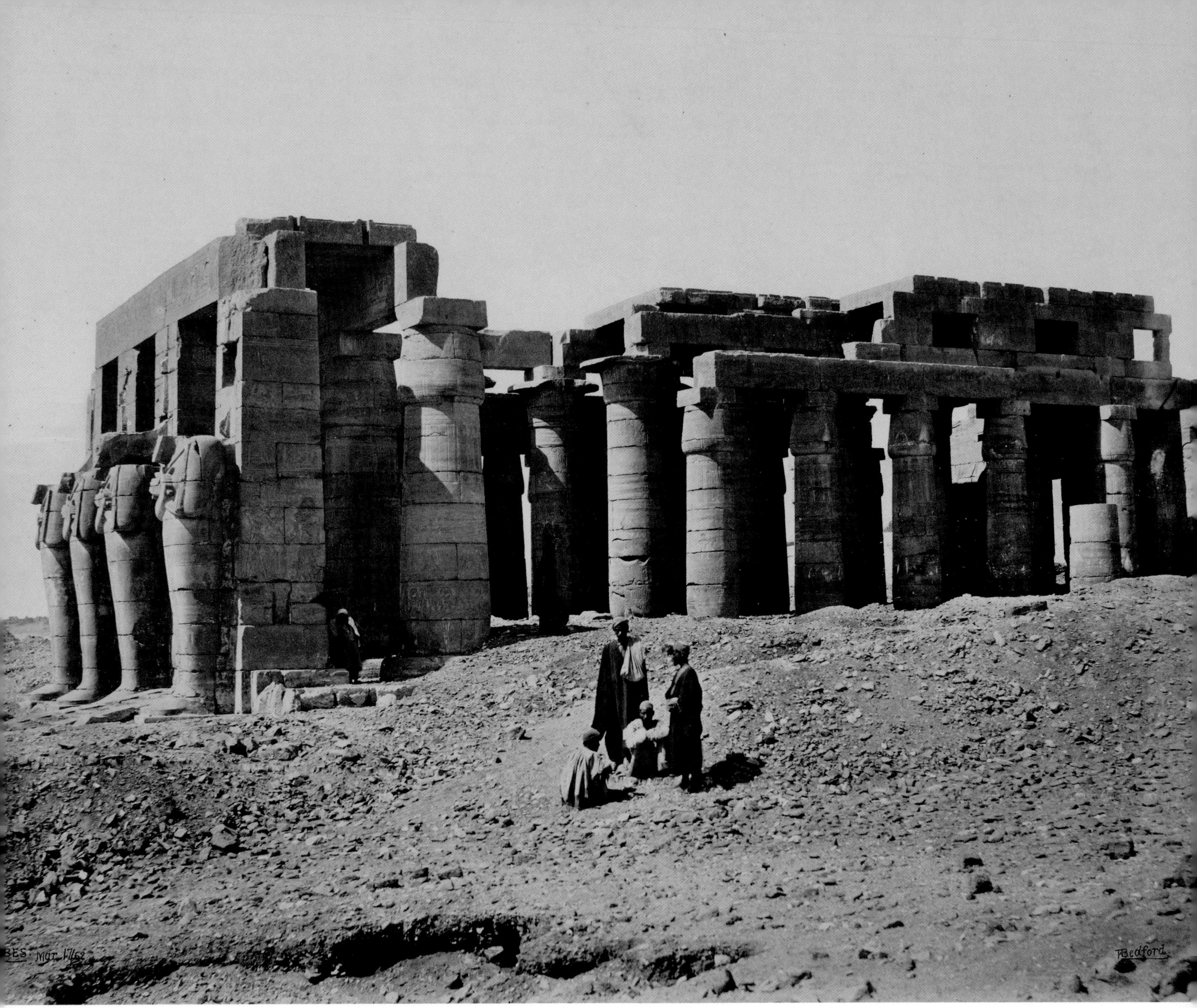

The Ramesseum, Luxor West Bank, 17 March 1862

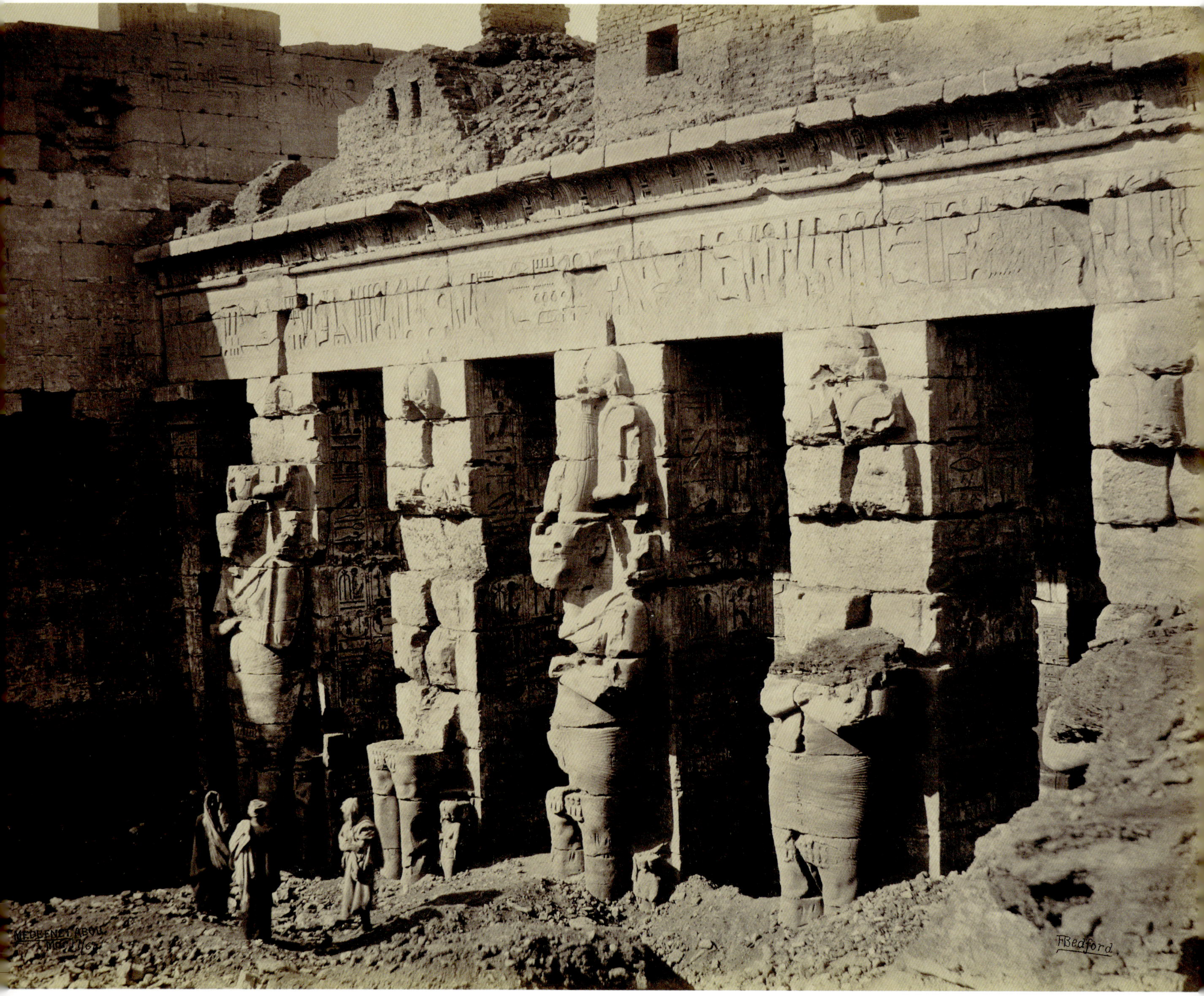

Medinat Habu, Luxor West Bank, 17 March 1862

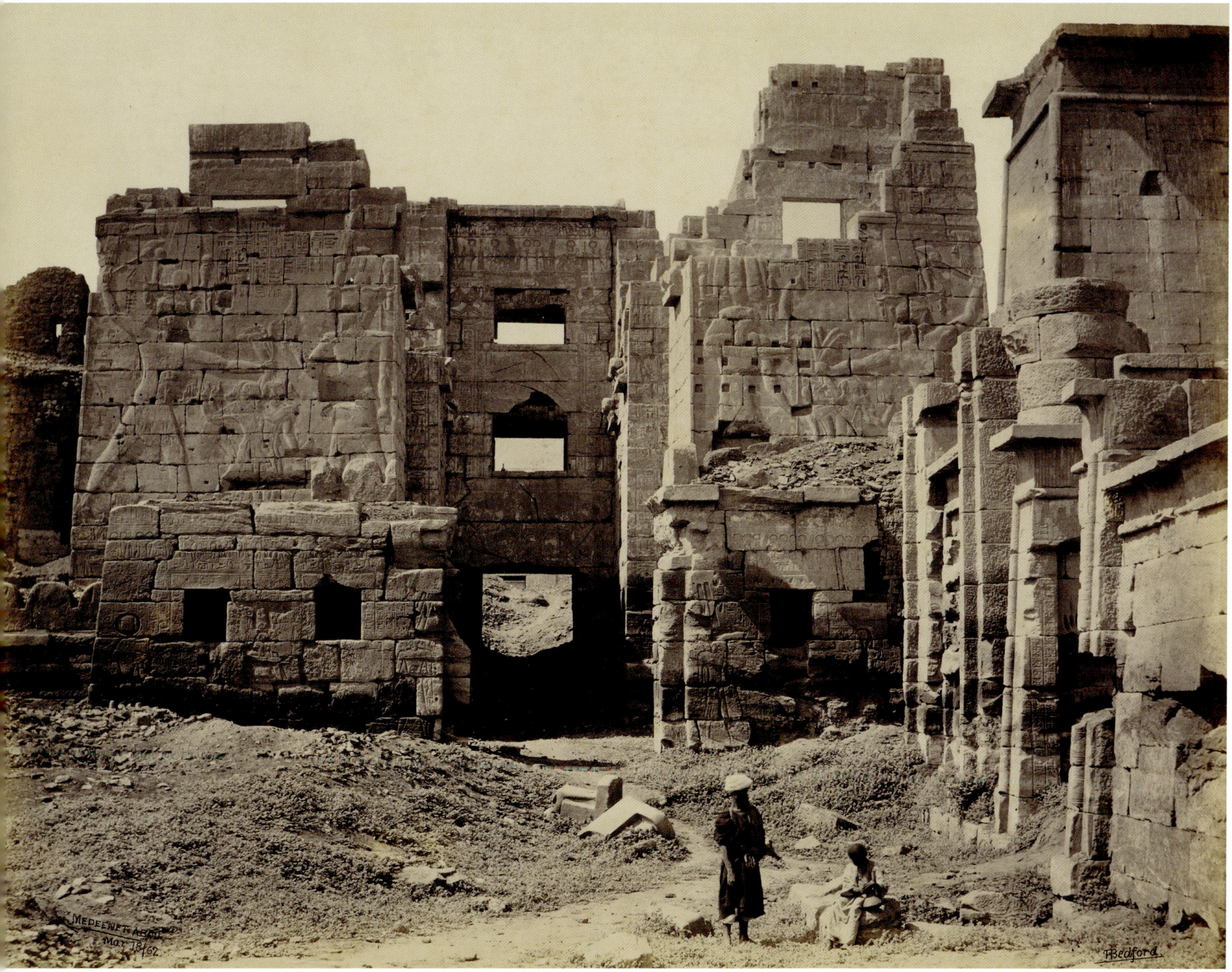

Medinat Habu, Luxor West Bank, 18 March 1862

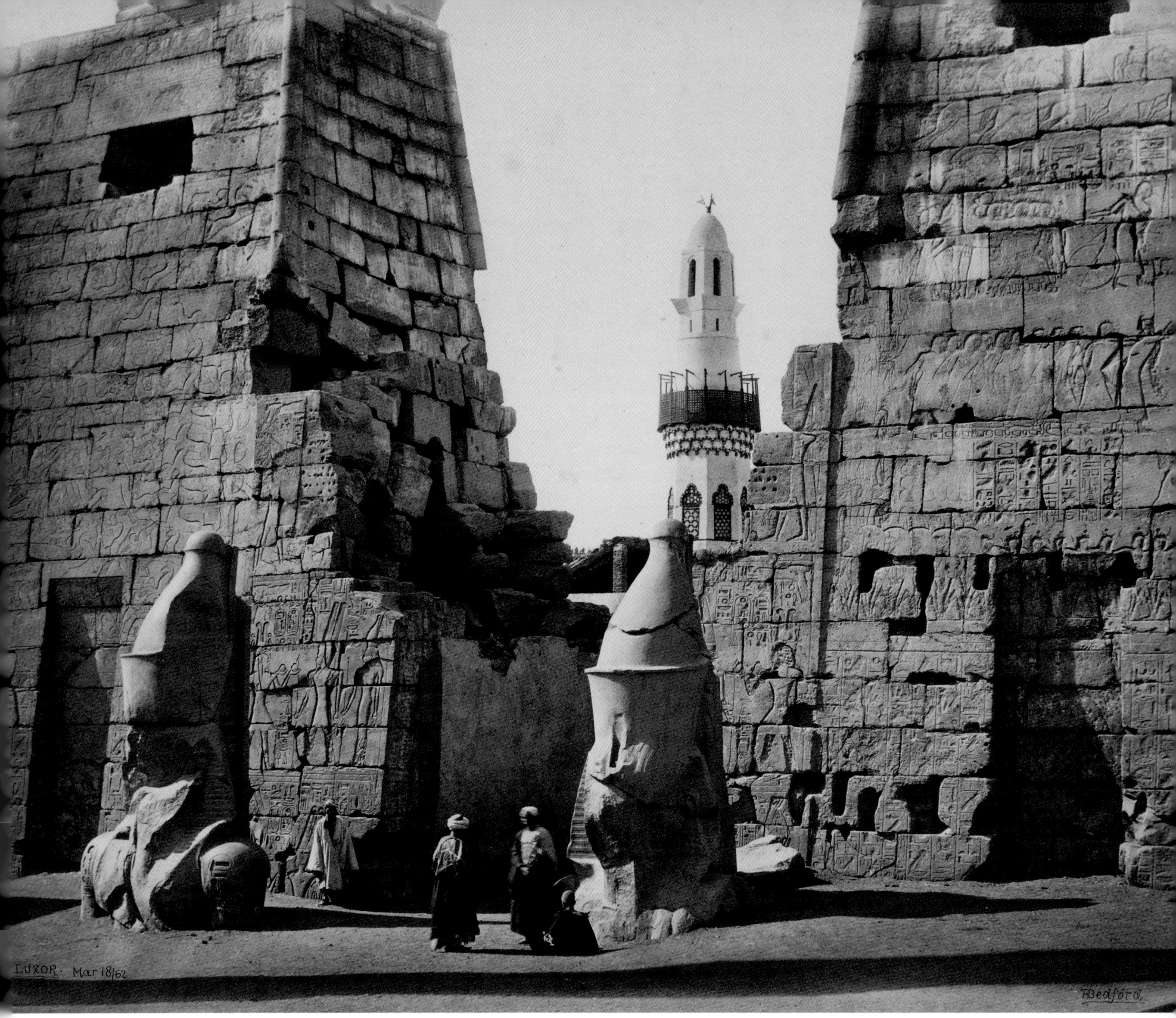

The first pylon, Luxor Temple, 18 March 1862

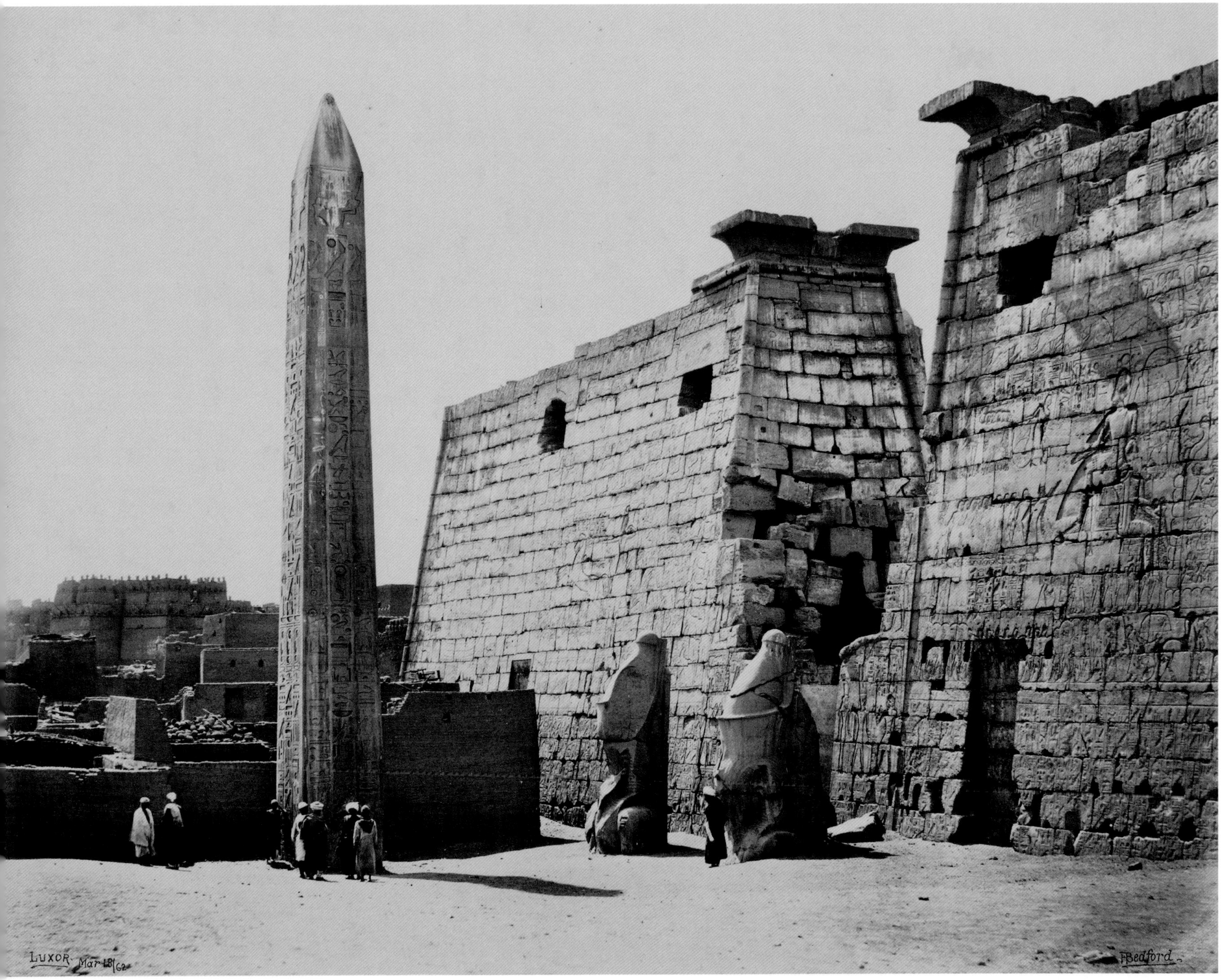

The first pylon and obelisk, Luxor Temple, 18 March 1862

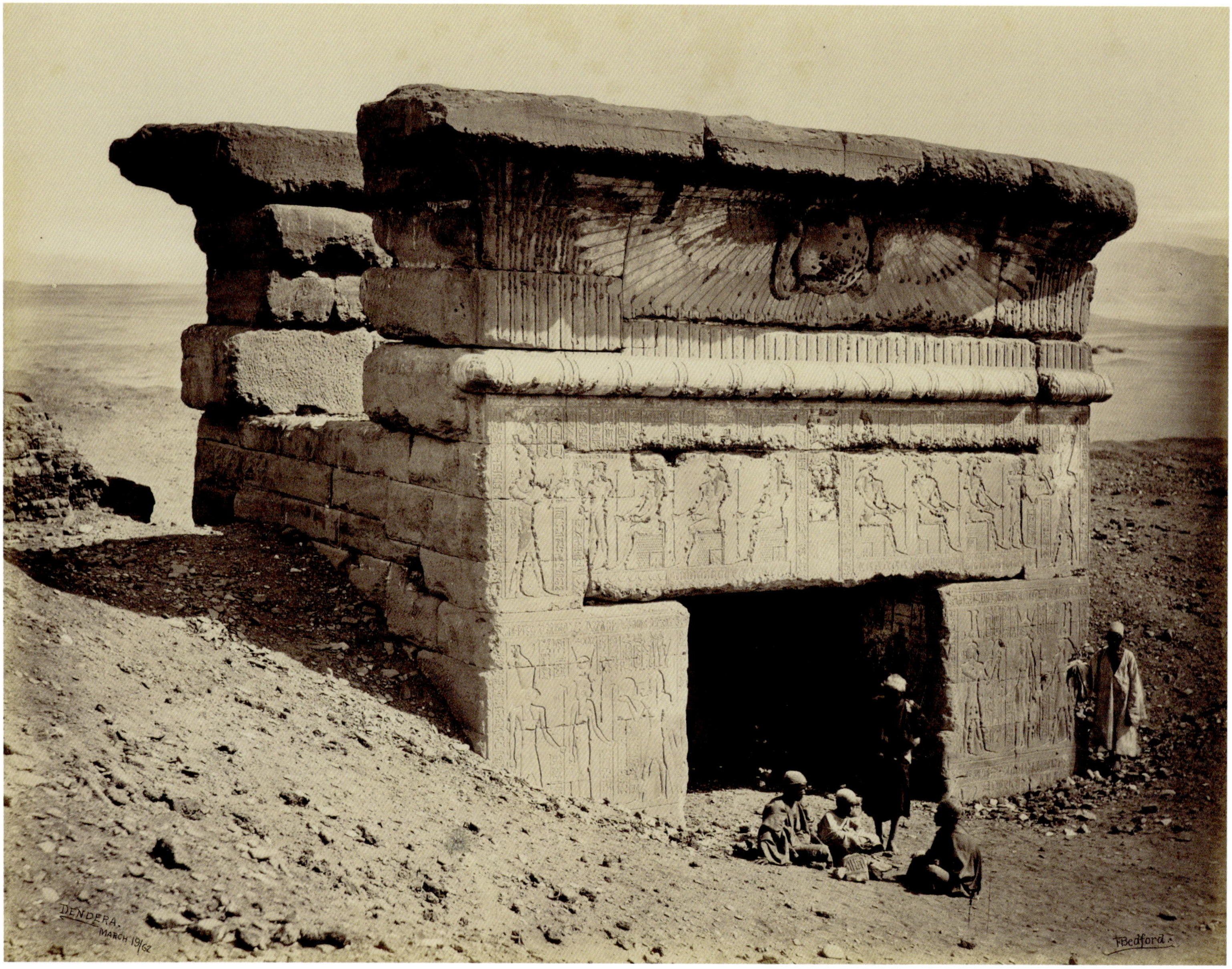

The Temple of Hathor, Dendera, 19 March 1862

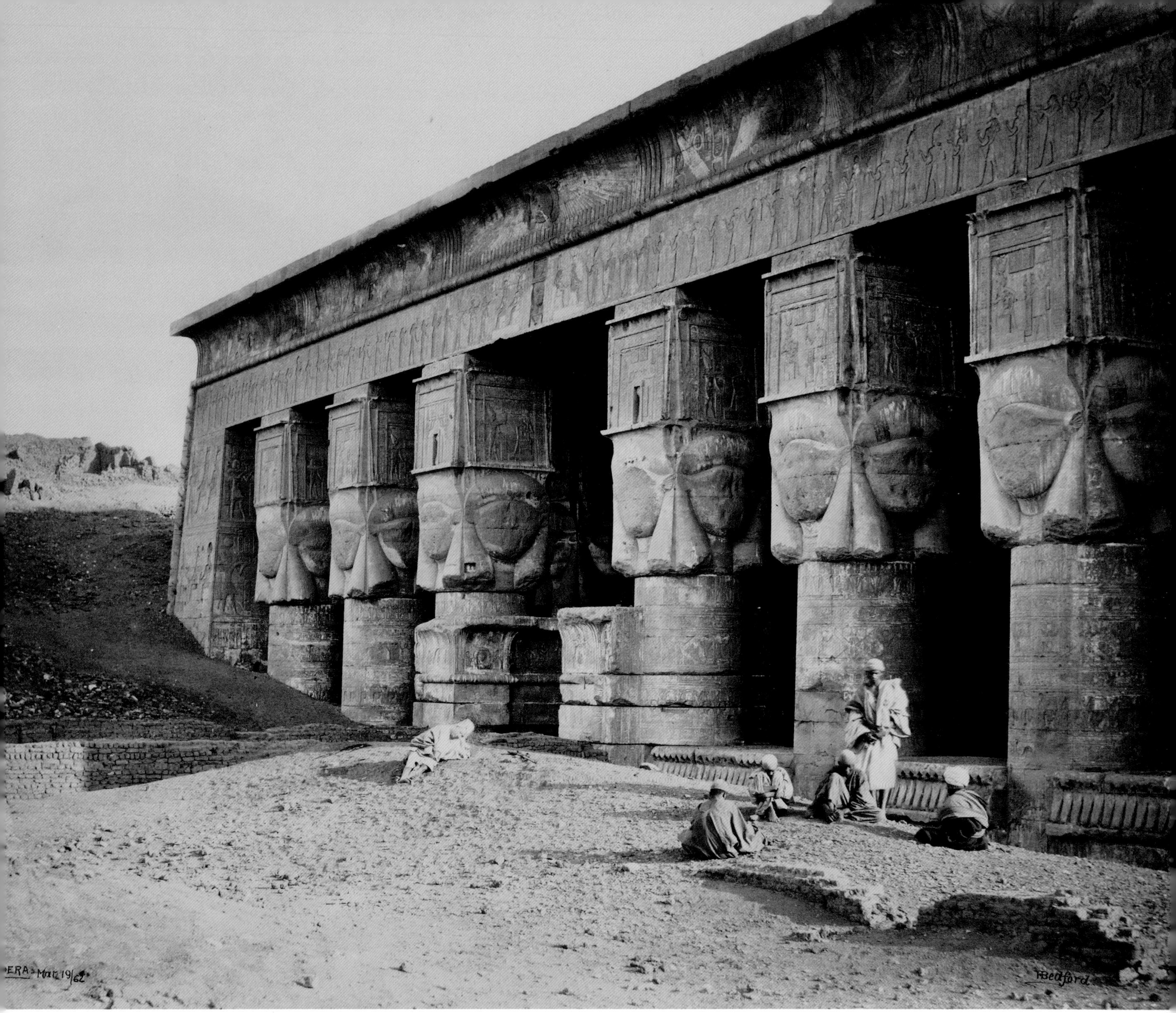

The Temple of Hathor, Dendera, 19 March 1862

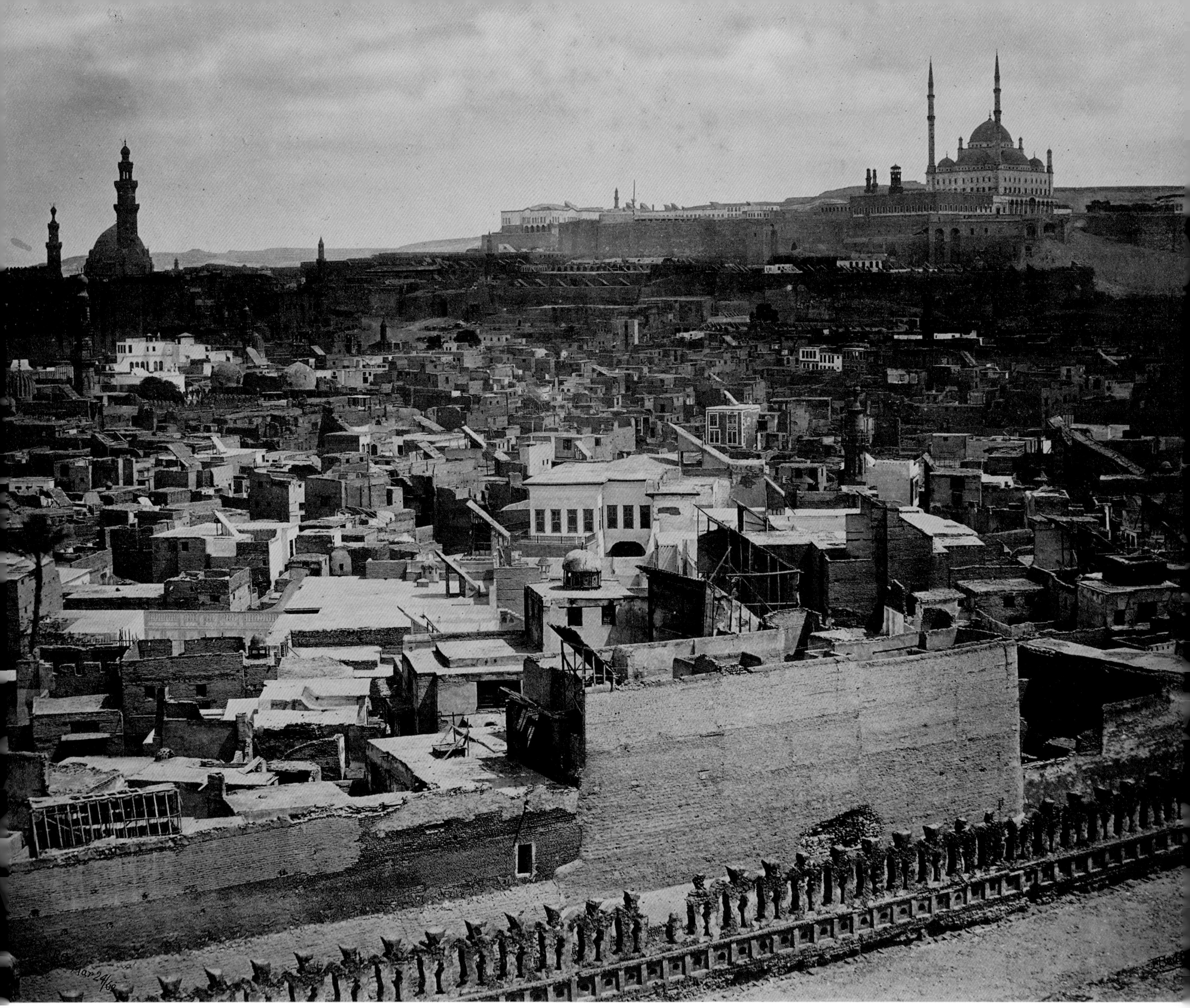

The Citadel and the Mosque of Sultan Hassan from the Mosque of Ibn Tulun, Cairo, 24 March 1862

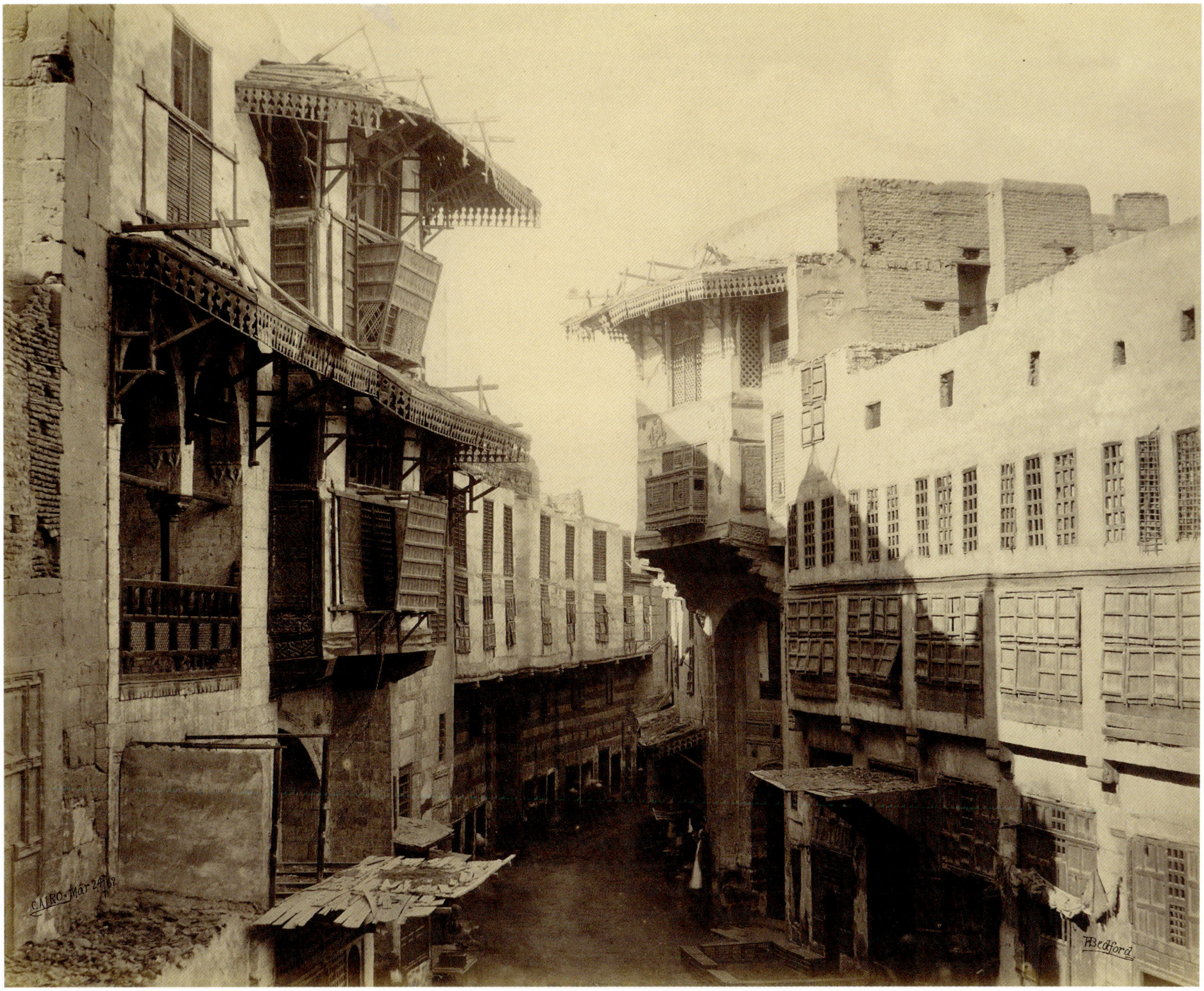

A street in Cairo, 24 March 1862

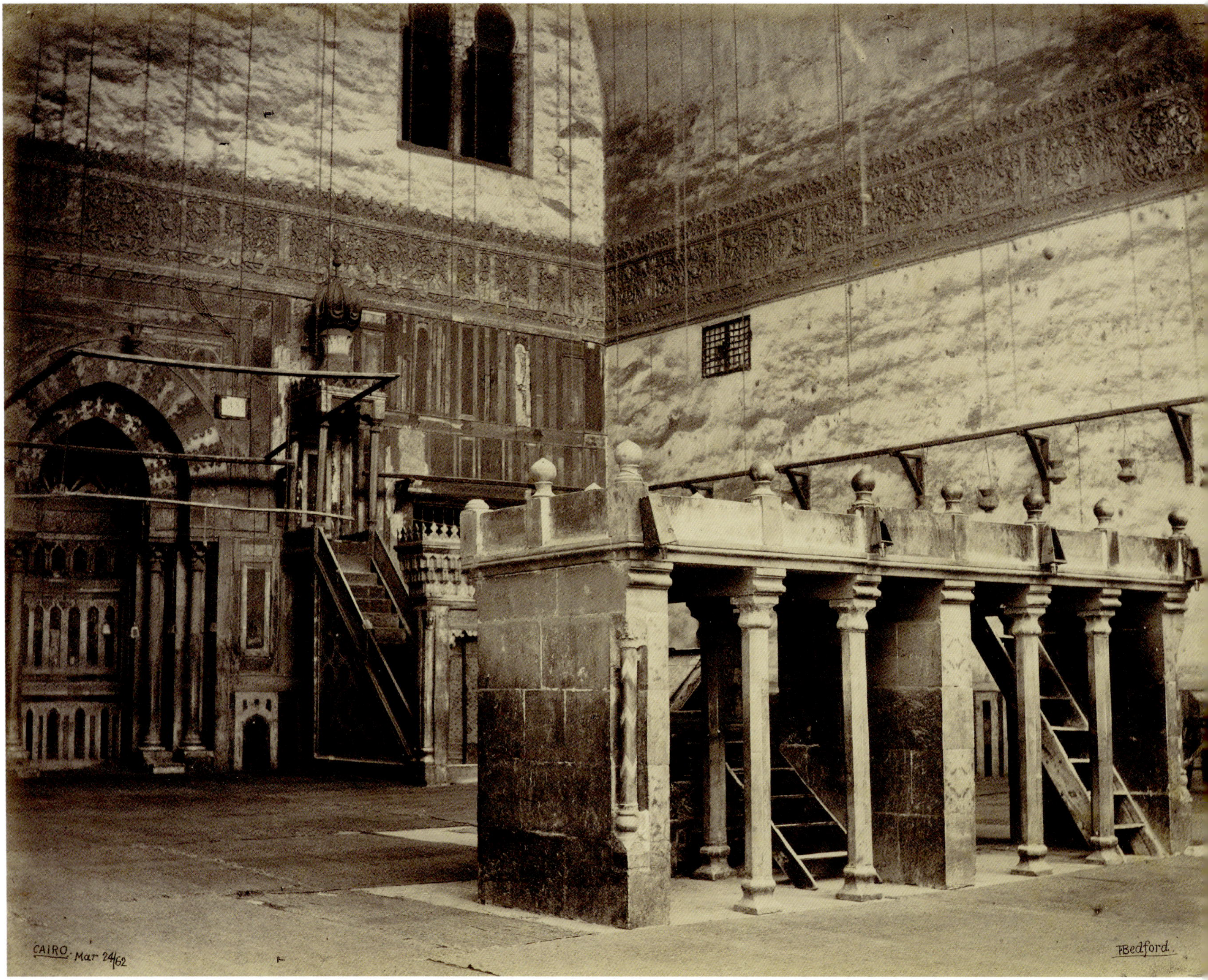

The Mosque of Sultan Hassan, Cairo, 24 March 1862

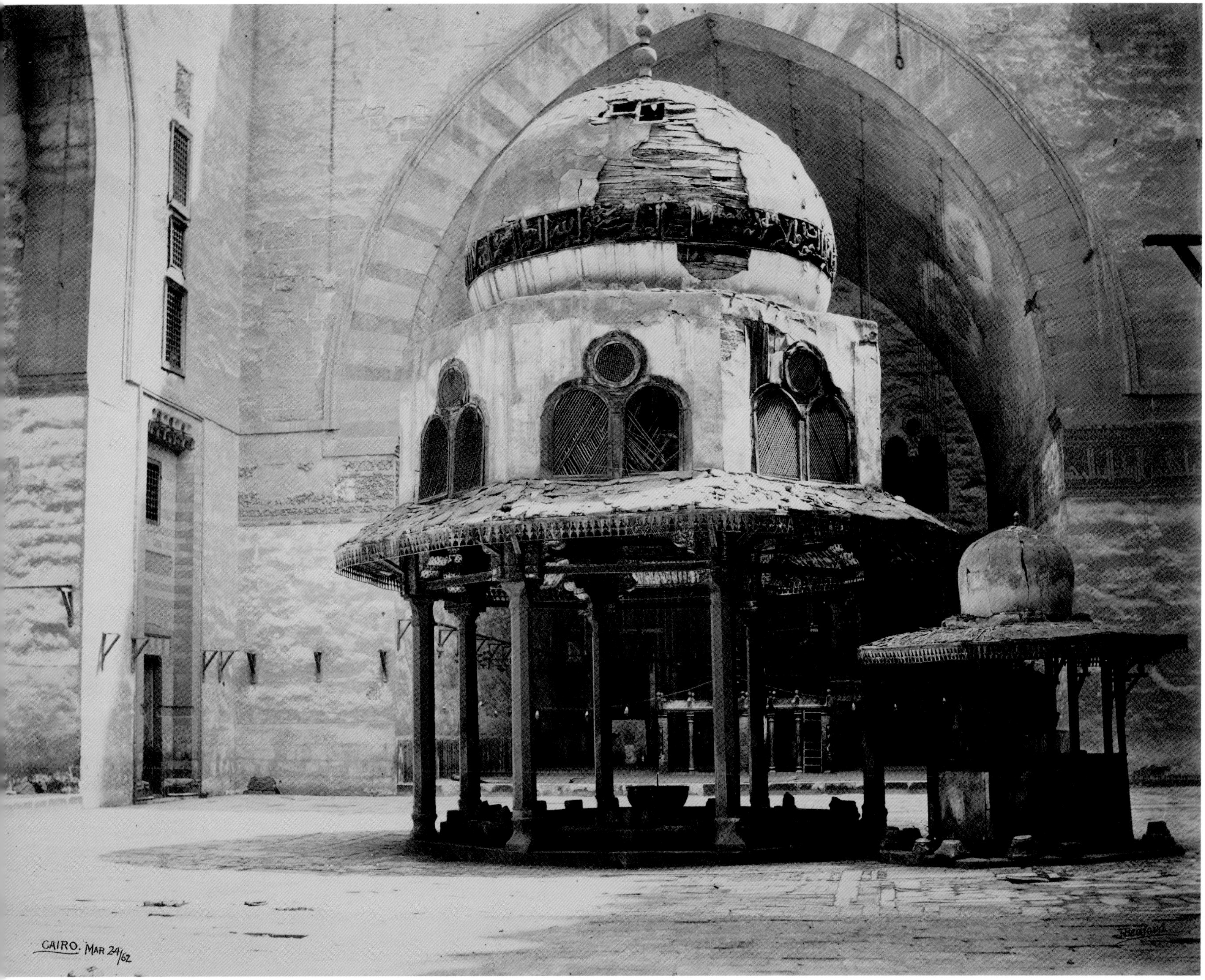

The Mosque of Sultan Hassan, Cairo, 24 March 1862

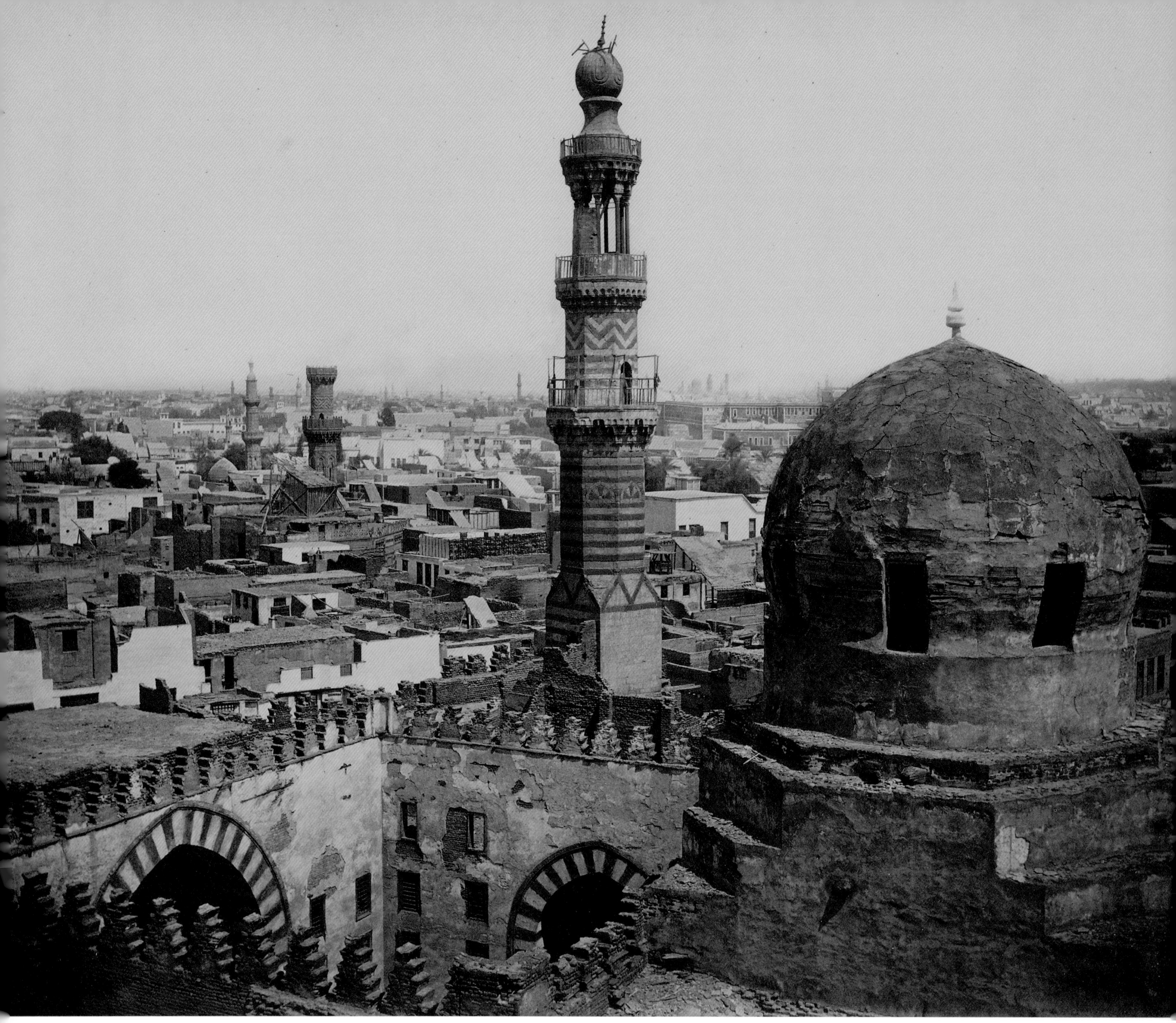

The Mosque–Madrasa of Sarghatmish, Cairo, 25 March 1862

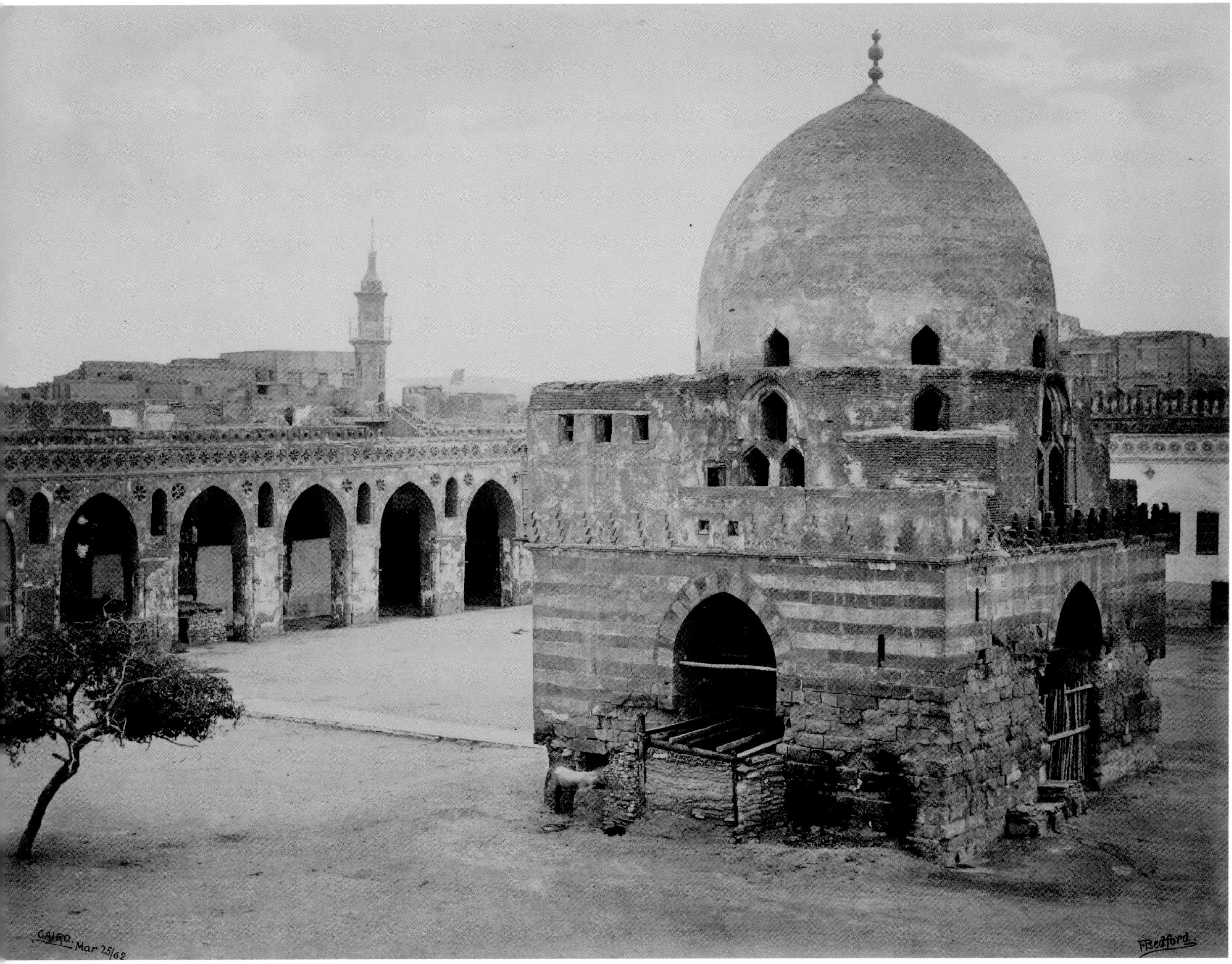

The Mosque of Ibn Tulun, Cairo, 25 March 1862

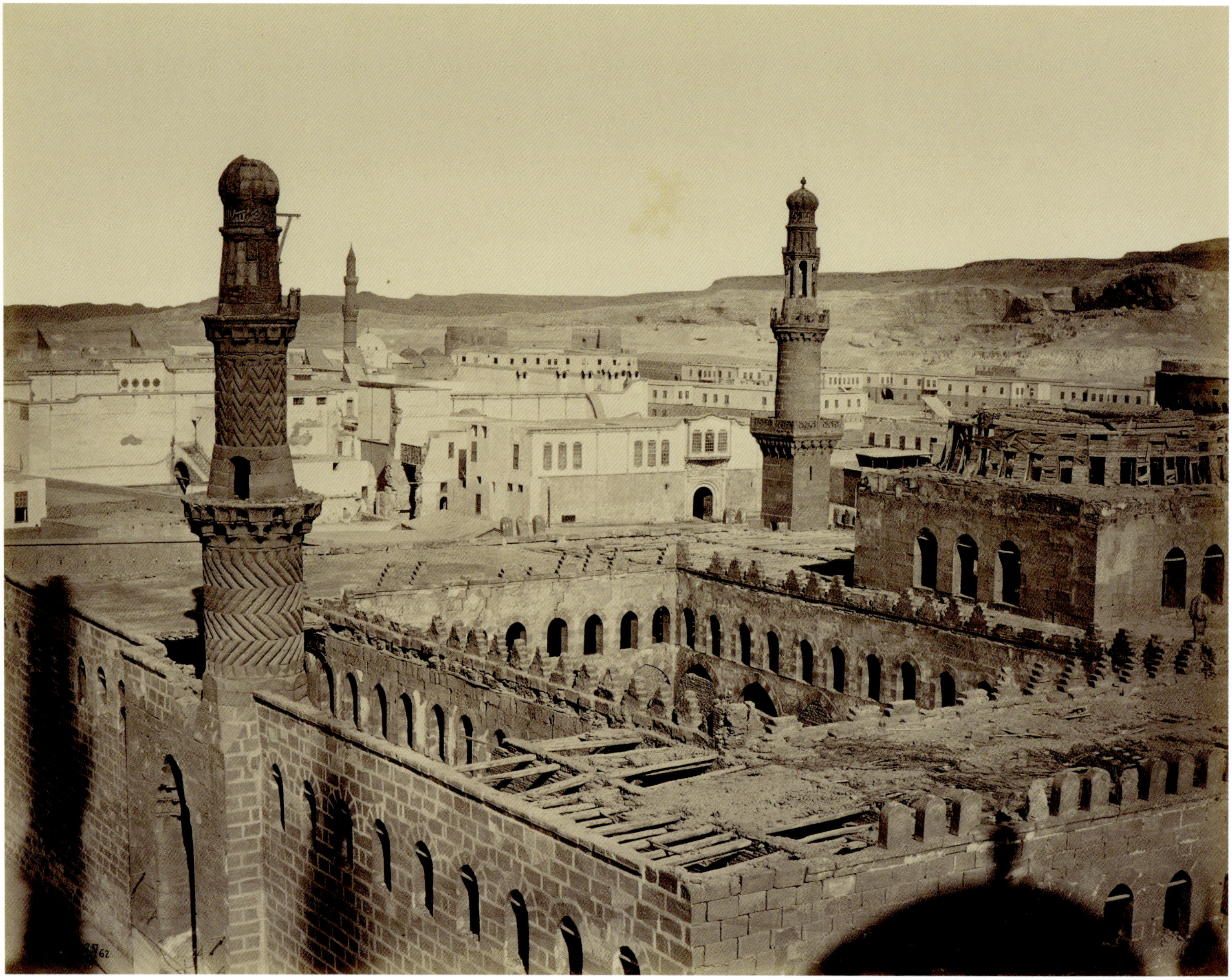

The Mosque of al-Nasir Muhammad, the Citadel, Cairo, 25 March 1862

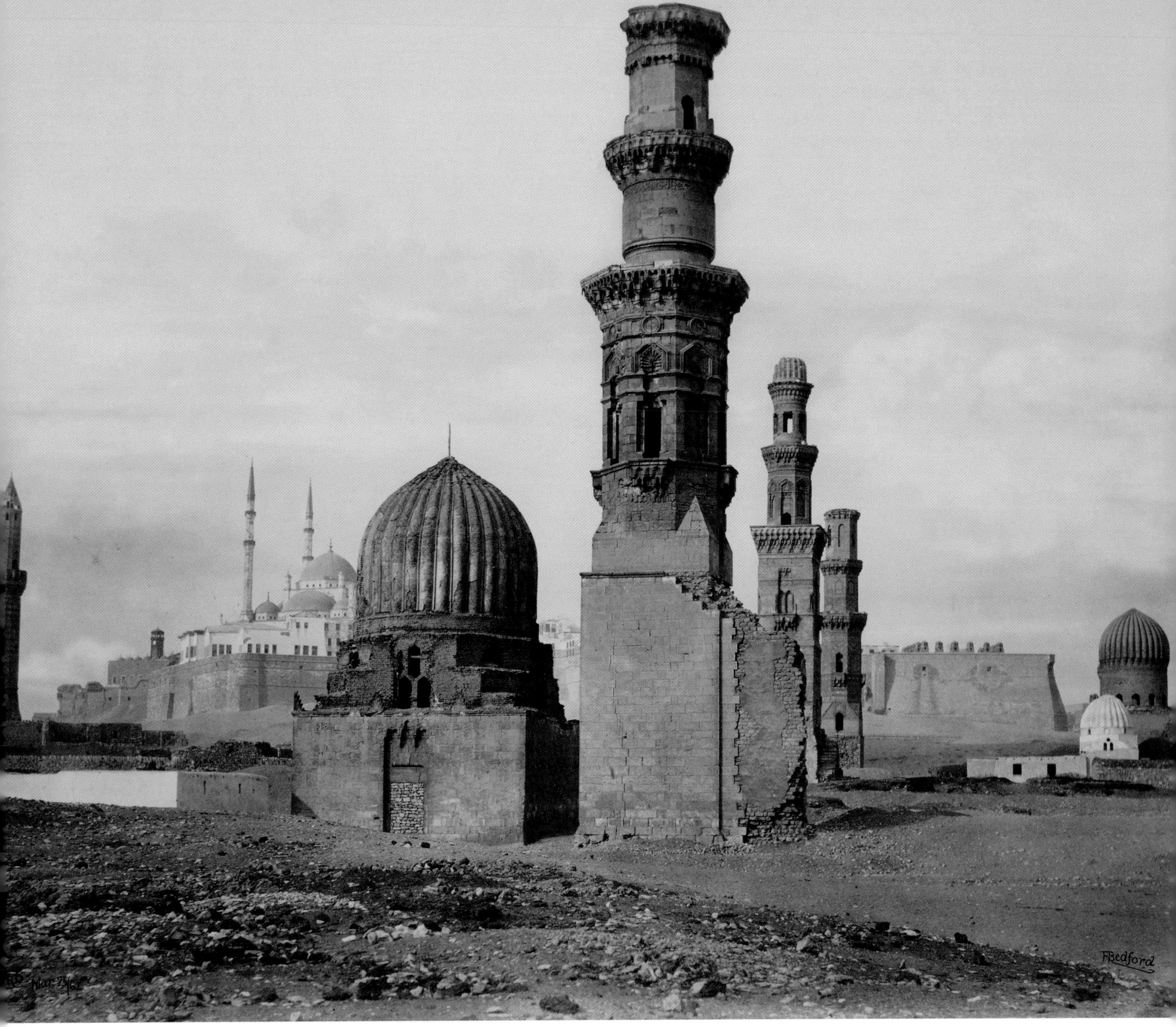

The Mausoleum and Khanqah of Qawsun, Cairo, 25 March 1862

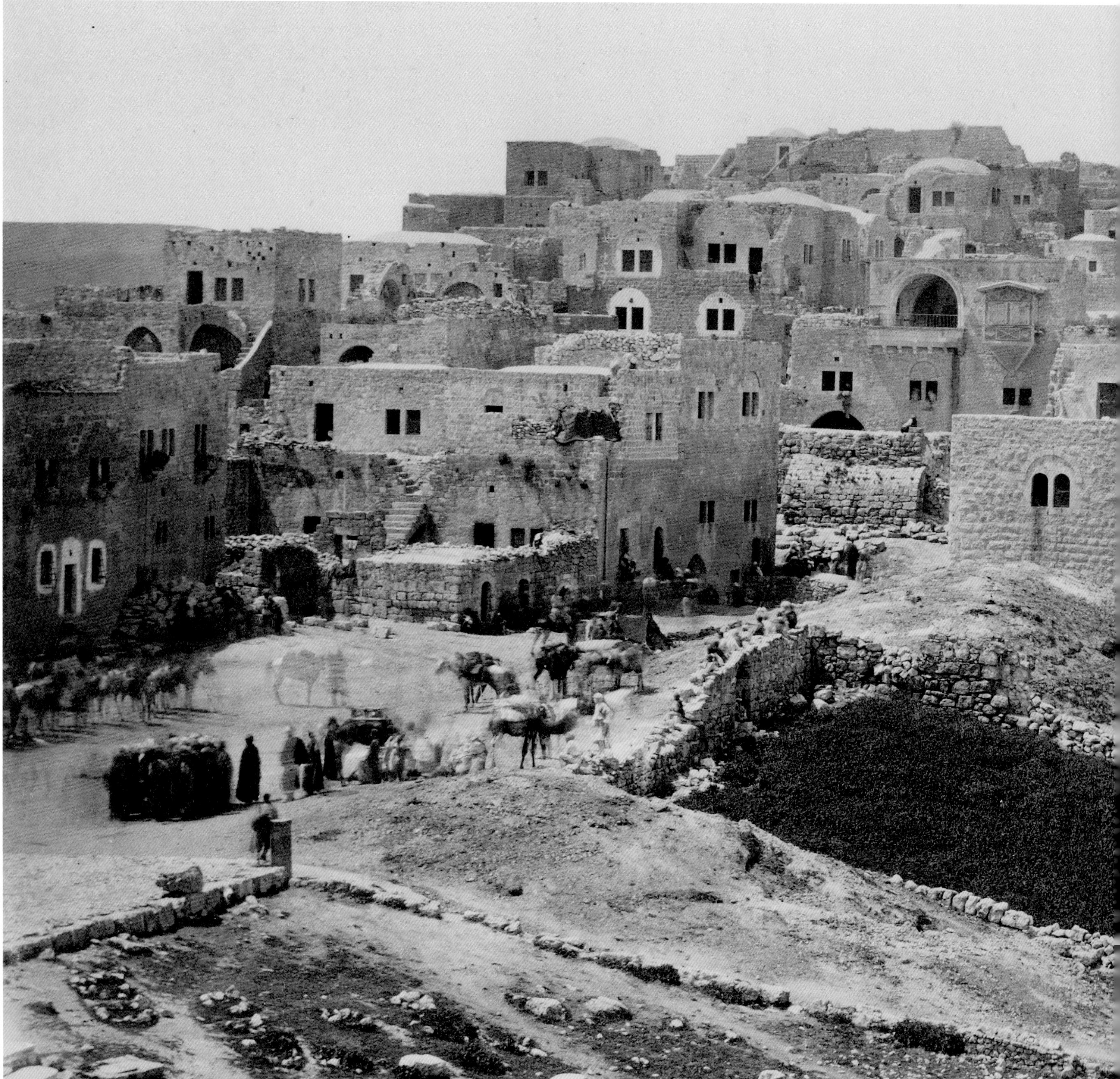

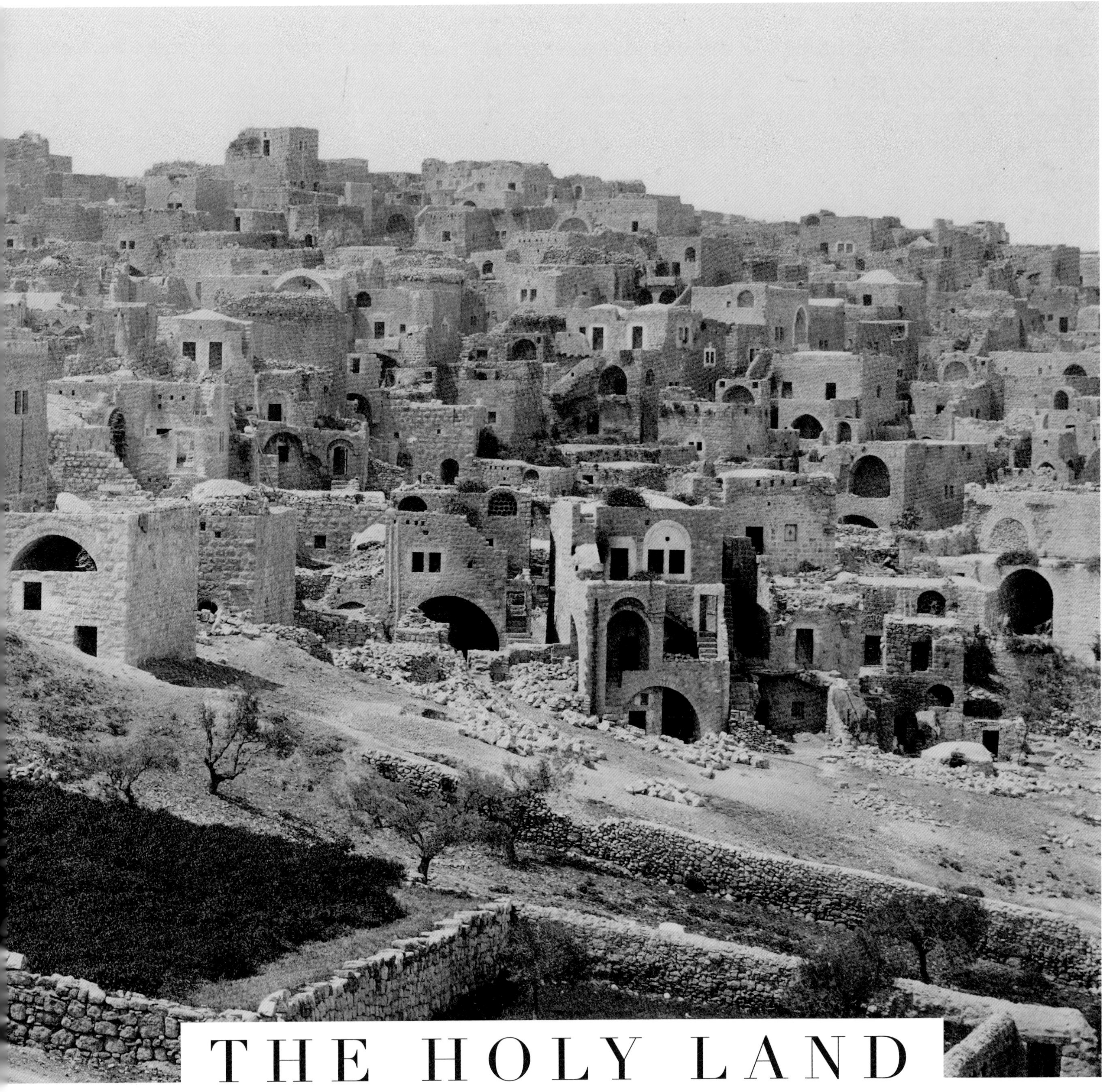

THE HOLY LAND

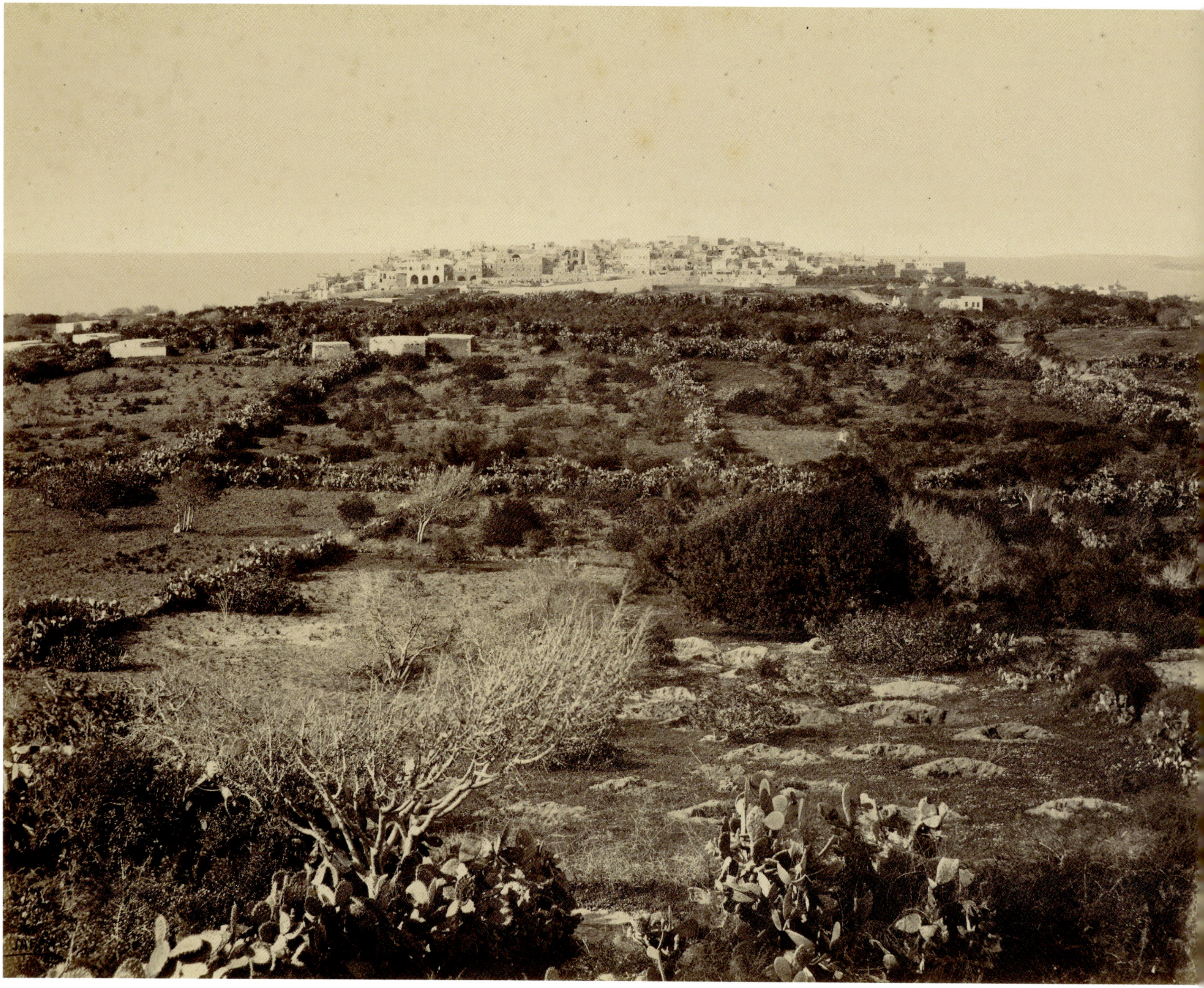

Jaffa from the south, 29 March 1862

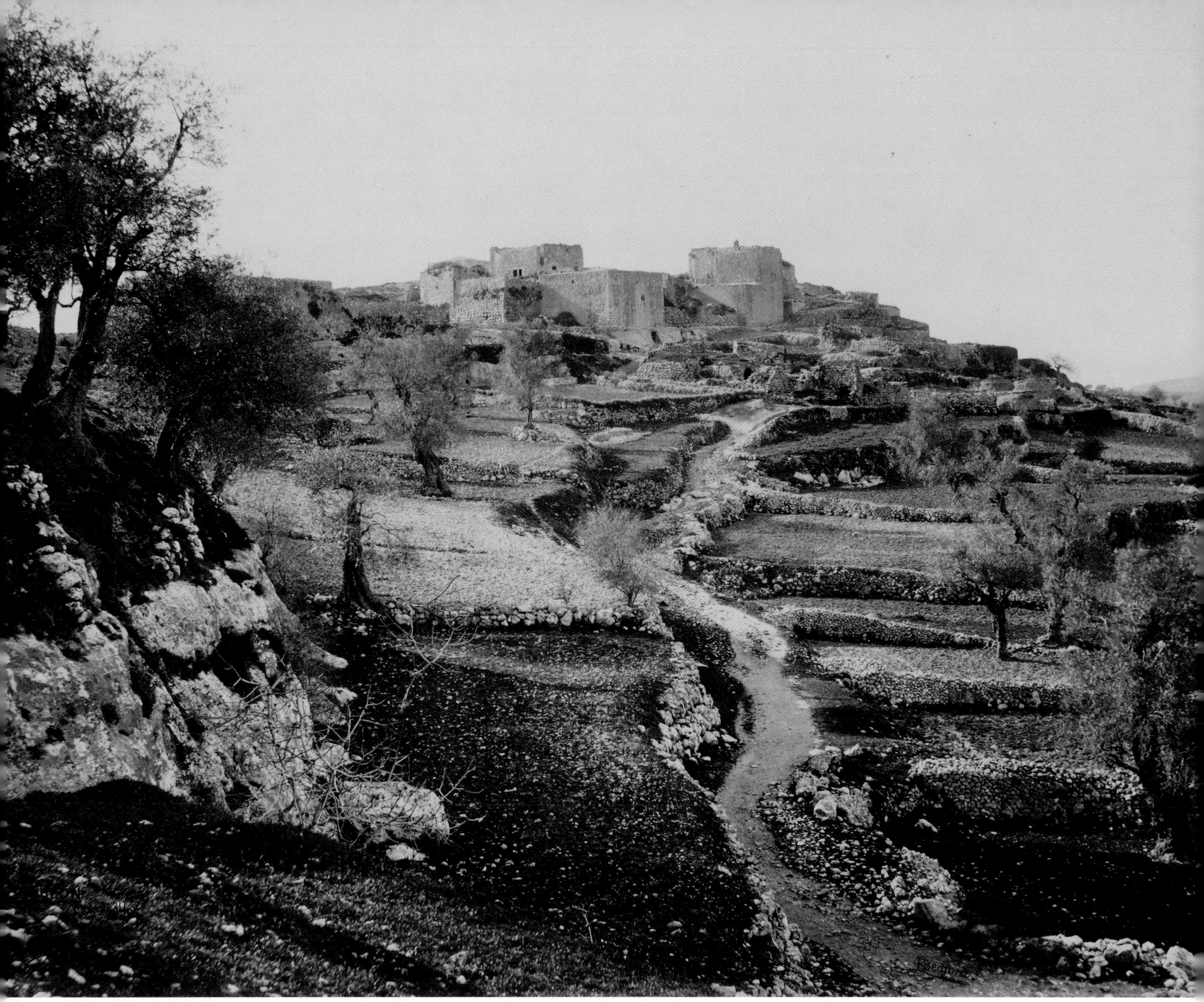

Gibeon, 31 March 1862

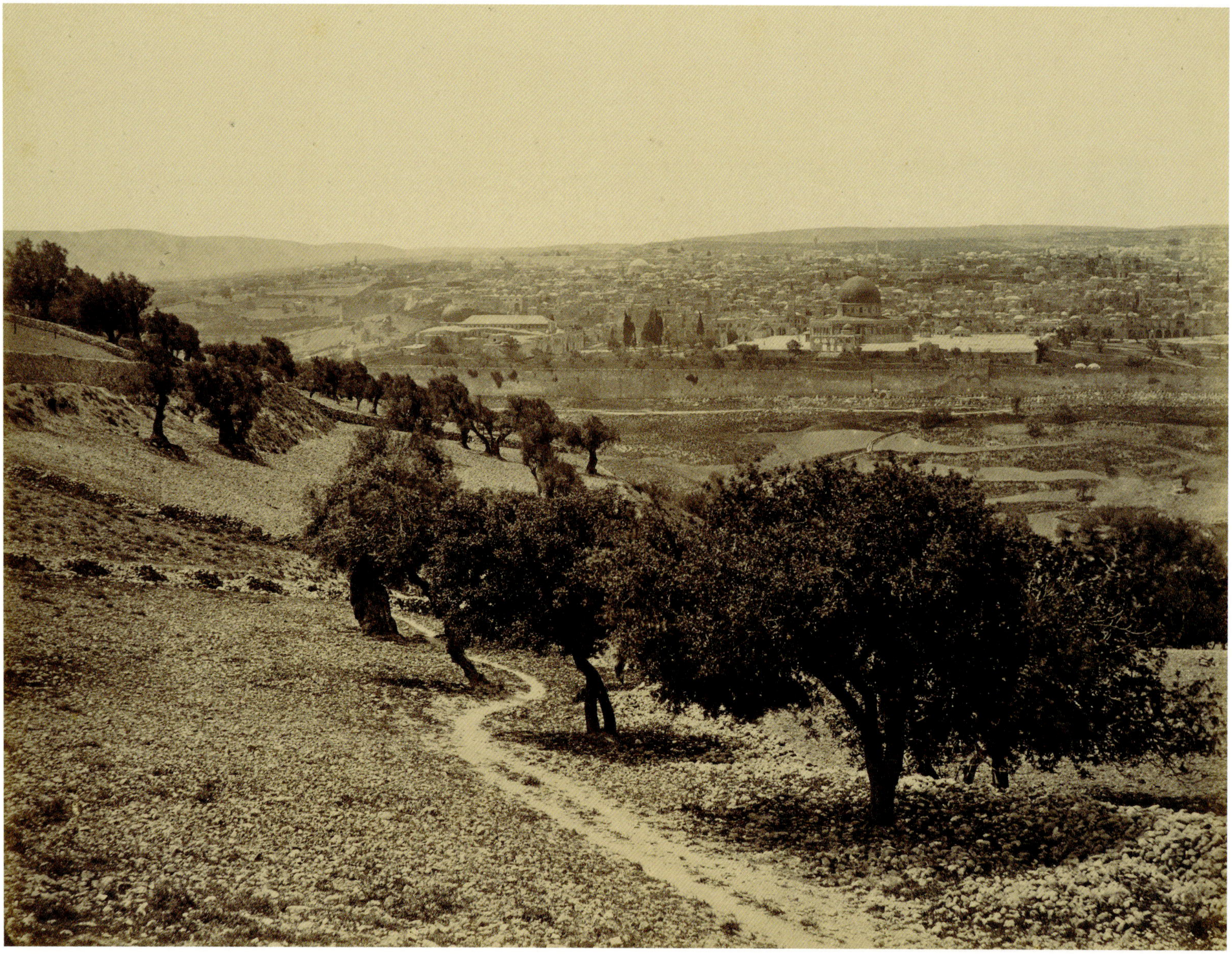

Jerusalem from the Mount of Olives, 1 April 1862

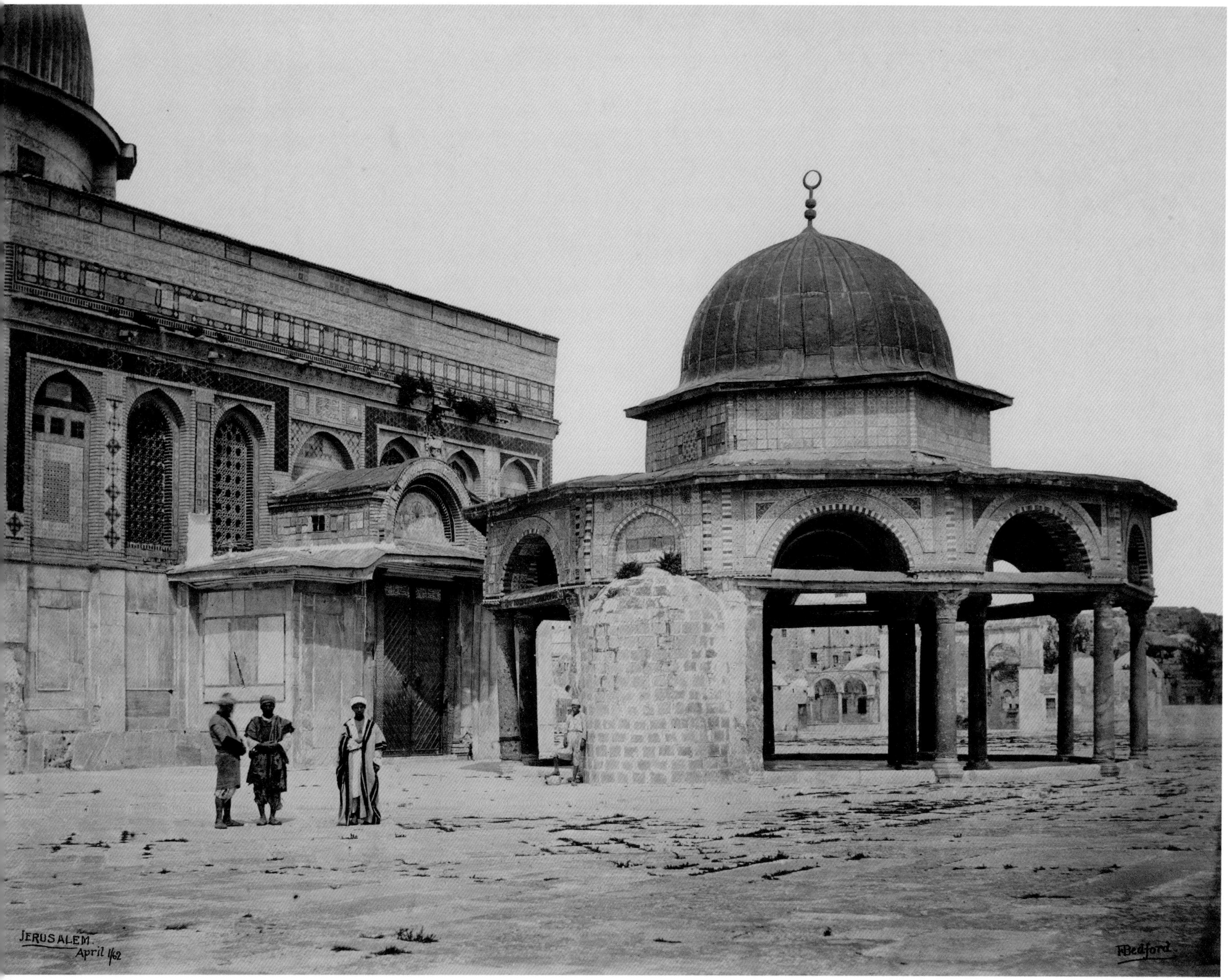

The Dome of the Rock, Jerusalem, 1 April 1862

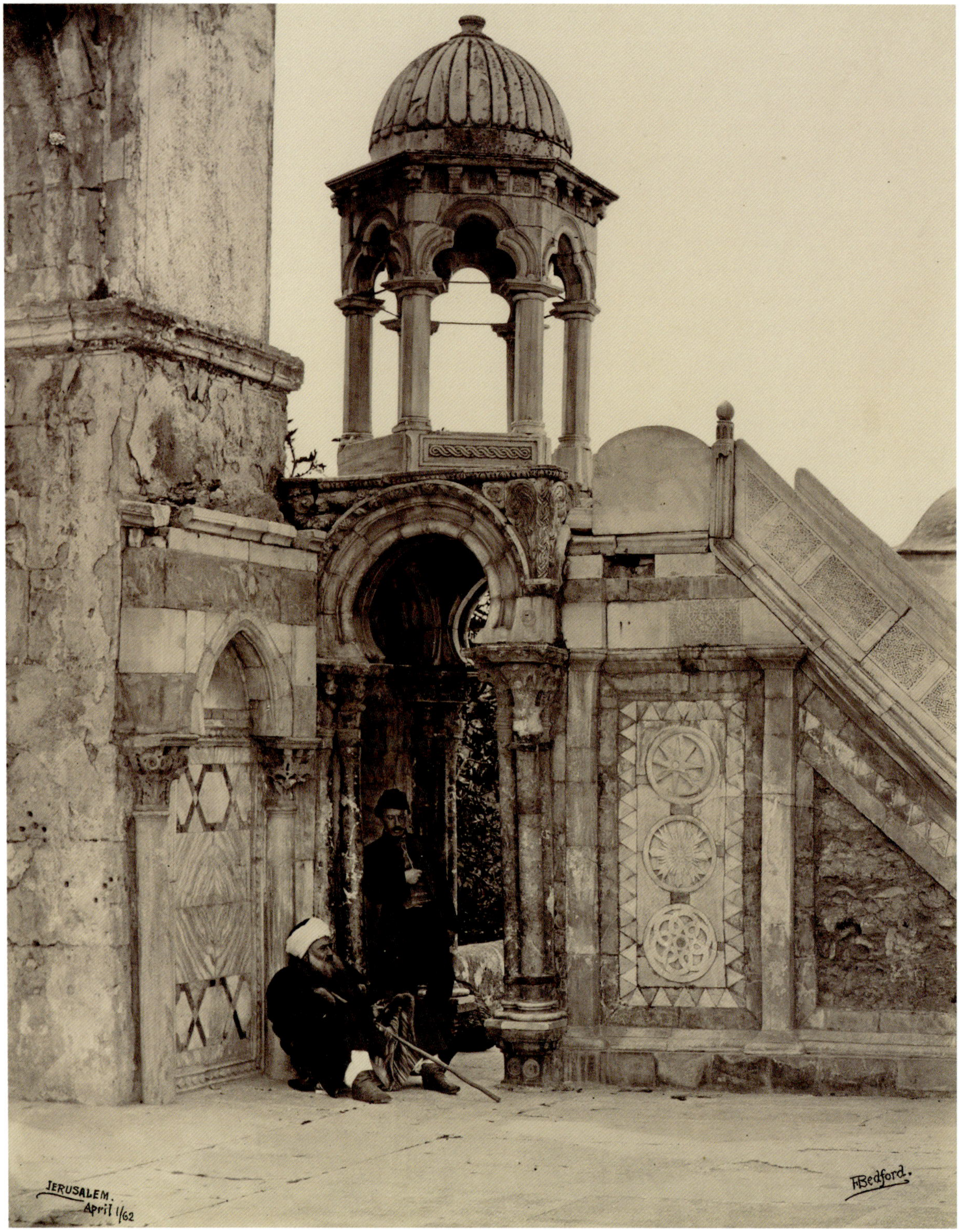

Minbar, Dome of the Rock, Jerusalem, 1 April 1862

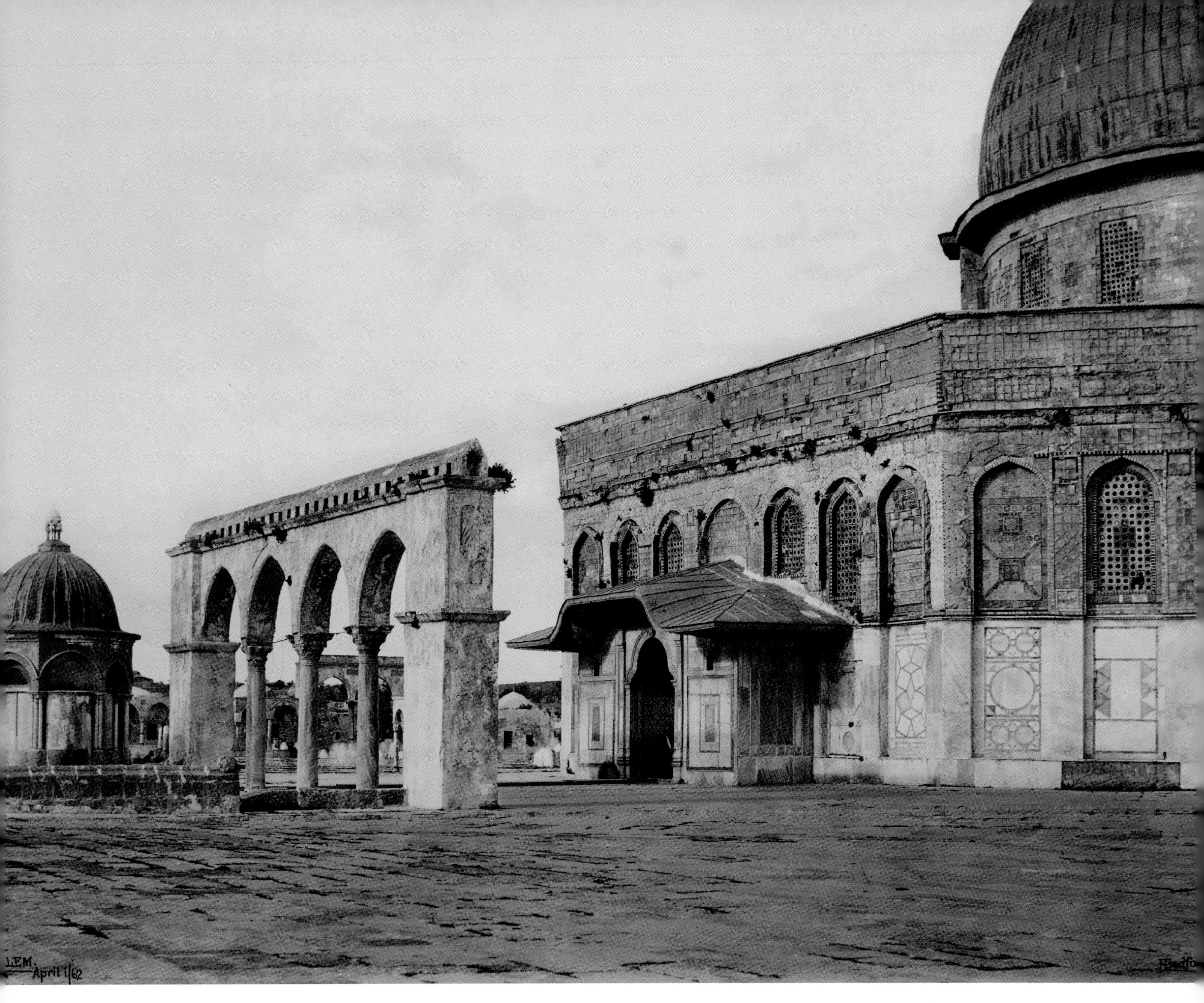

The Dome of the Rock, Jerusalem, 1 April 1862

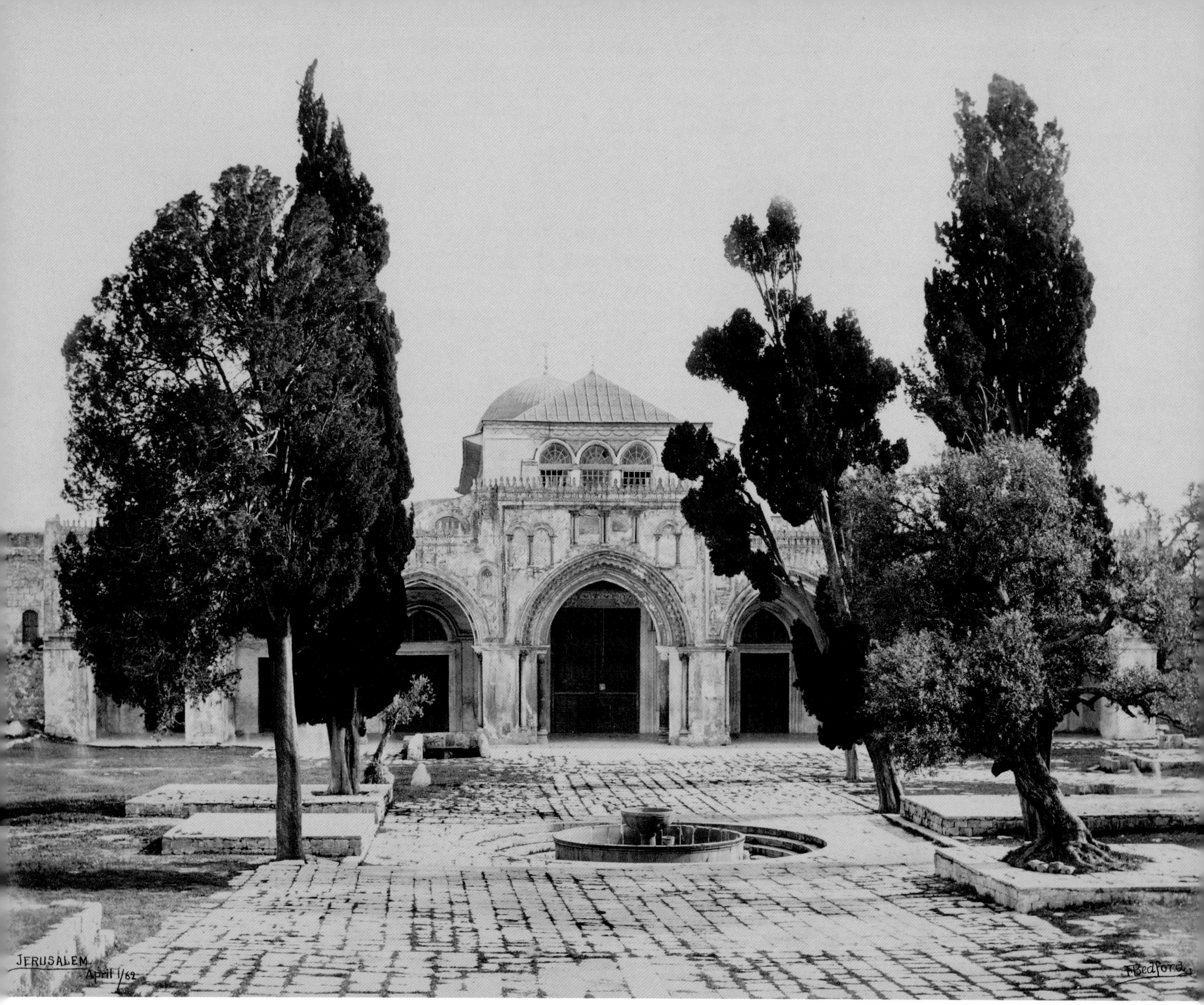

Al-Aqsa Mosque, Jerusalem, 1 April 1862

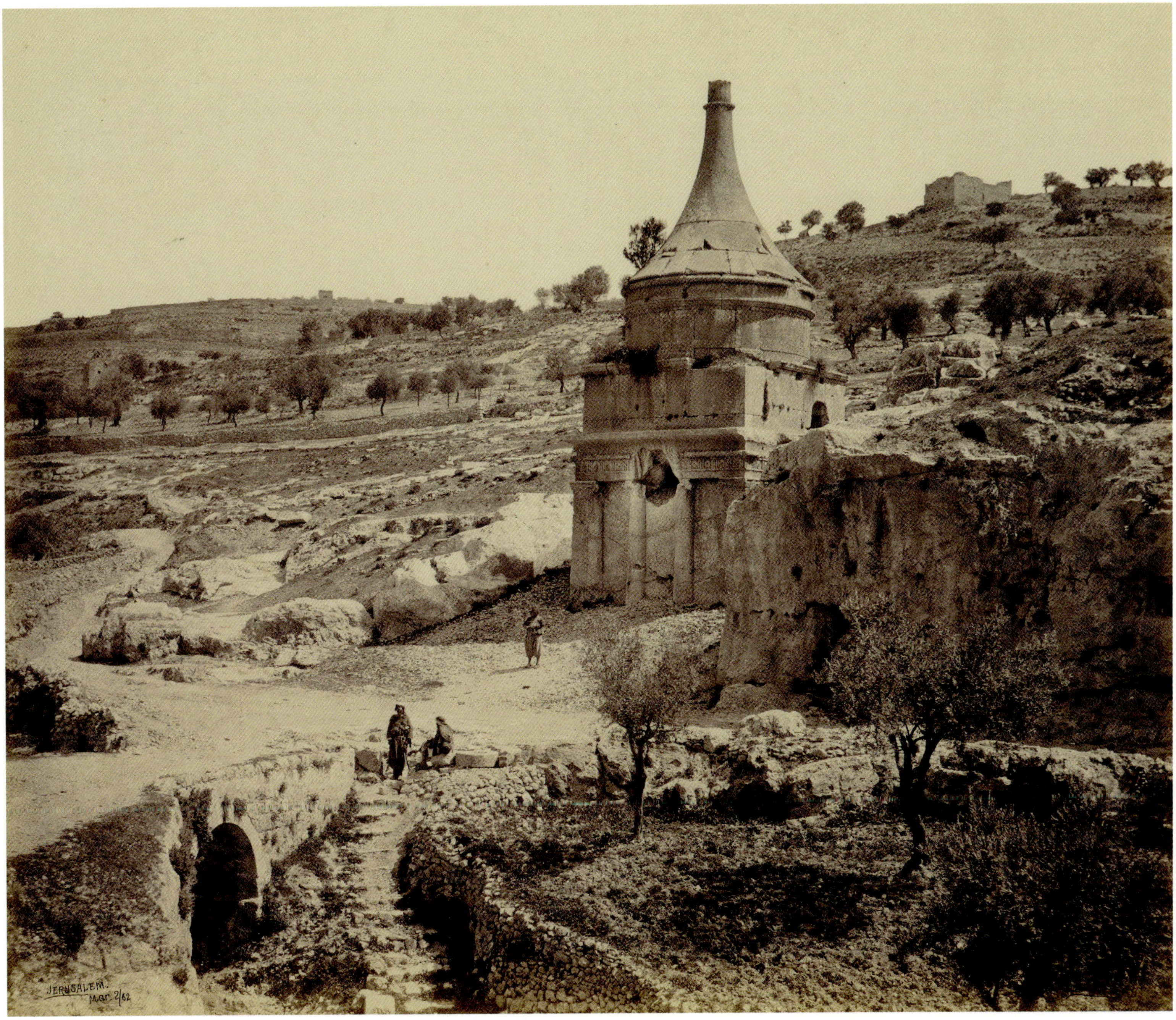

The Tomb of Absalom, Kidron Valley, Jerusalem, 2 April 1862

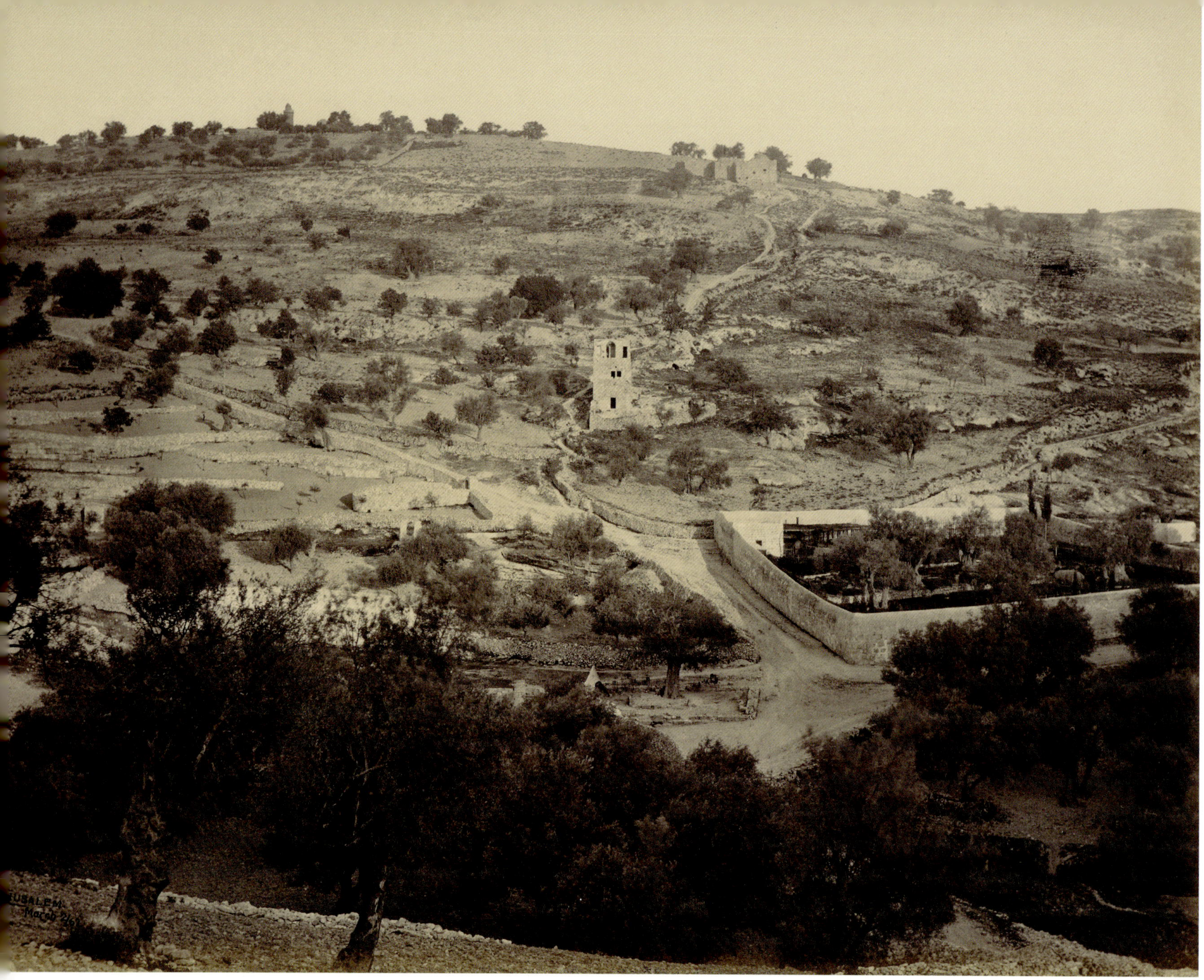

The Mount of Olives and the Garden of Gethsemane, Jerusalem, 2 April 1862

"We rode to the Garden of Gethsemane, in wh[ich] there [are] 8 olive trees, & a very nicely kept garden . . . . From thence, we rode up to the Mount of Olives (the olive trees are very scanty just now, but fresh ones are being planted) & had a splendid view fr[om] the Minaret wh[ich] is on the top. We saw Jerusalem to perfection, & also the Dead Sea & the mountain ranges to perfection."
Prince of Wales's Journal, 2 April 1862

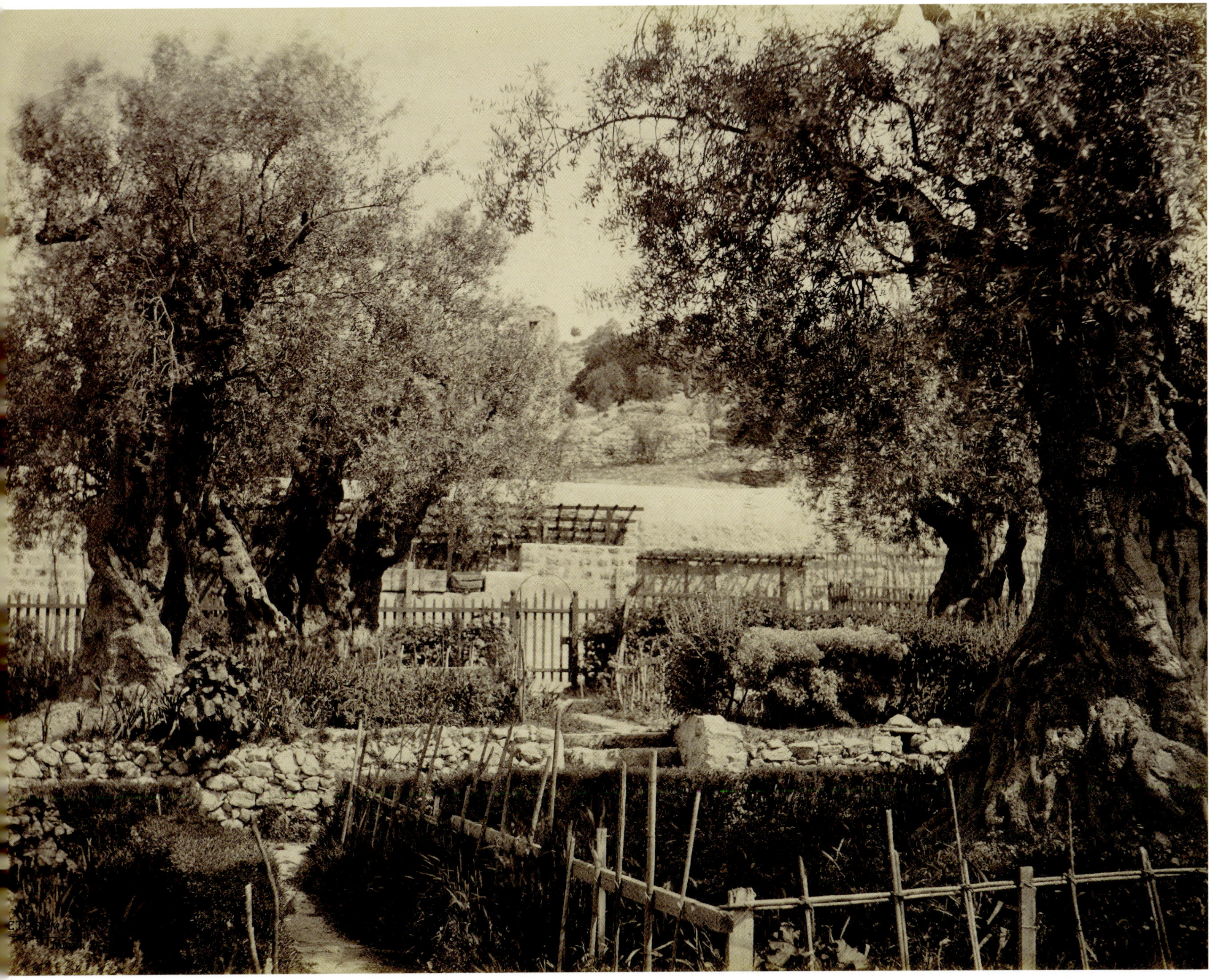

The Garden of Gethsemane, Jerusalem, 2 April 1862

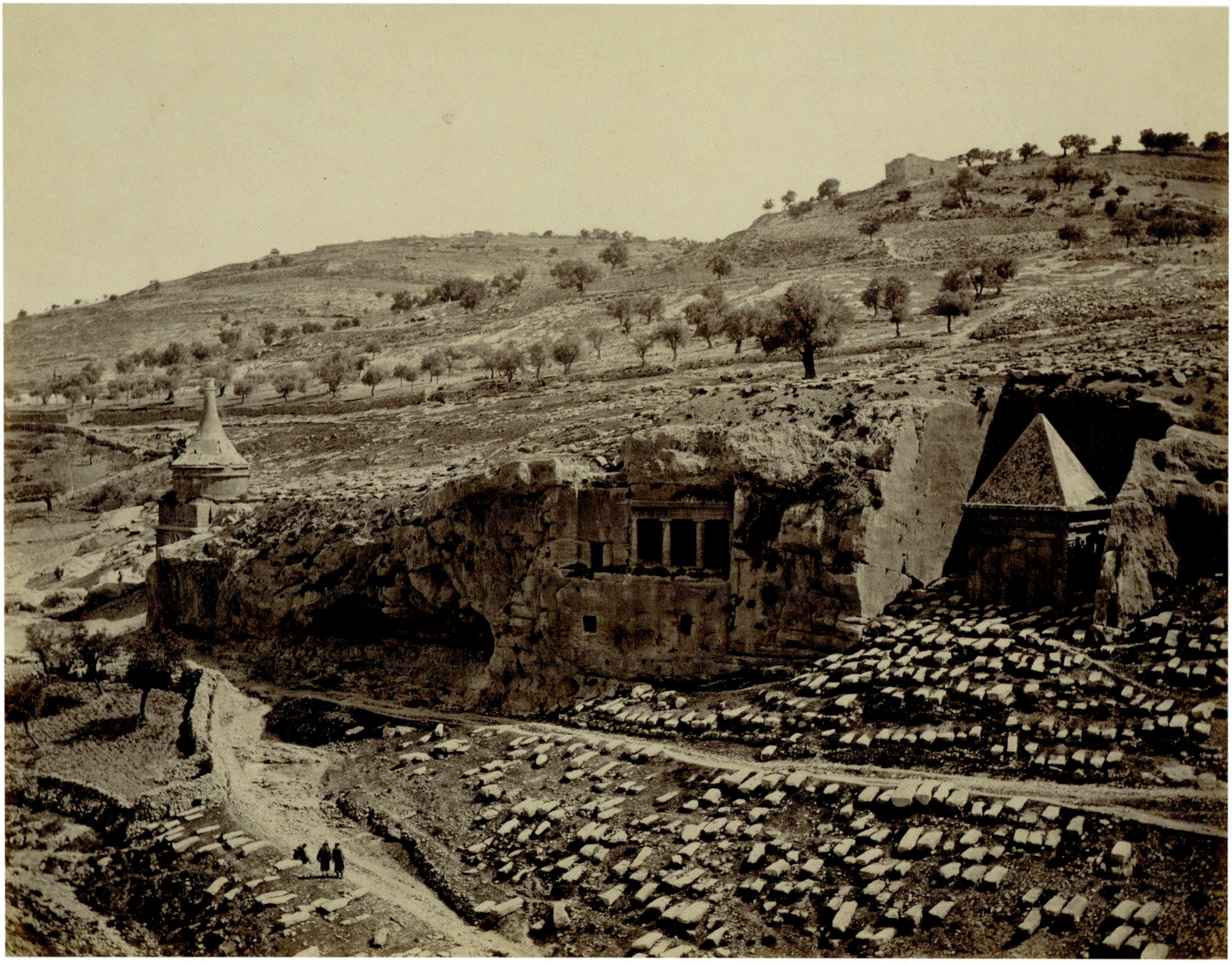

The Tomb of Absalom and the Tomb of Zechariah, Kidron Valley, Jerusalem, 2 April 1862

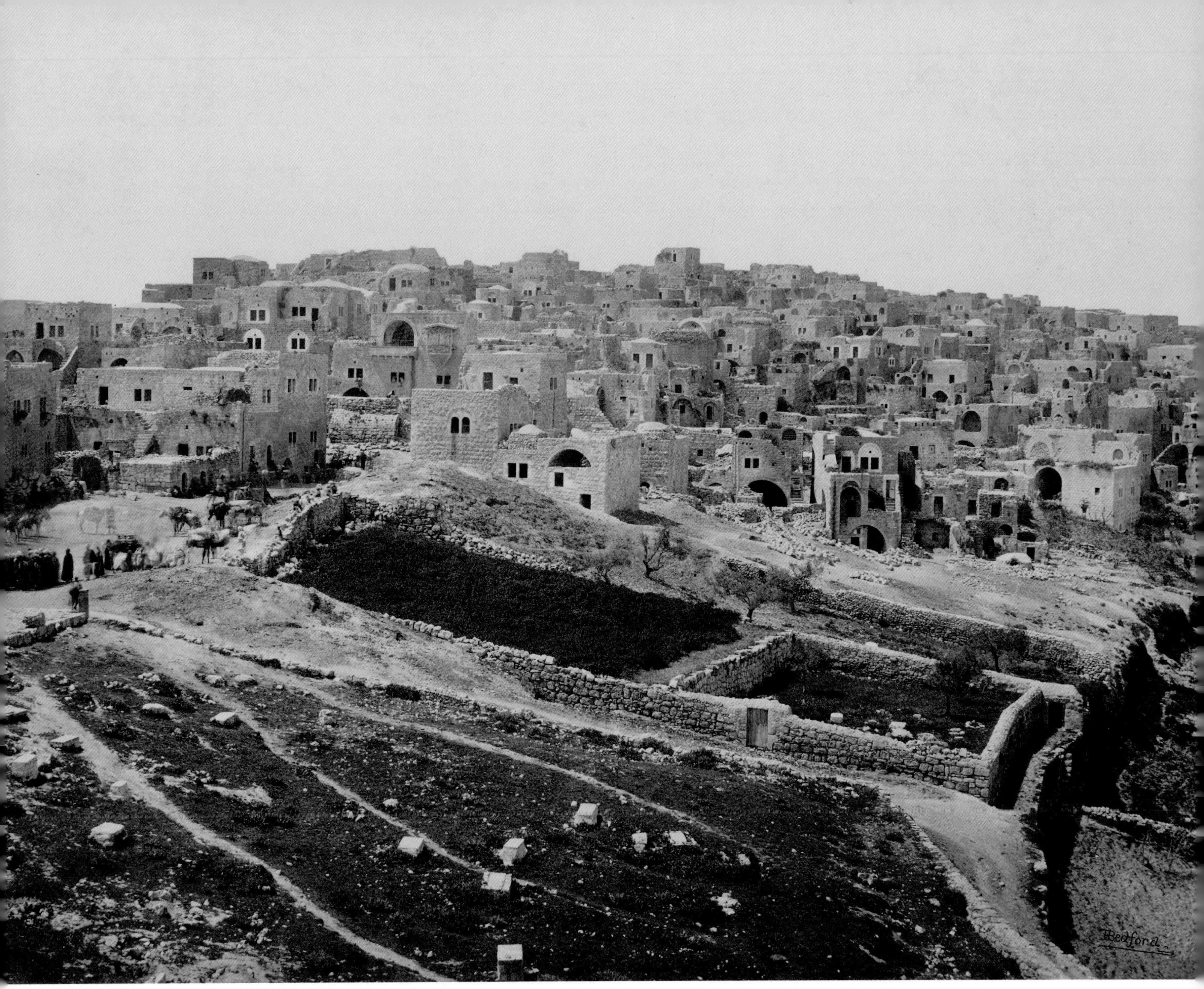

Bethlehem, 3 April 1862

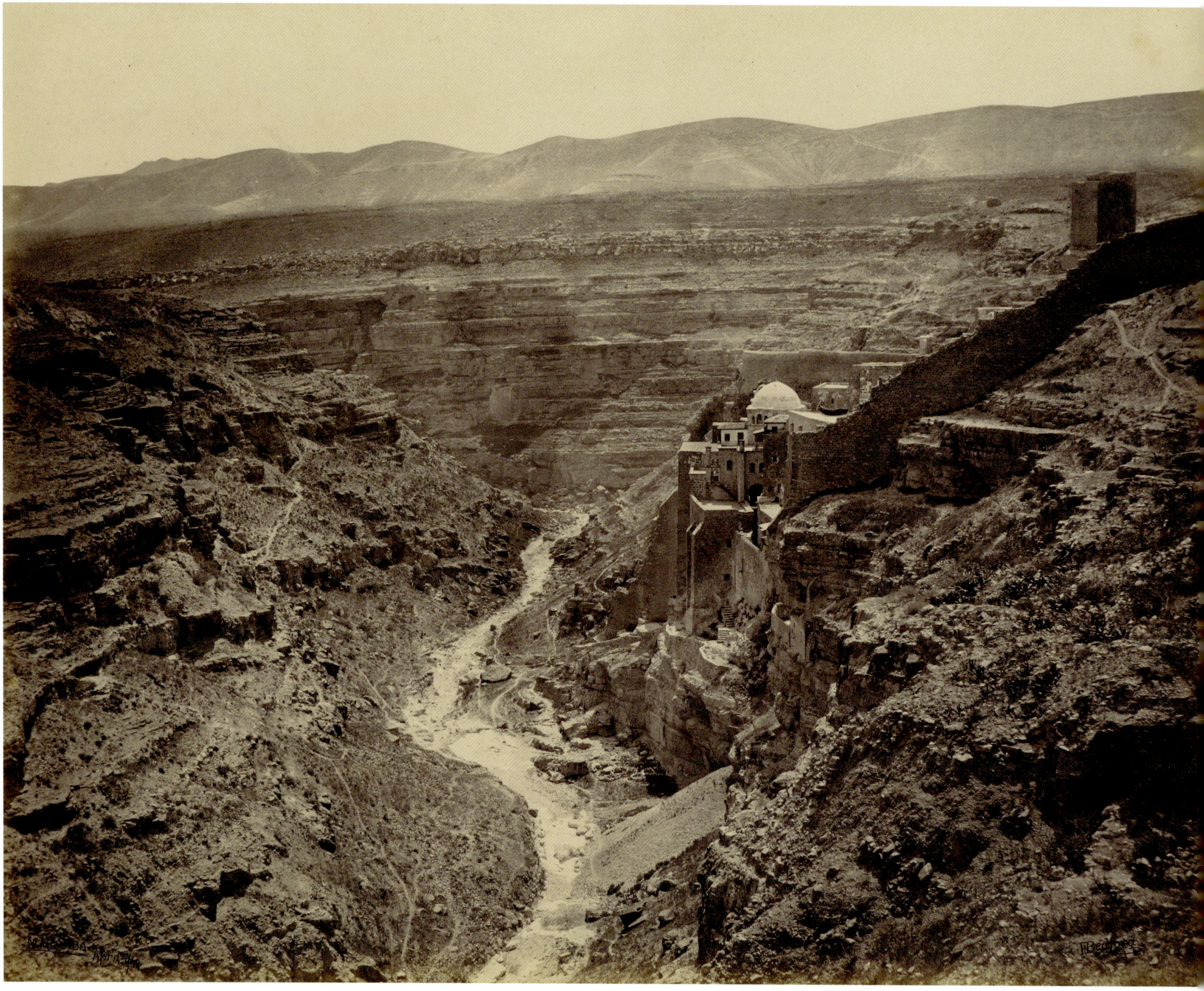

The Mar Saba Monastery, above the Kidron River, 4 April 1862

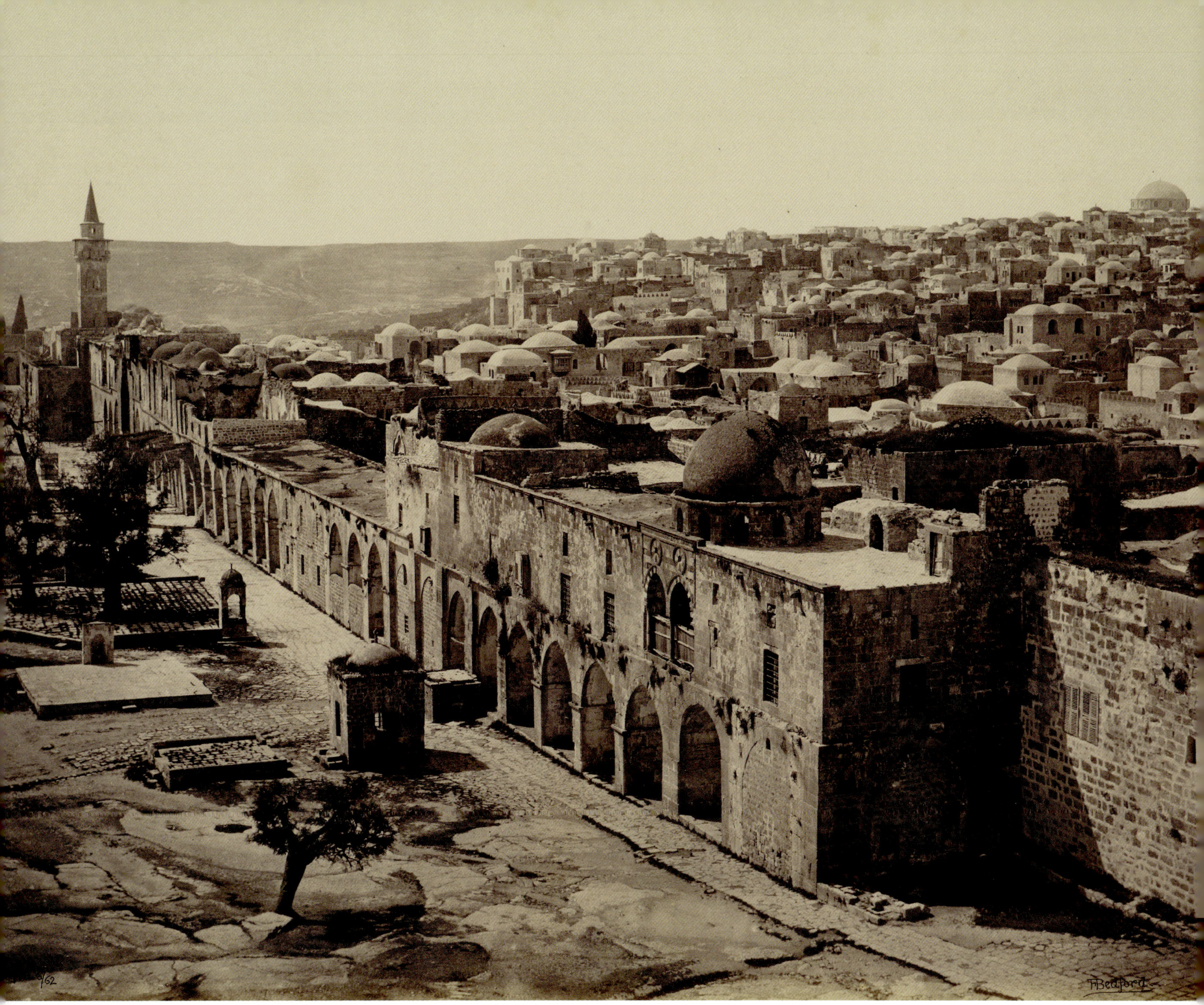

Mount Zion from the Governor's House, Jerusalem, 6 April 1862

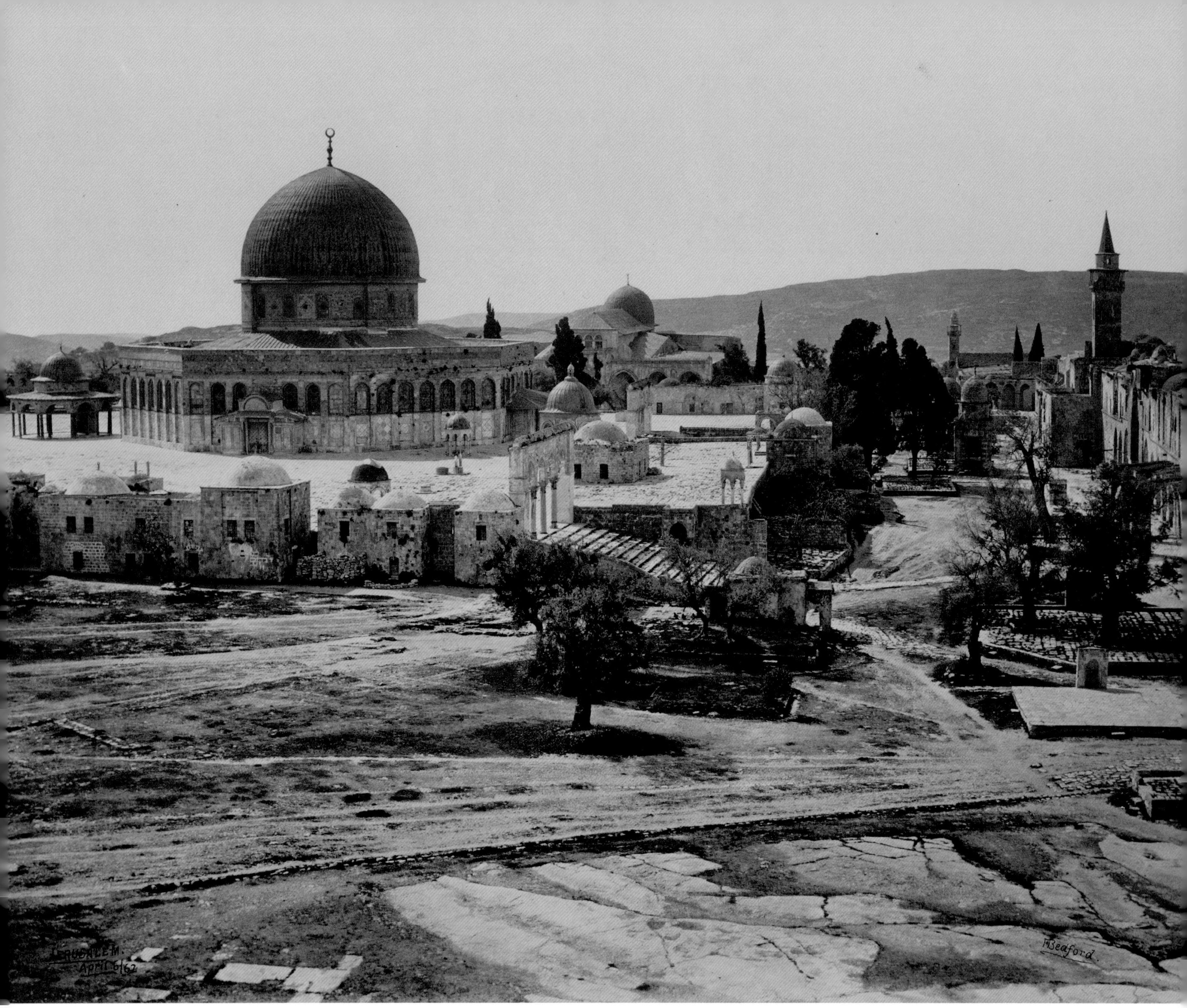

The Dome of the Rock, Jerusalem, 6 April 1862

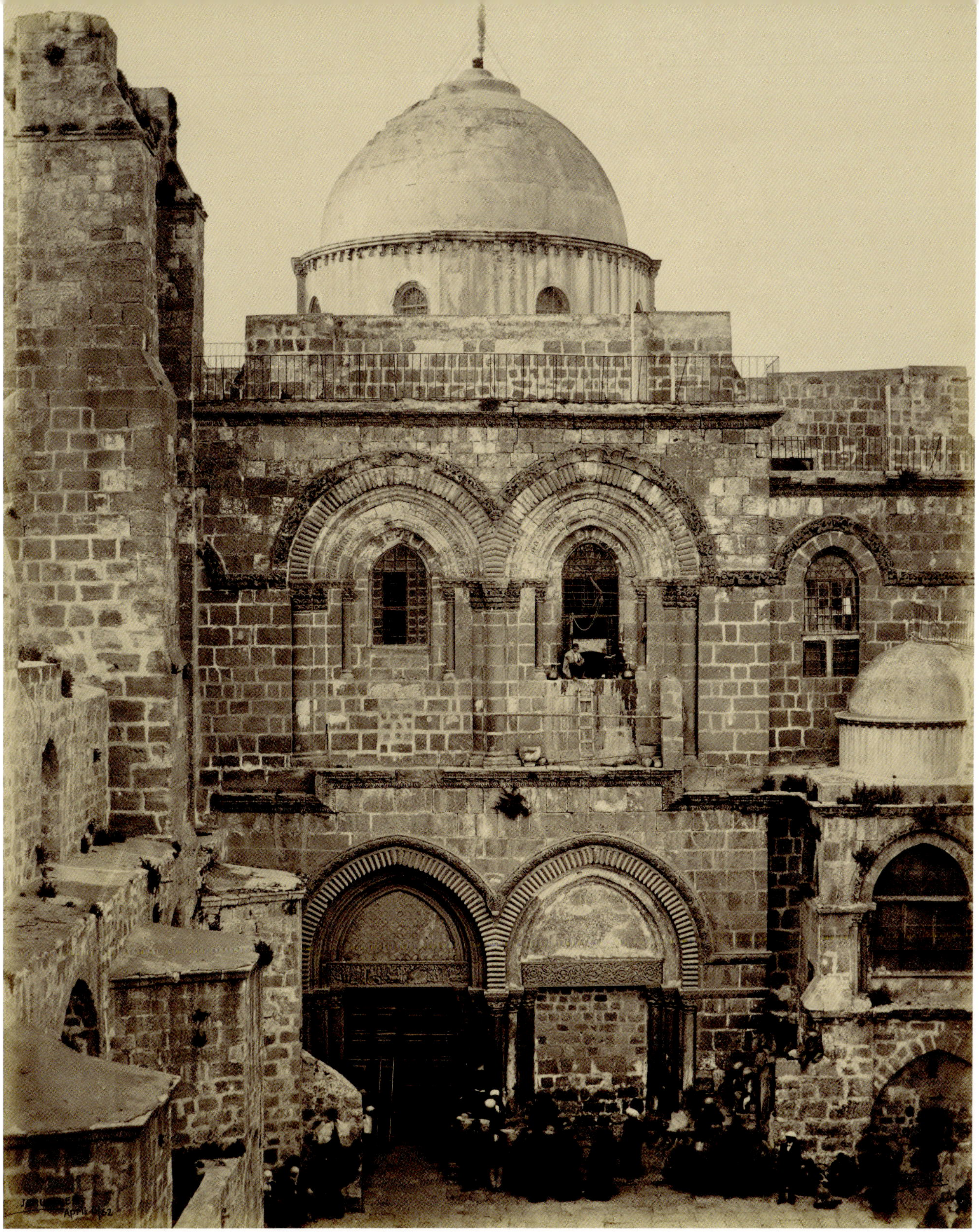

The Church of the Holy Sepulcher, Jerusalem, 6 April 1862

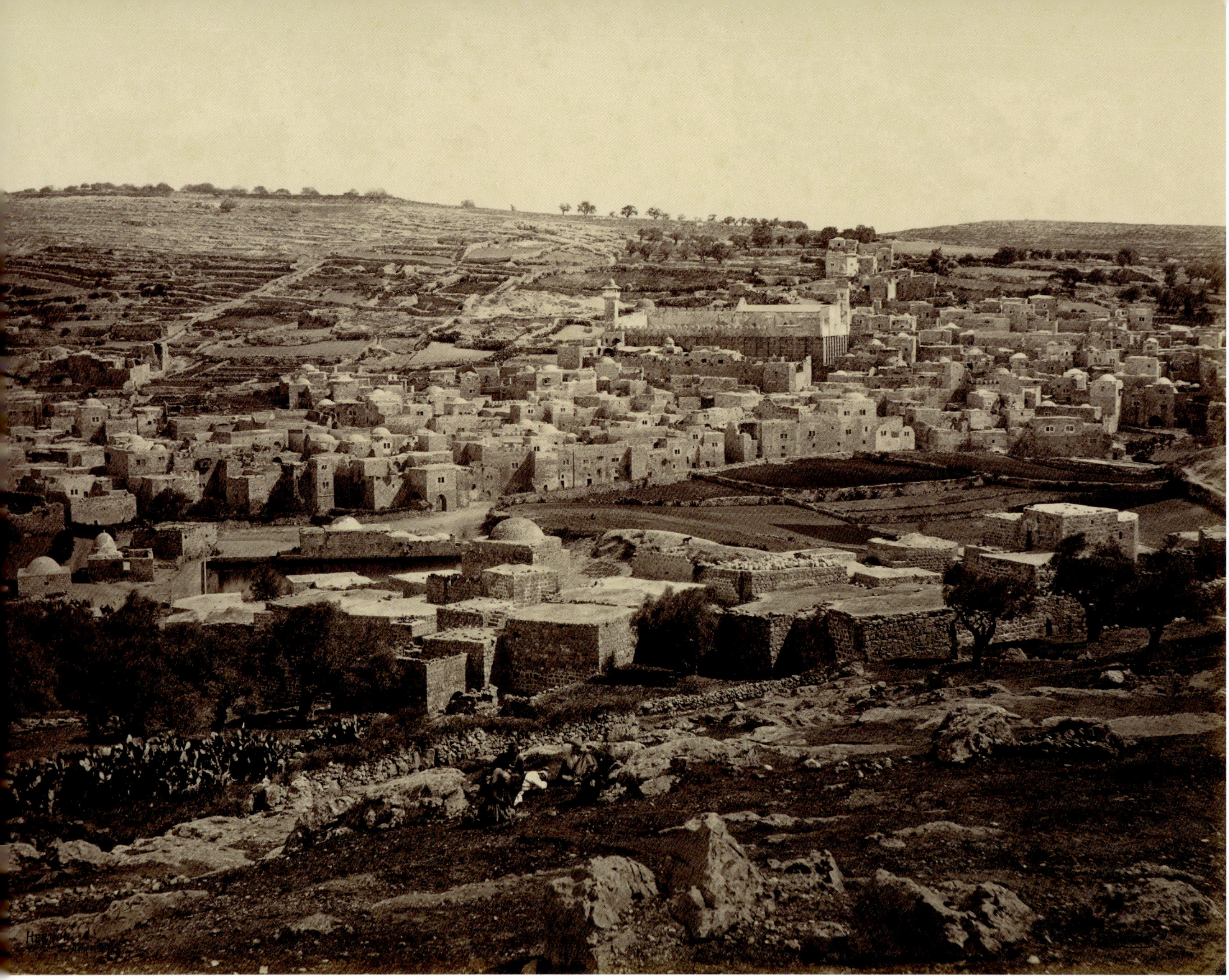

Al-Khalil (Hebron), with the Mosque of al-Khalil, 8 April 1862

"This Mosque is very interesting as no Xtian before us had ever been in it, & there was a g[rea]t difficulty in our going in. We went accompanied by a large guard of soldiers, & entered the Mosque where we were shown the Tombs of Abraham, & Sarah, on one side of the entrance, then that of Isaac & Rebecca inside the Mosque & then that of Jacob & Lear [sic] & that of Joseph. The Mahometans venerate these immensely, and hitherto have prevented any Xtian going in, but with the help of the Pasha, as a g[rea]t favour I & my party . . . were let in."
Prince of Wales's Journal, 7 April 1862

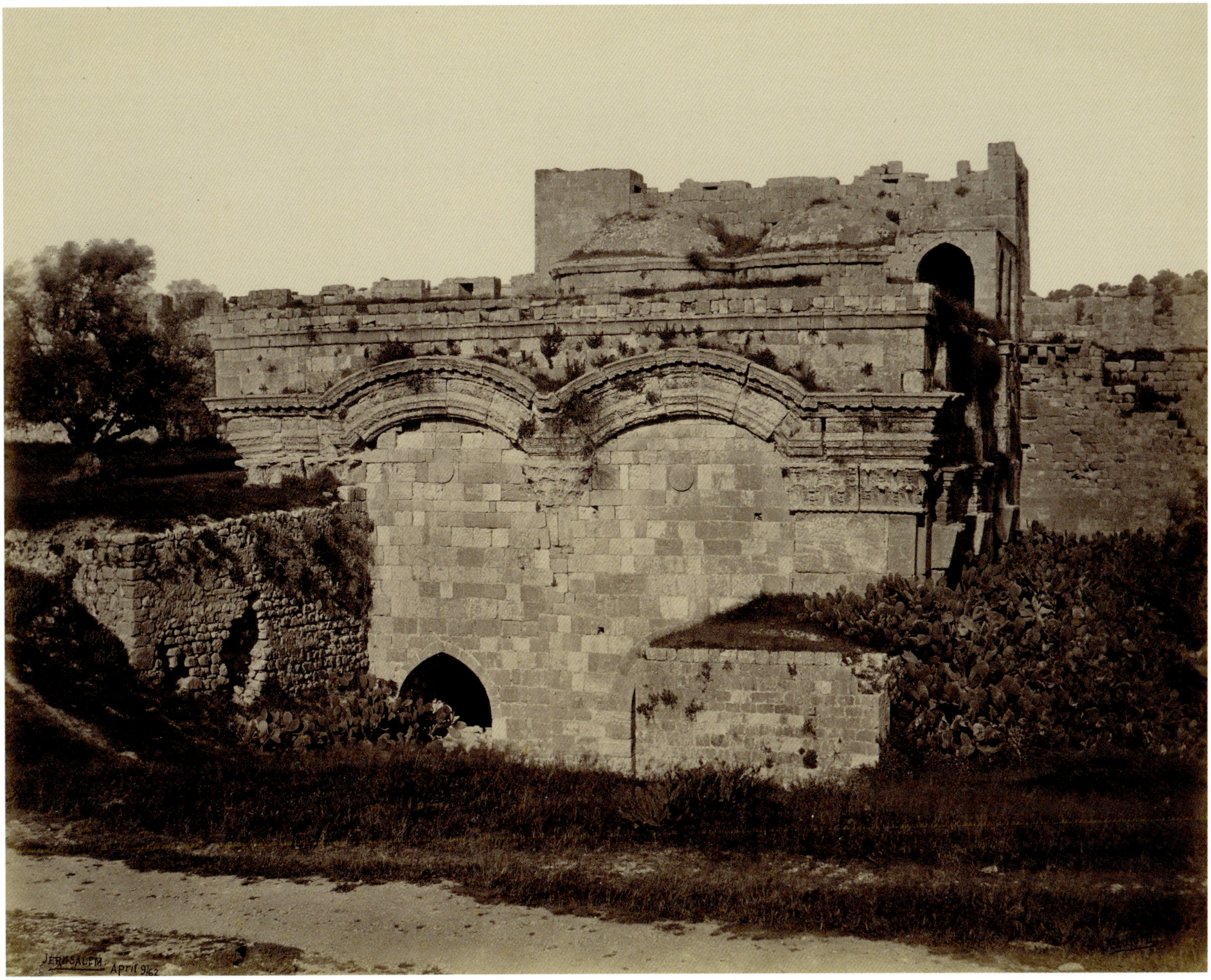

The Golden Gate, Jerusalem, 9 April 1862

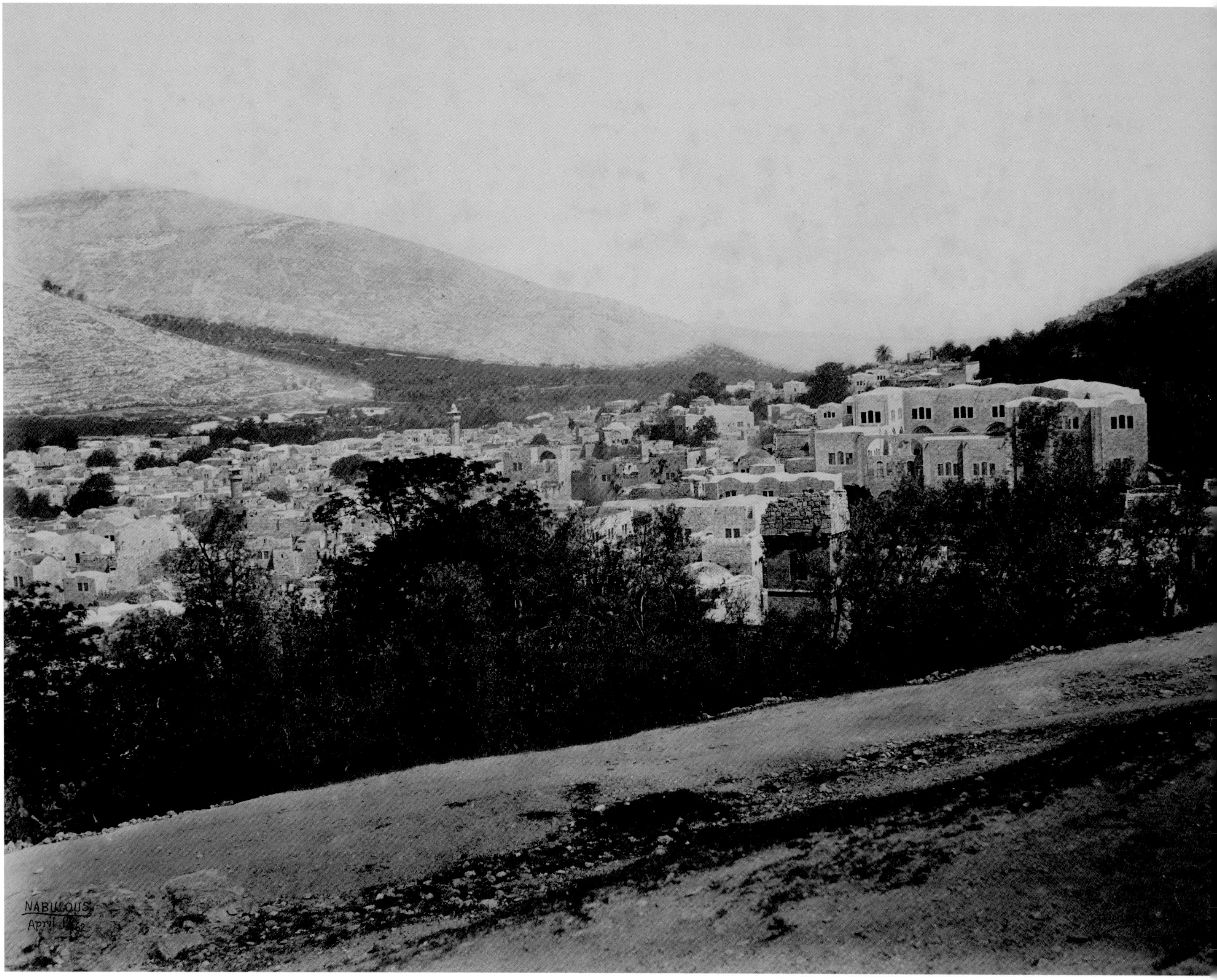

Nablus, 12 April 1862

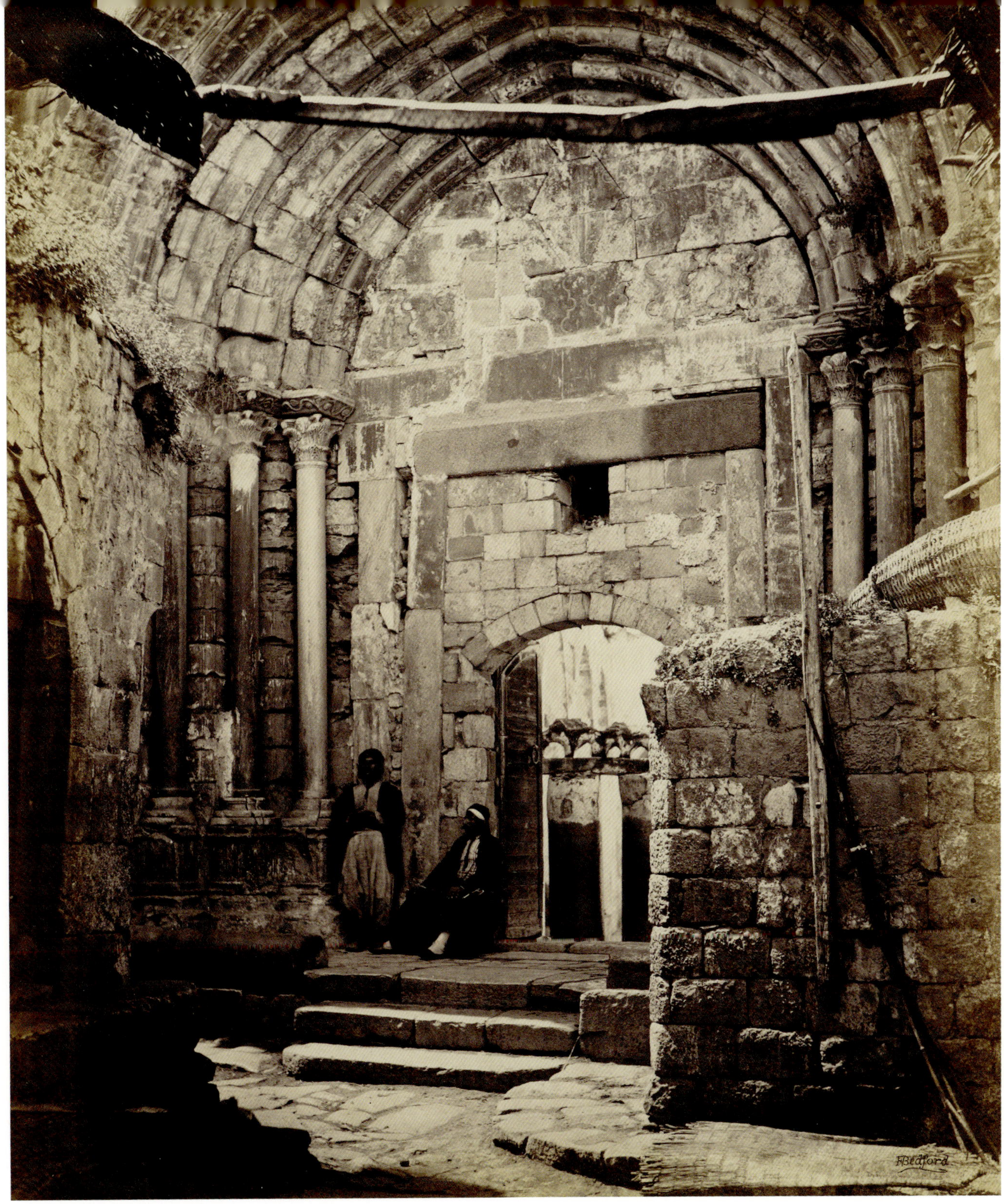

The Great Mosque, Nablus, 12 April 1862

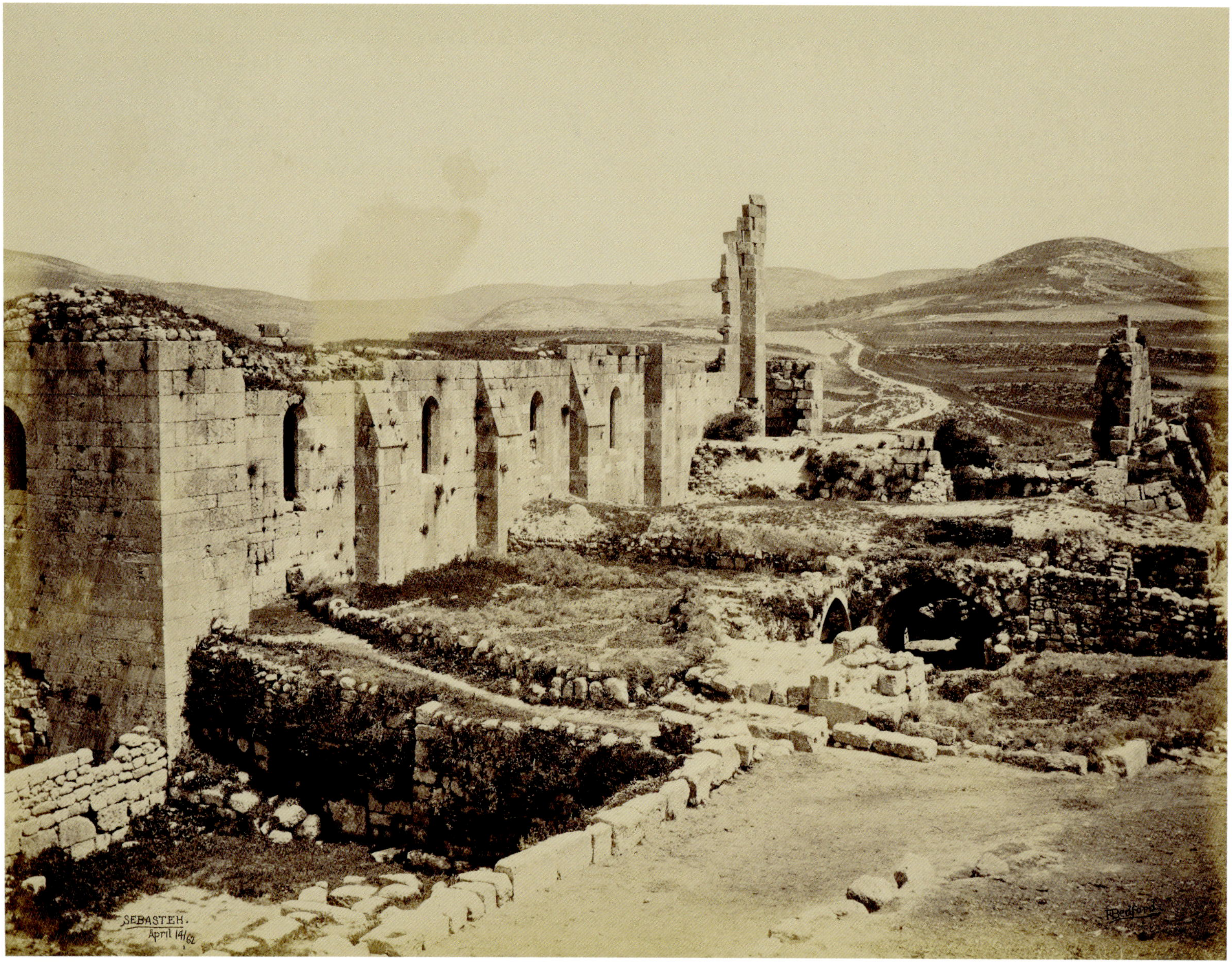

The Church of St. John, Sebastiya, 14 April 1862

"We started at 8am & in two hours reached Sebastieh, wh[ich] is on the site of the town of Samaria. We saw the ruins of a Xtian Church there, & the tomb of John the Babtist [sic] was show to us, & it is possble that it may be correct."
Prince of Wales's Journal, 14 April 1862

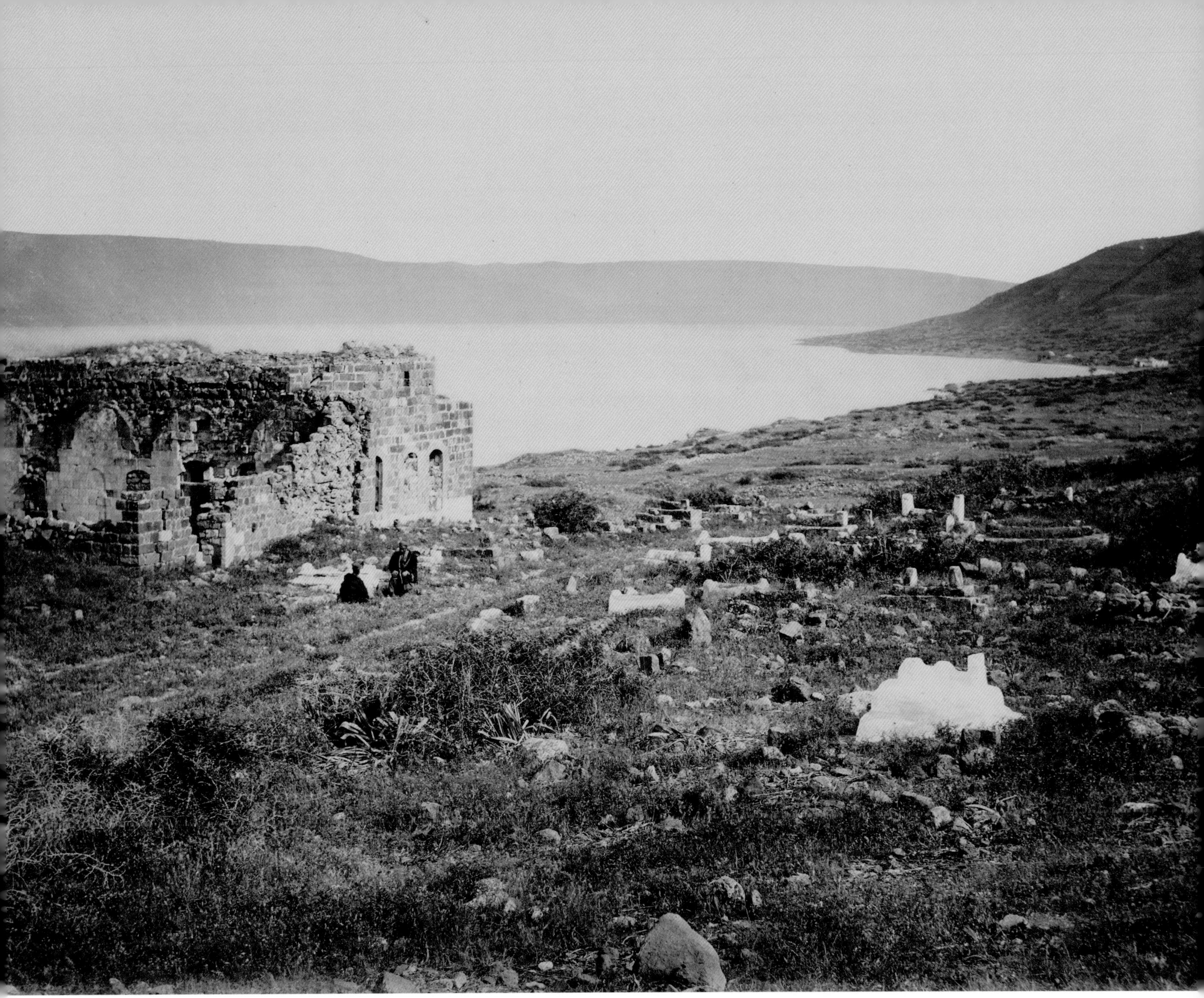

The Sea of Galilee, near Tiberias, 20 April 1862

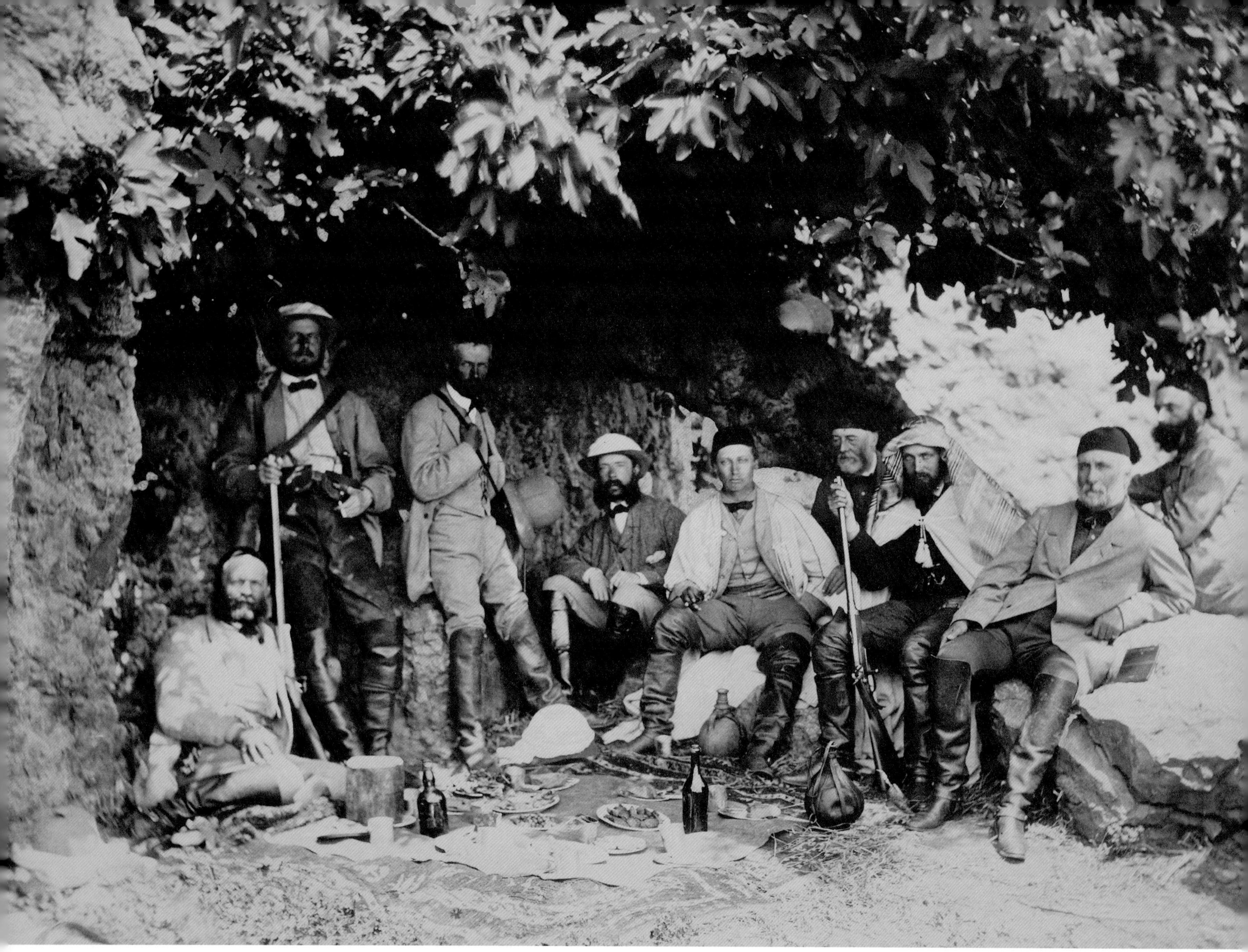

The Prince of Wales (center) and his group at Capernaum, 21 April 1862

"We lunched under a fig tree at 12 o'clock on the site of where once the city of Capernaum is said to have stood, & Mr. Bedford photographed us 'en groupe.'"
Prince of Wales's Journal, 21 April 1862

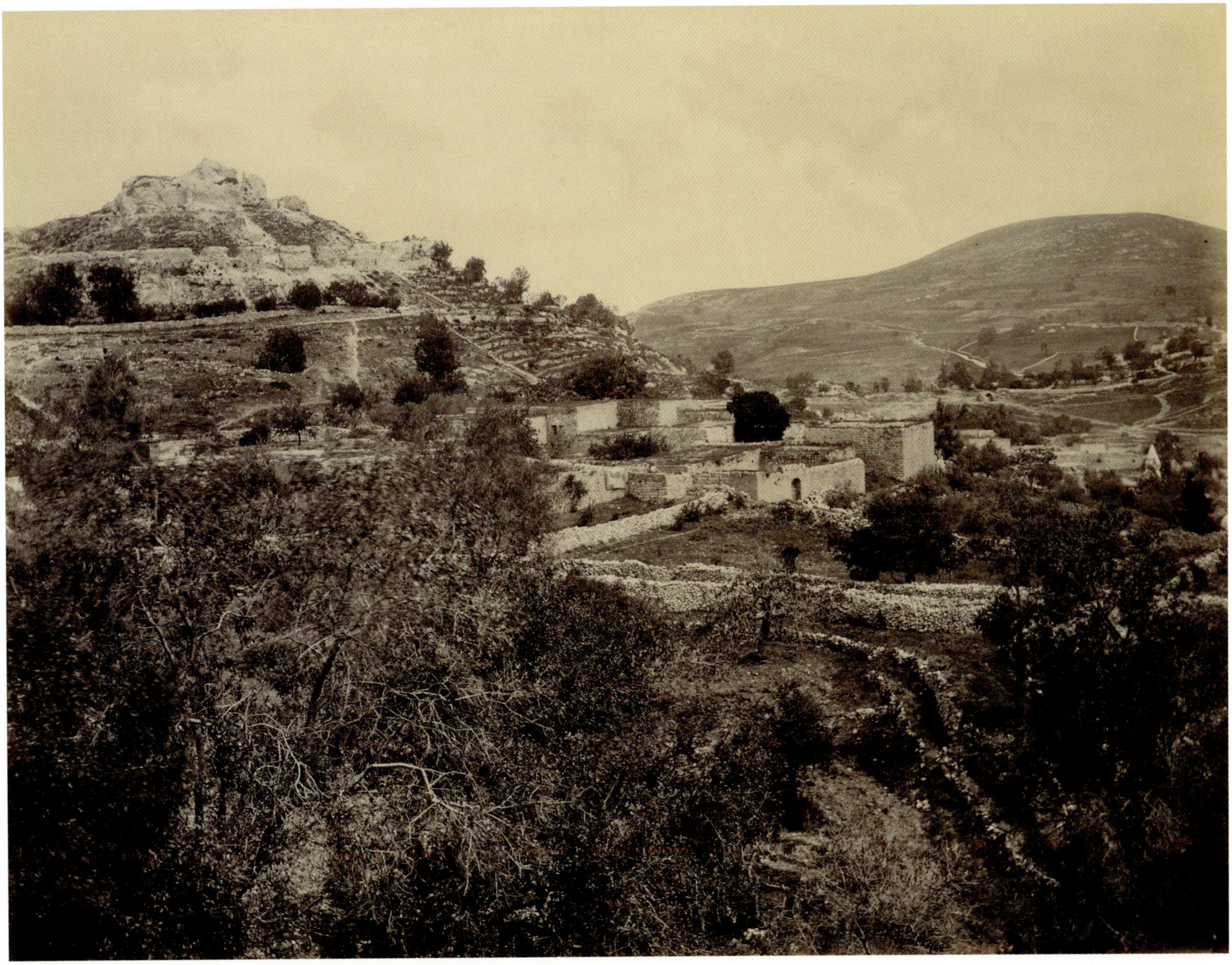

The castle at Safed, 22 April 1862

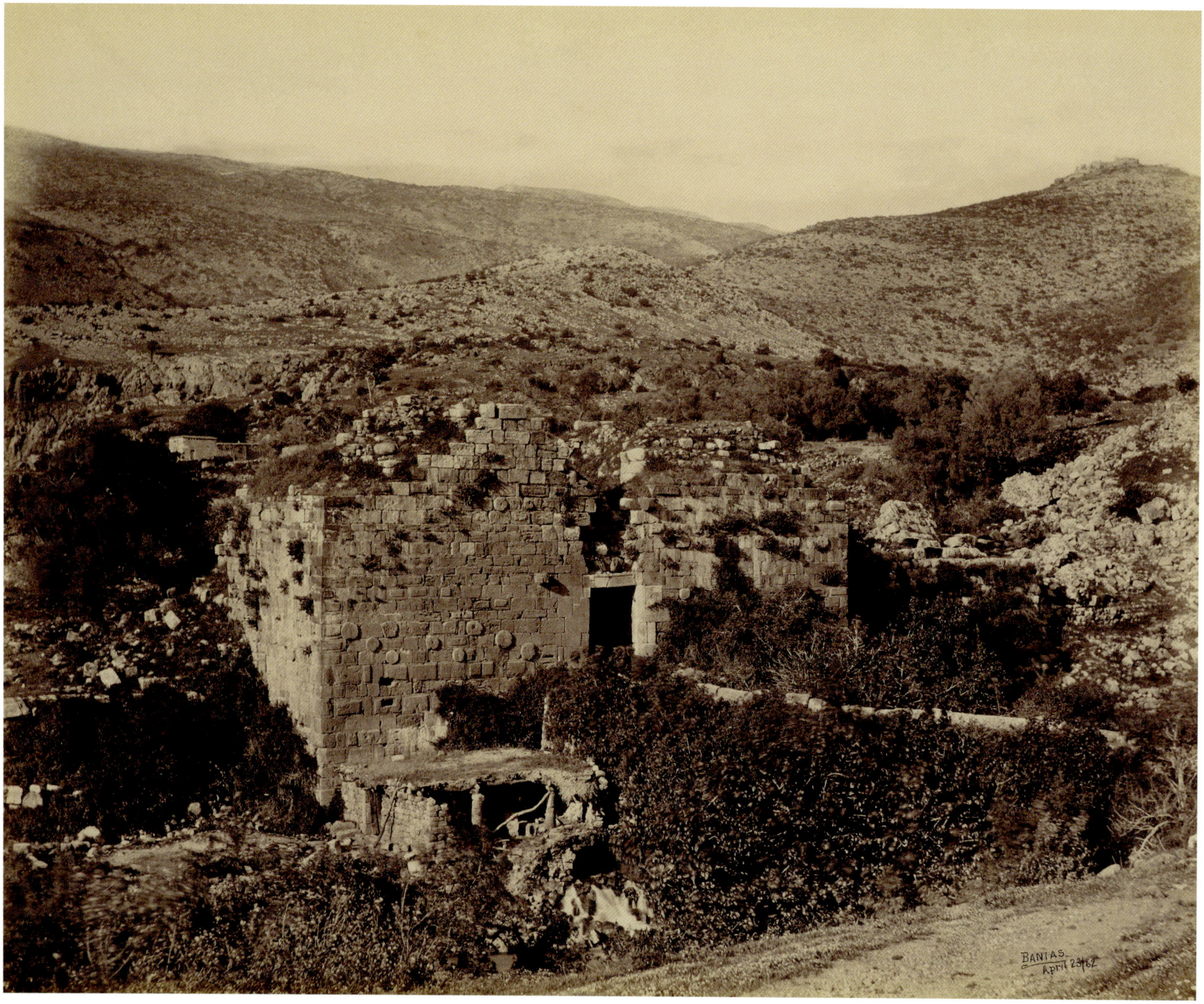

The Citadel, Banias, 23 April 1862

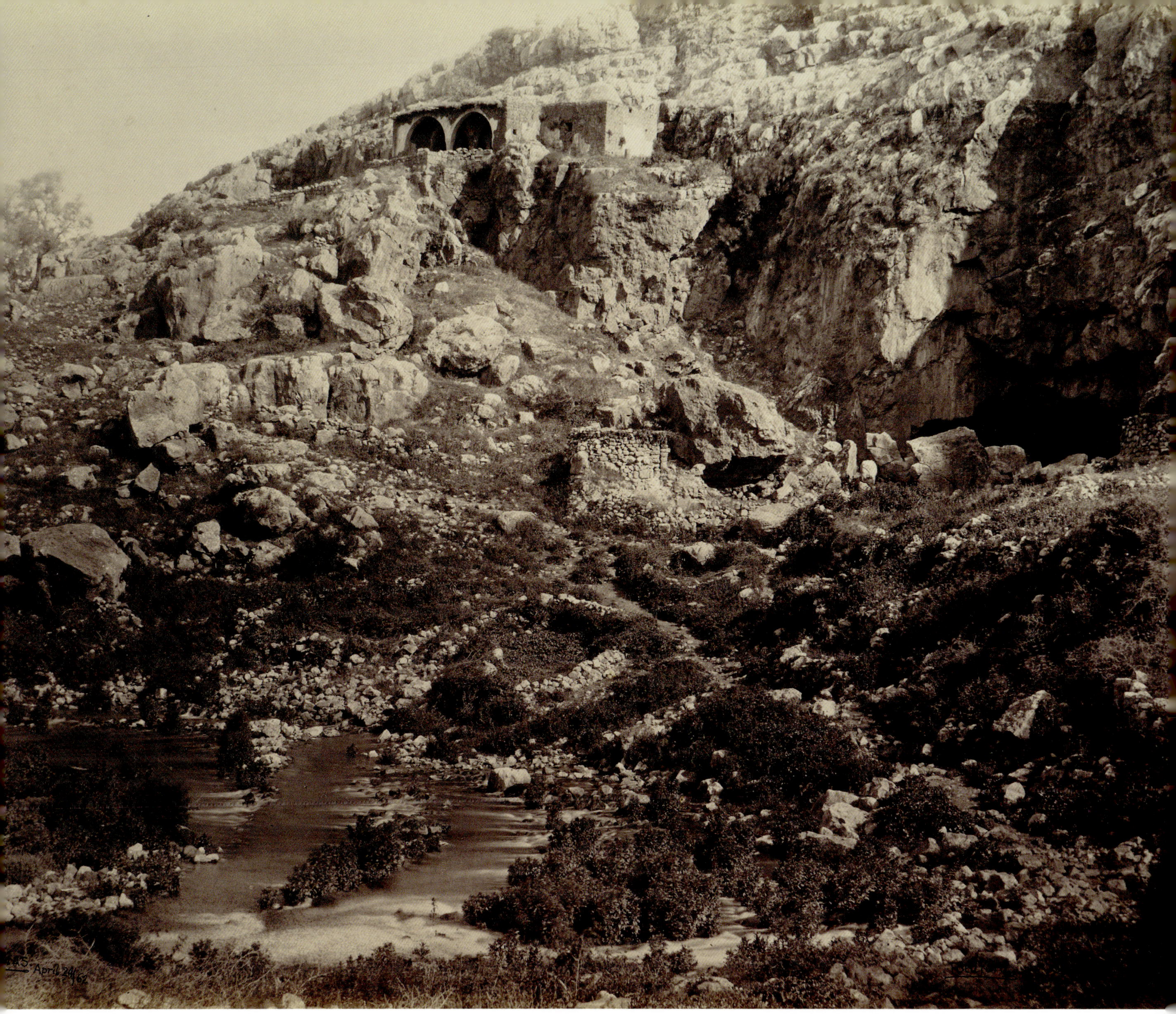

The upper source of the Jordan River, Banias, 24 April 1862

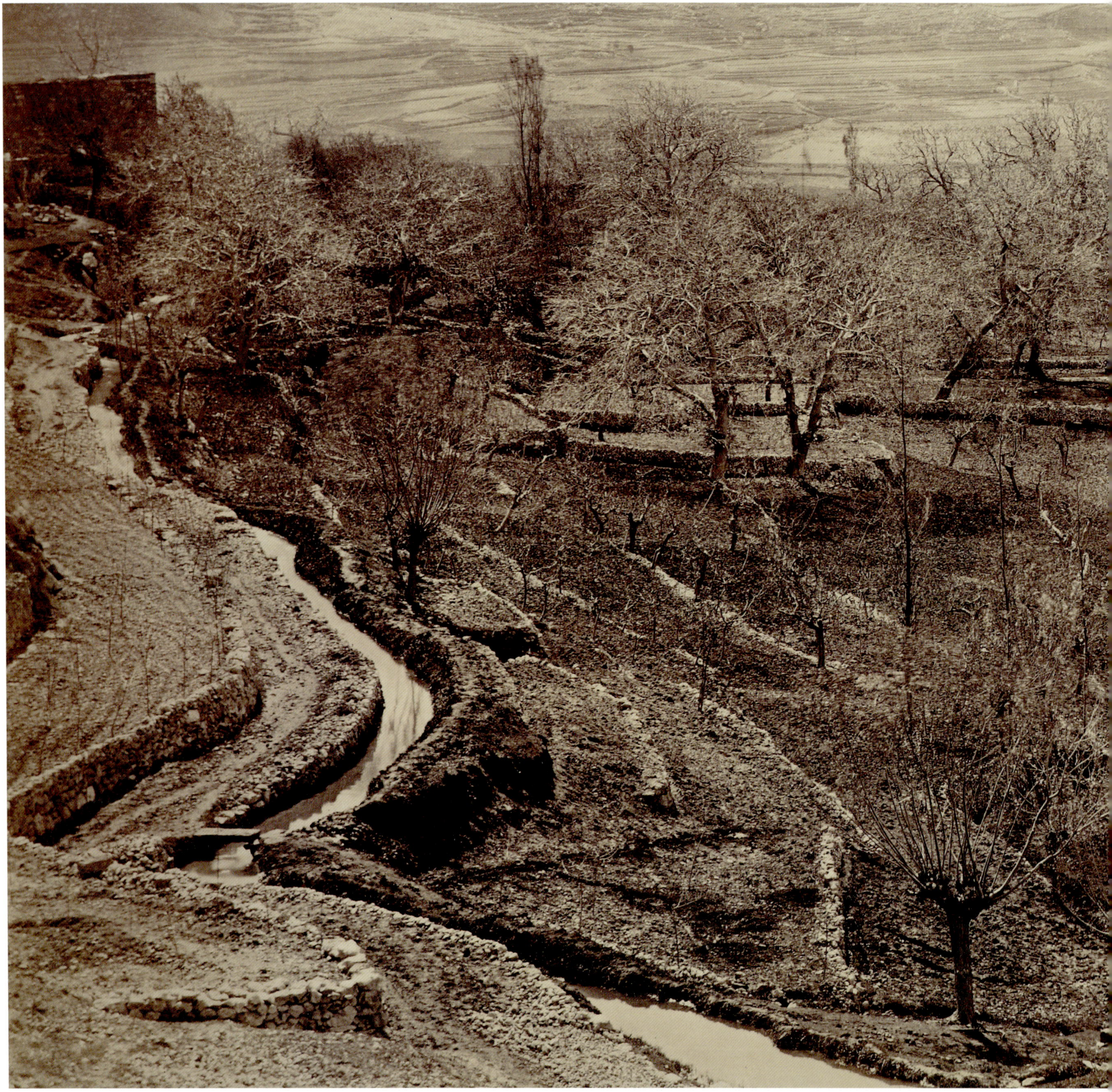

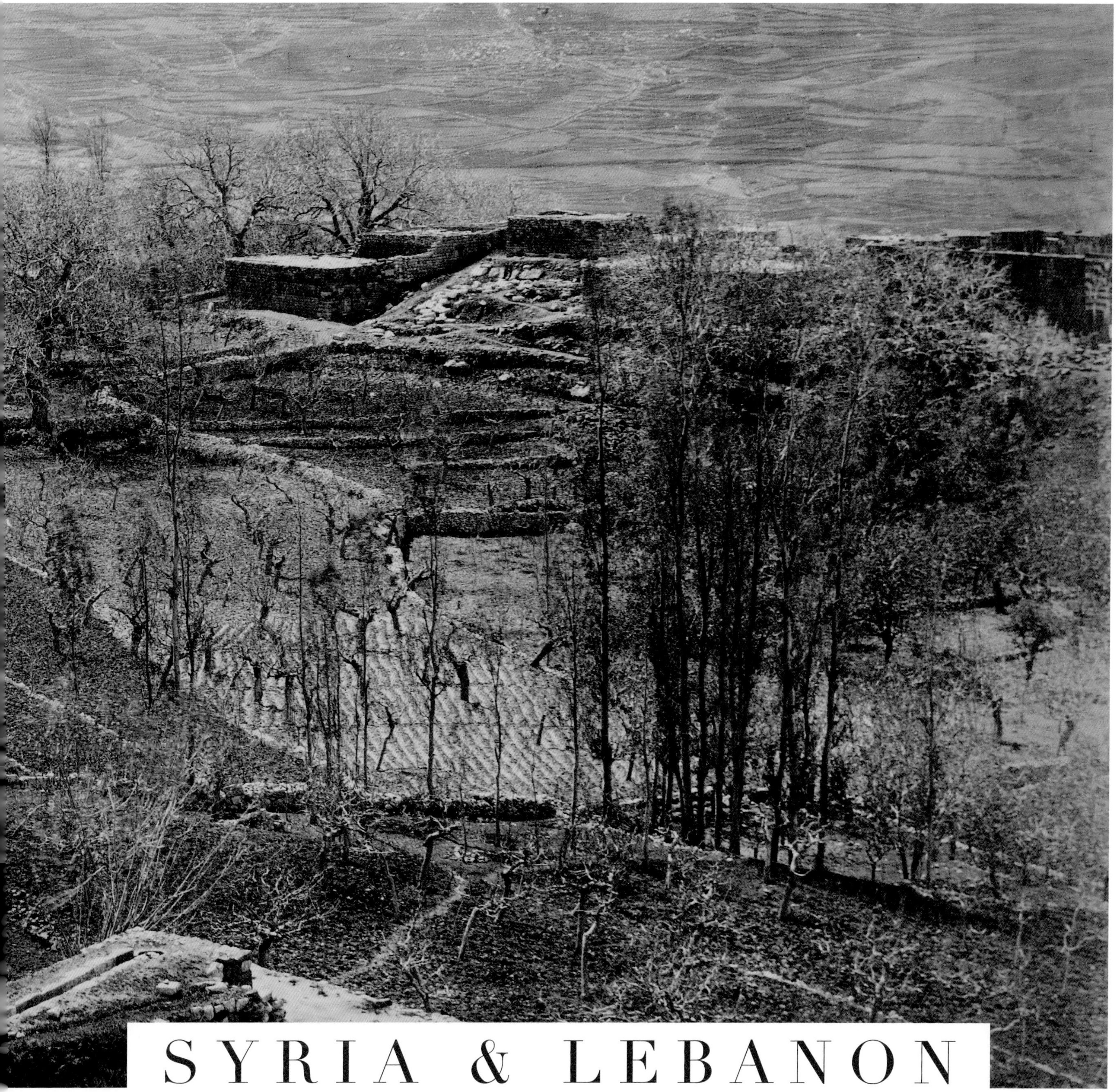

SYRIA & LEBANON

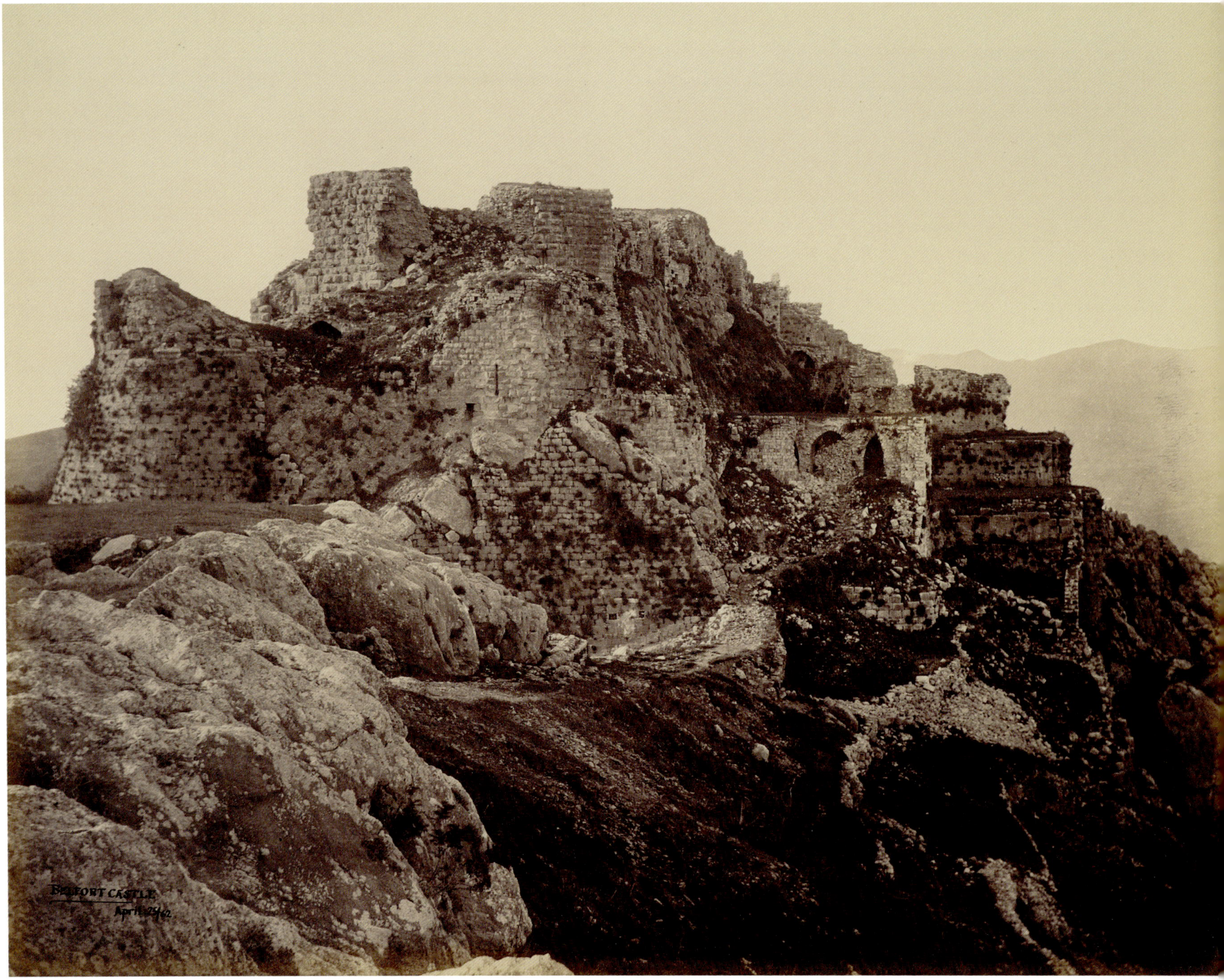

Beaufort Castle, Lebanon, 25 April 1862

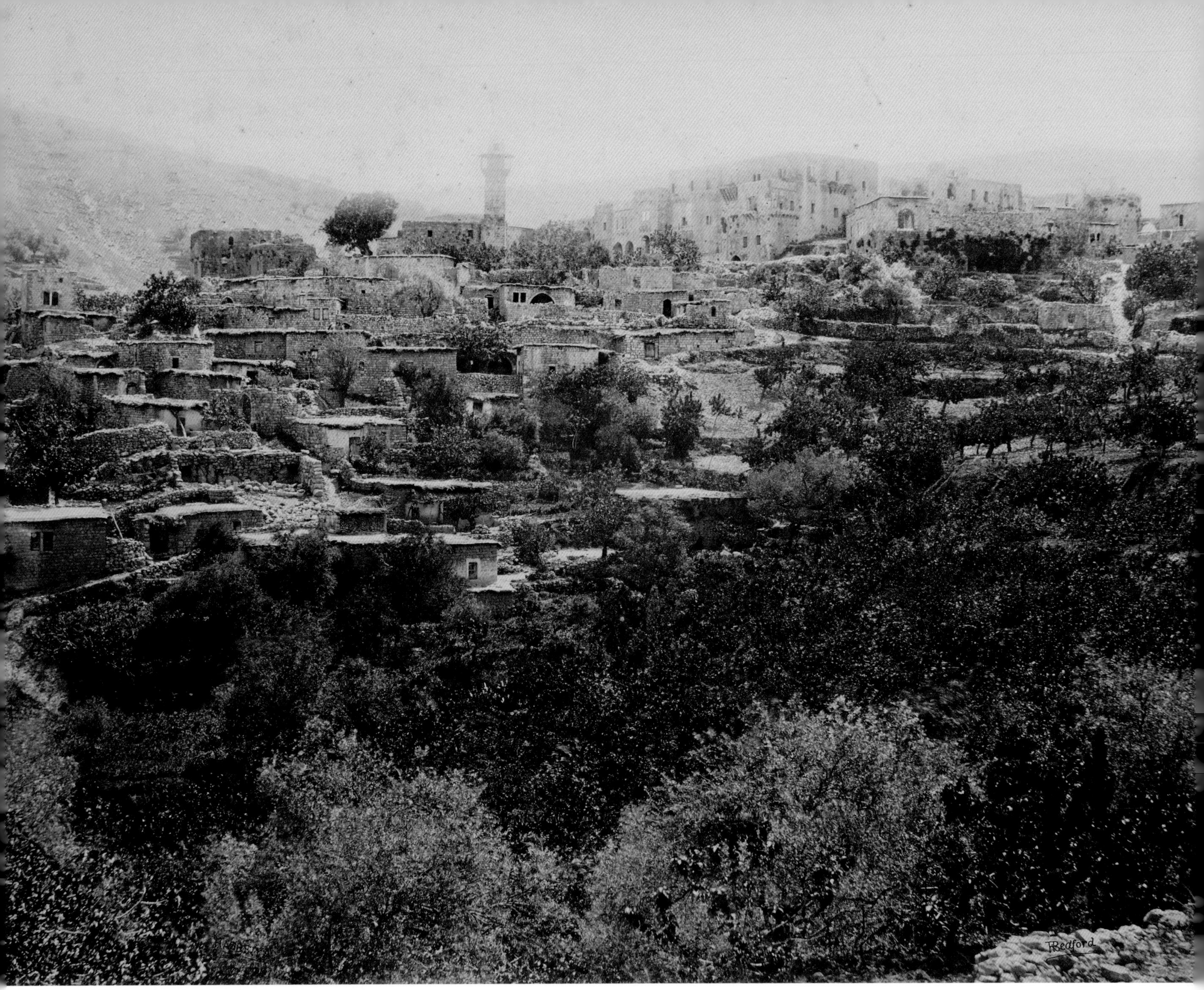

Hasbaya, Lebanon, 26 April 1862

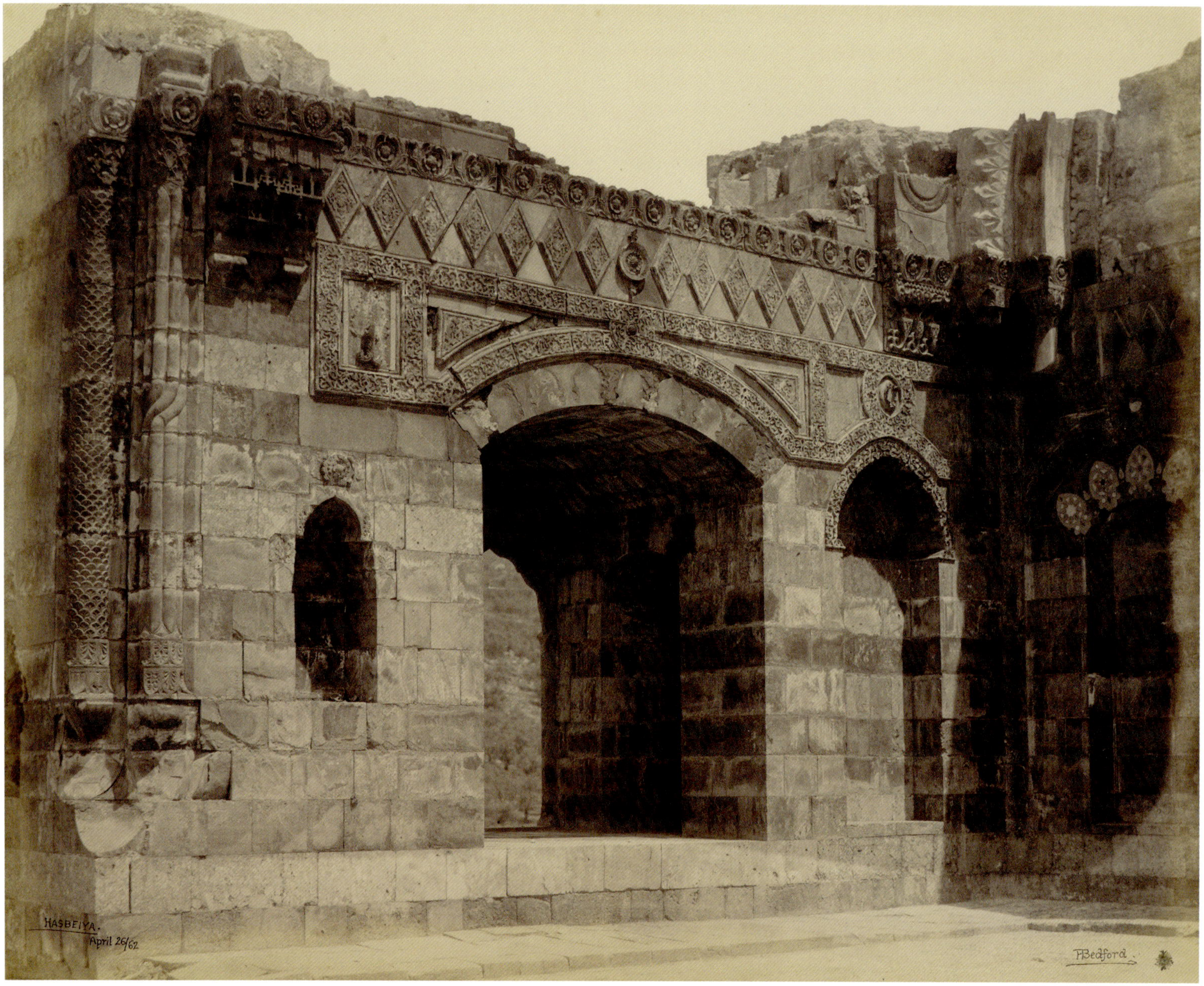

The Citadel, Hasbaya, Lebanon, 26 April 1862

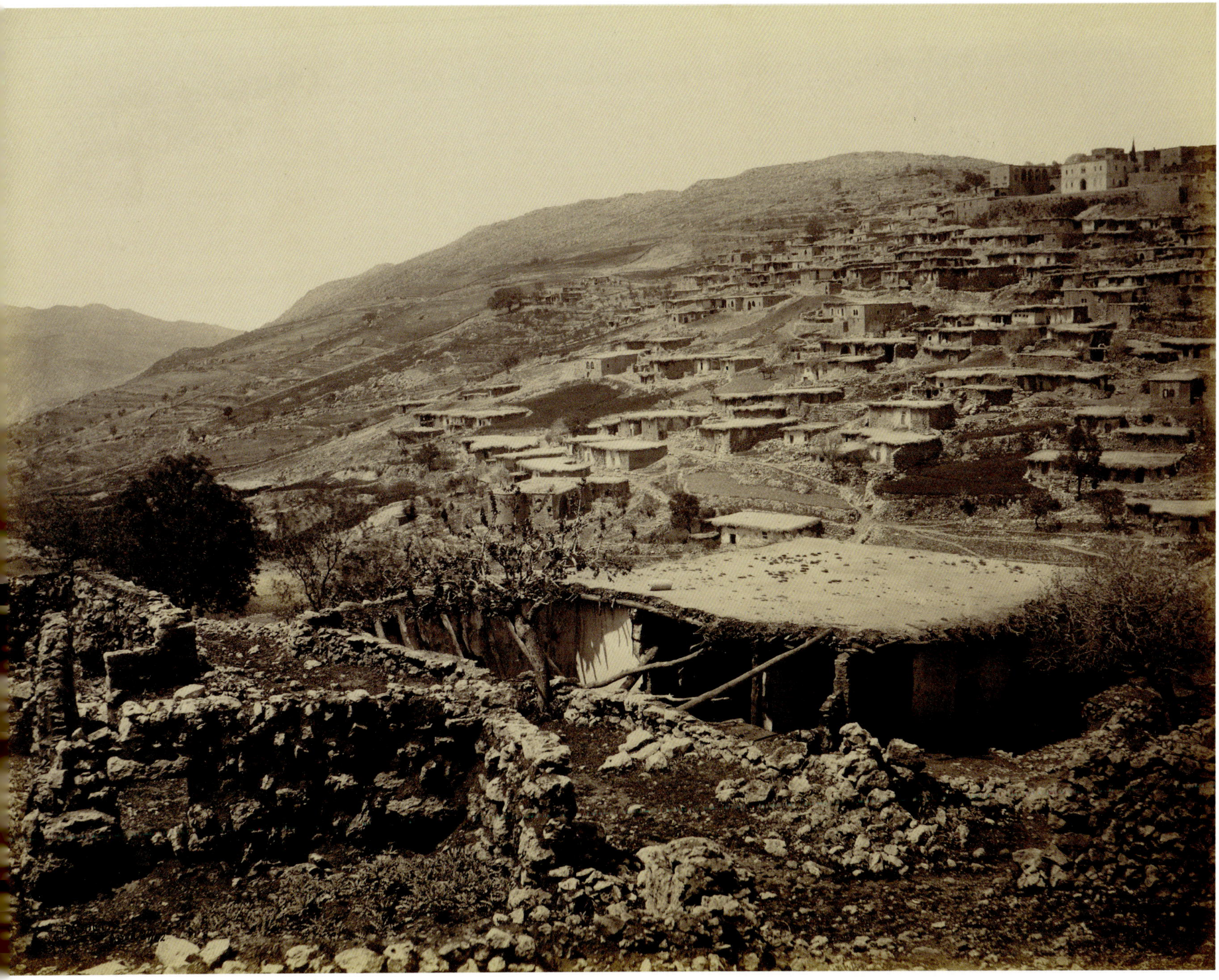

Rashaya, Lebanon, 27 April 1862

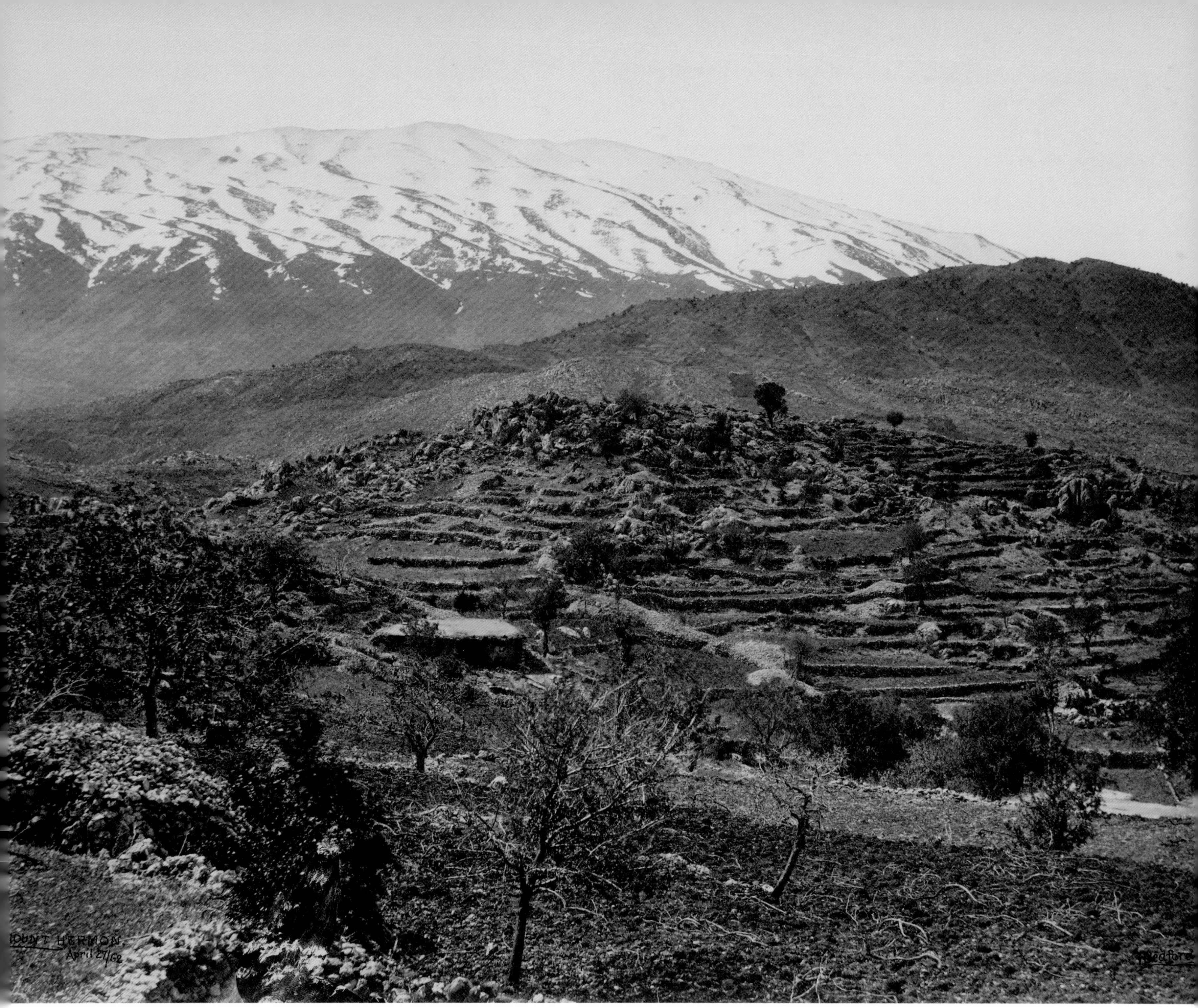

Mount Hermon from Rashaya, Lebanon, 27 April 1862

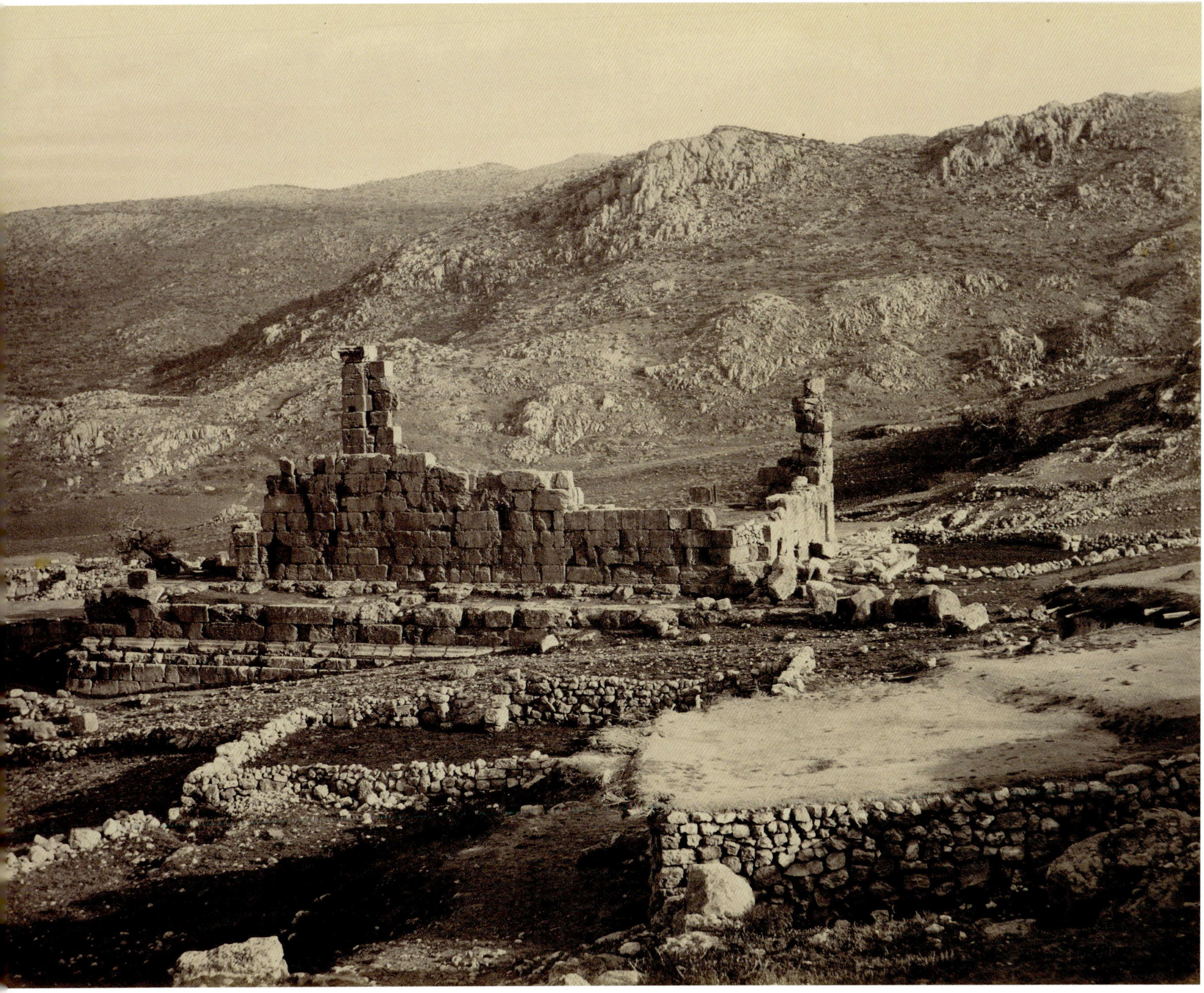

Temple ruins, Deir al-Asha'ir, Lebanon, 27 April 1862

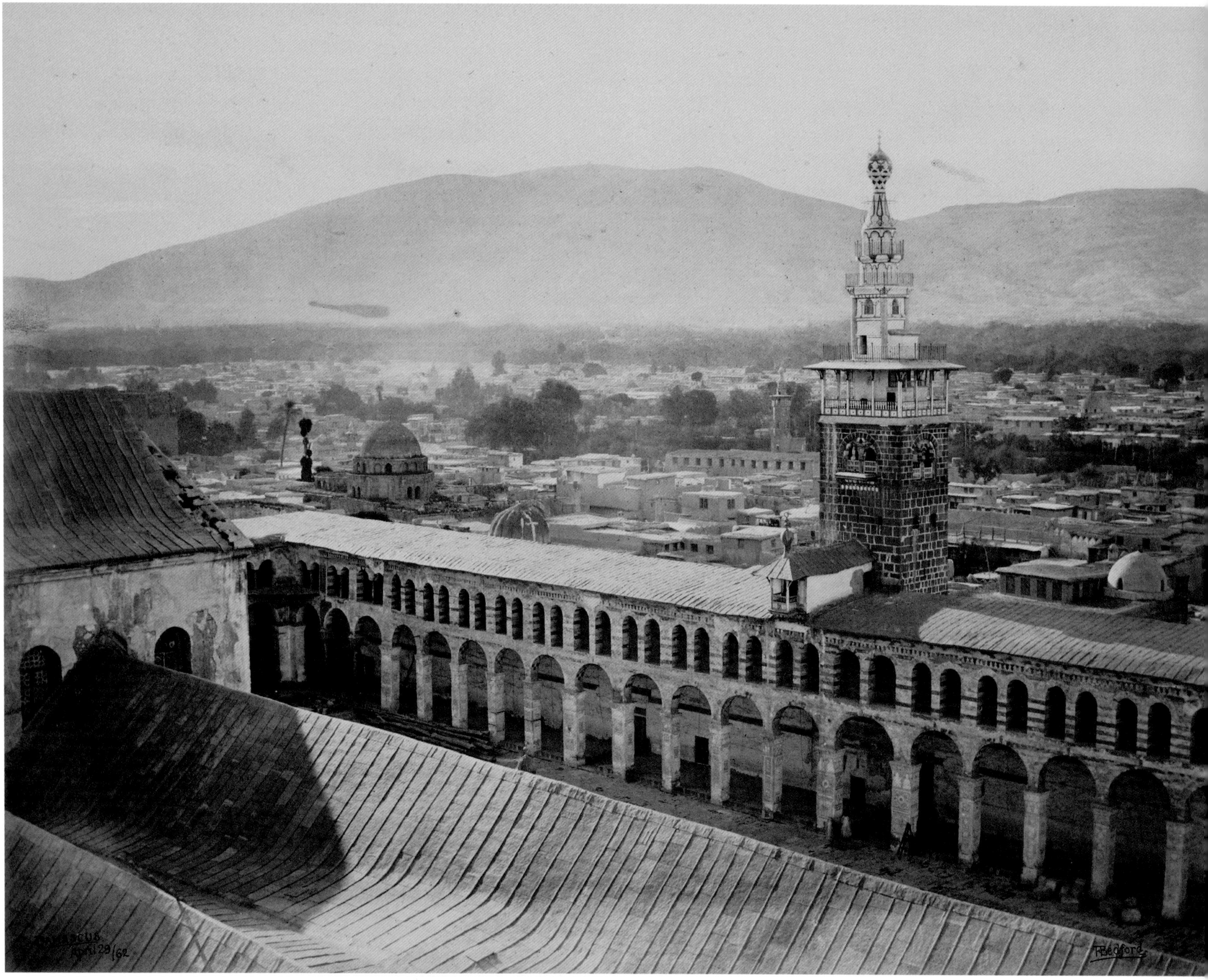

The Great Mosque, Damascus, 29 April 1862

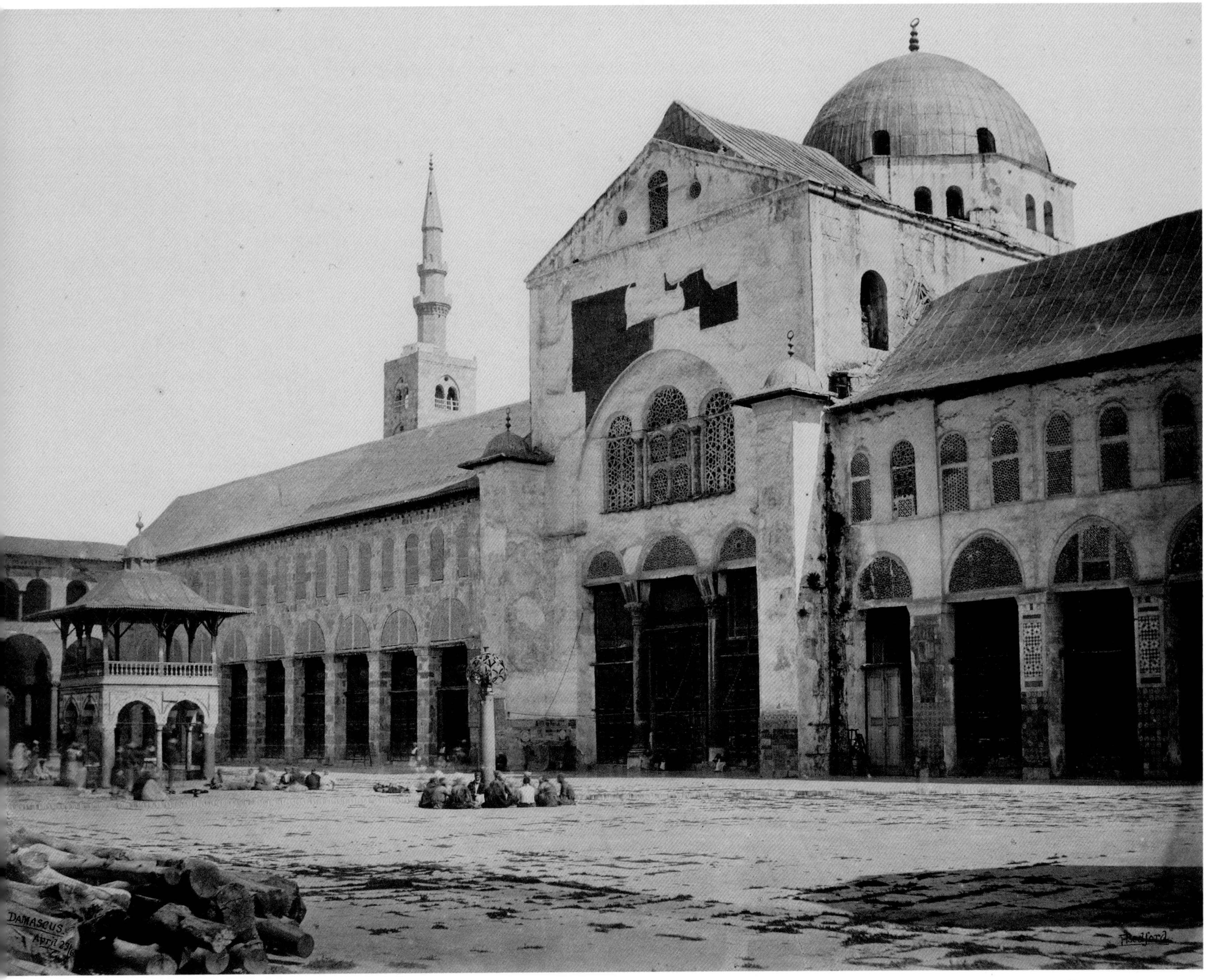

The Great Mosque, Damascus, 29 April 1862

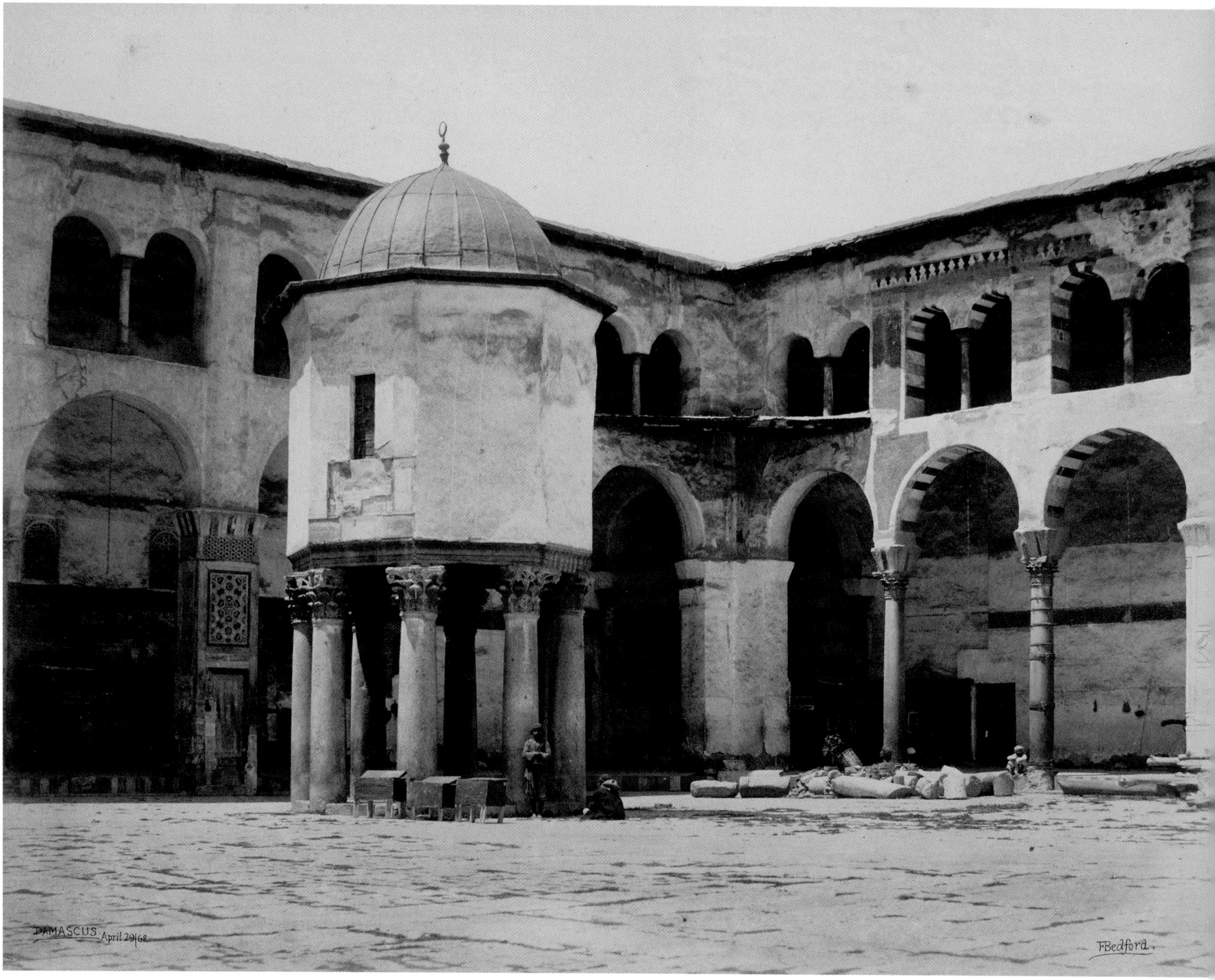

The Great Mosque, Damascus, 29 April 1862

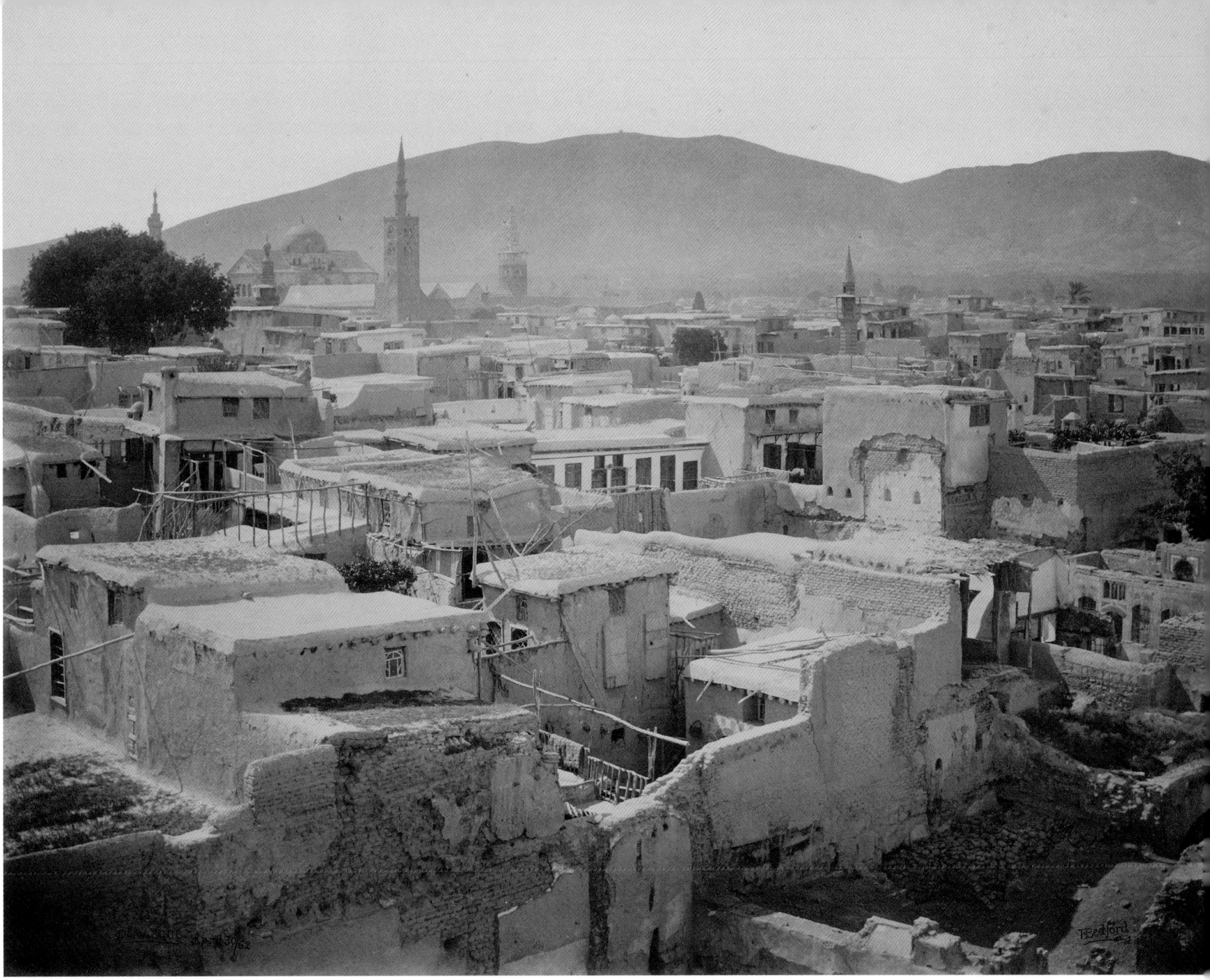

Damascus from a minaret in the Christian Quarter, 30 April 1862

"After luncheon we visited the Xtian quarter, wh[ich] is now all in ruins, since the terrible massacres in 1860 . . . . We saw specifically the ruins of the Greek Churches & the house of a rich Xtian wh[ich] once were beautiful, & are now a heap of ruins. We also went up an old Minaret, & had a good view of the desolate houses, w[h]ere once 25,000 Xtians lived prosperously."
Prince of Wales's Journal, 29 April 1862

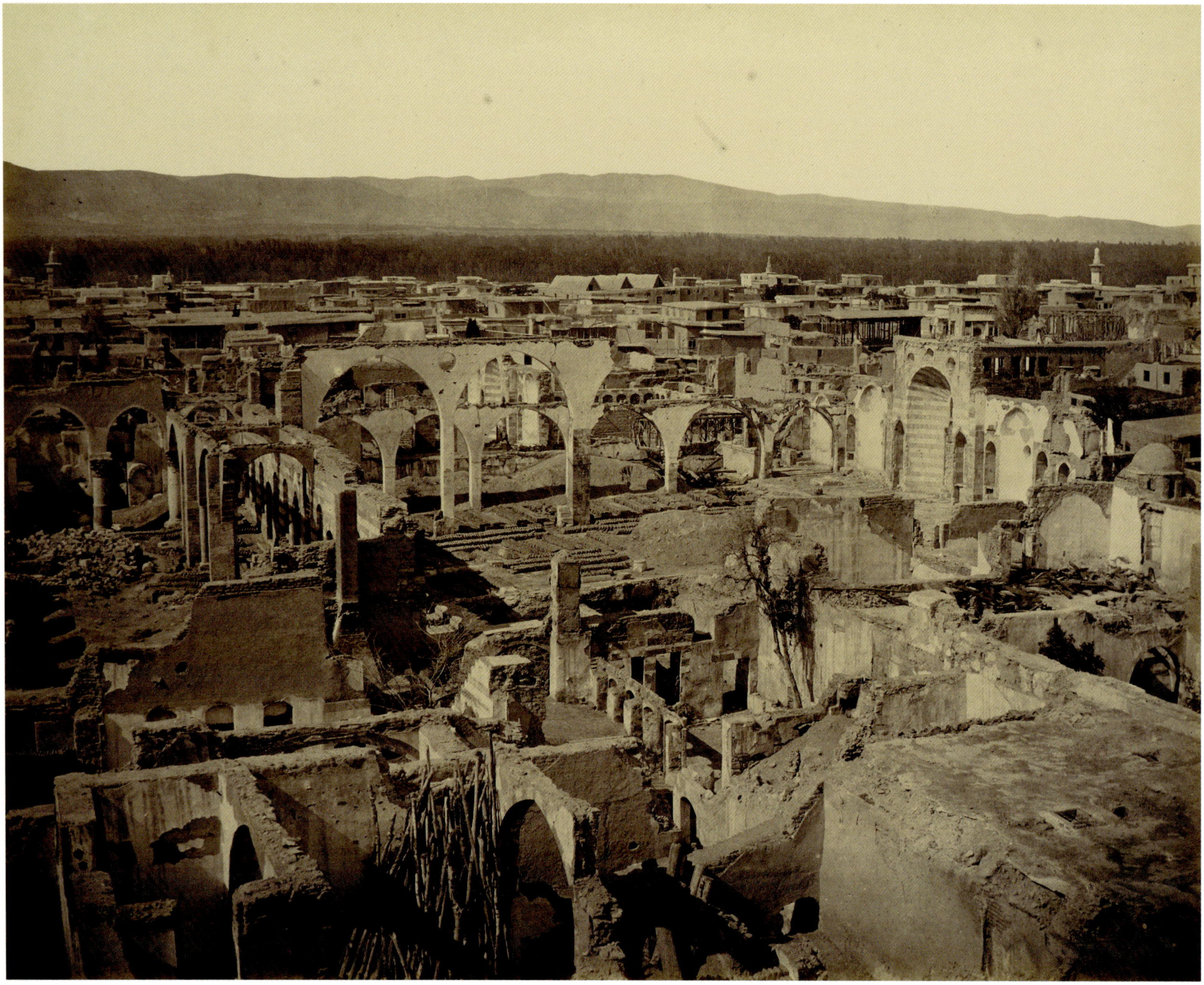

Ruins of the Greek church in the Christian Quarter, Damascus, 30 April 1862

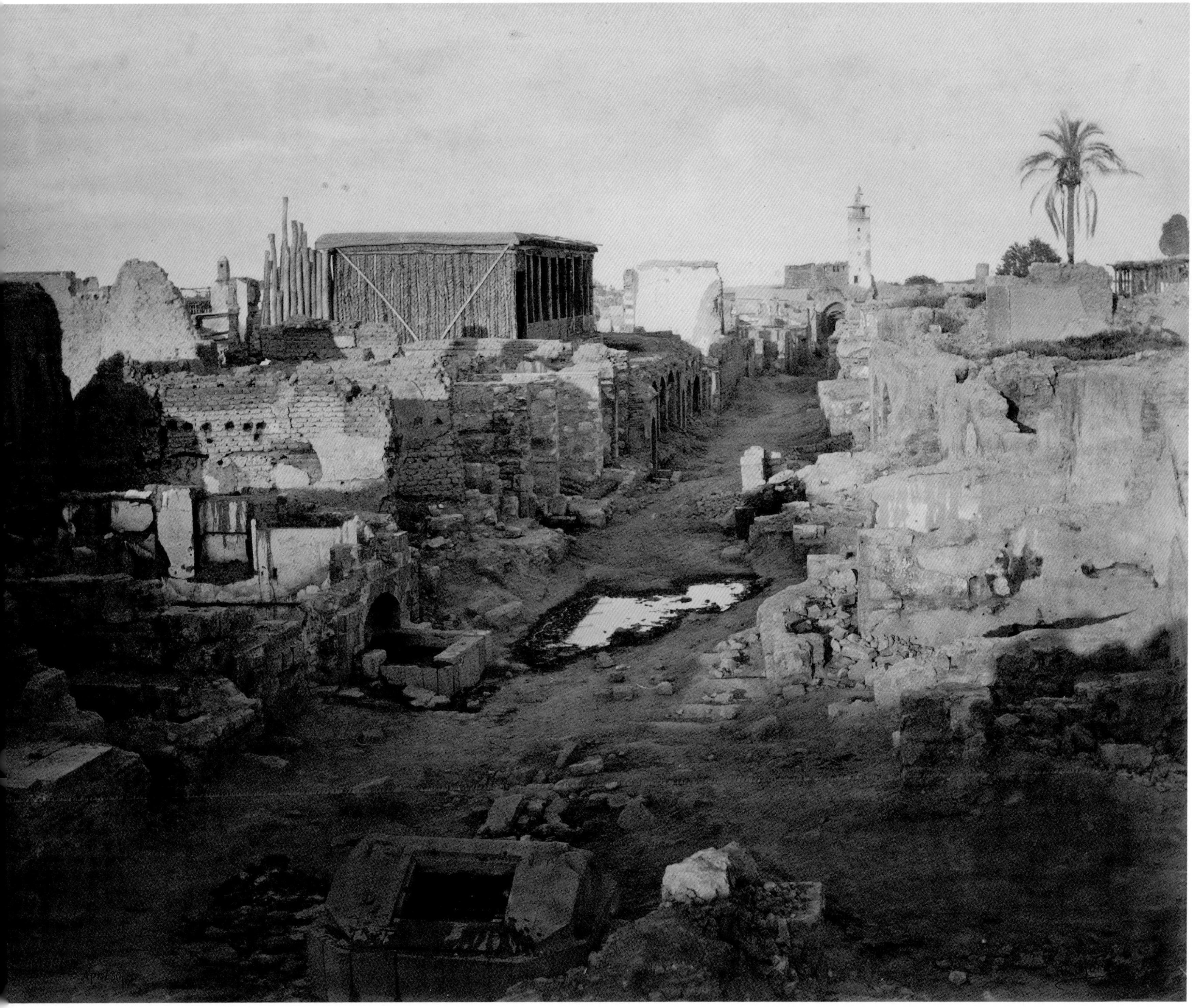

Straight Street, Damascus, 30 April 1862

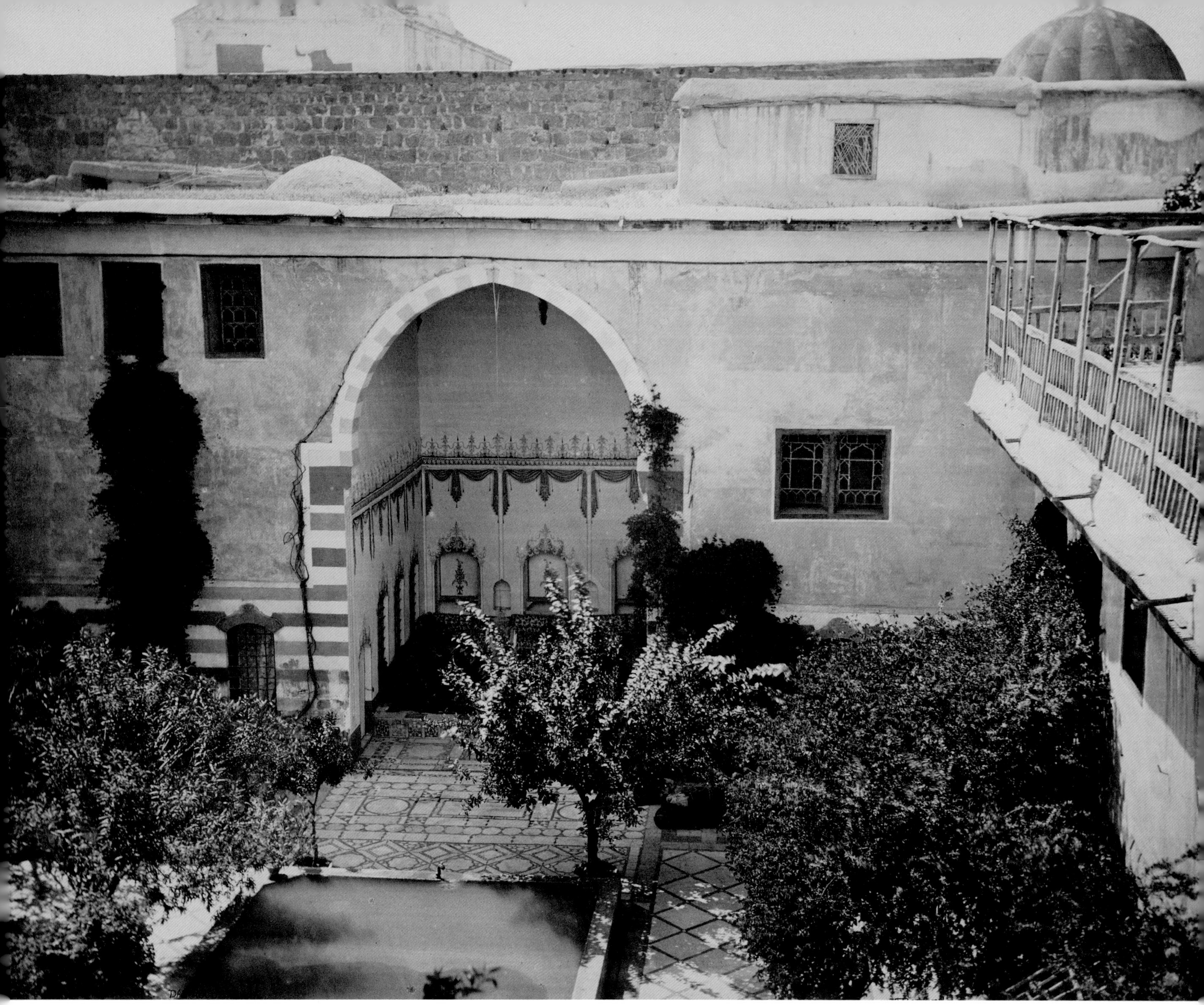

The British Consulate, Damascus, 1 May 1862

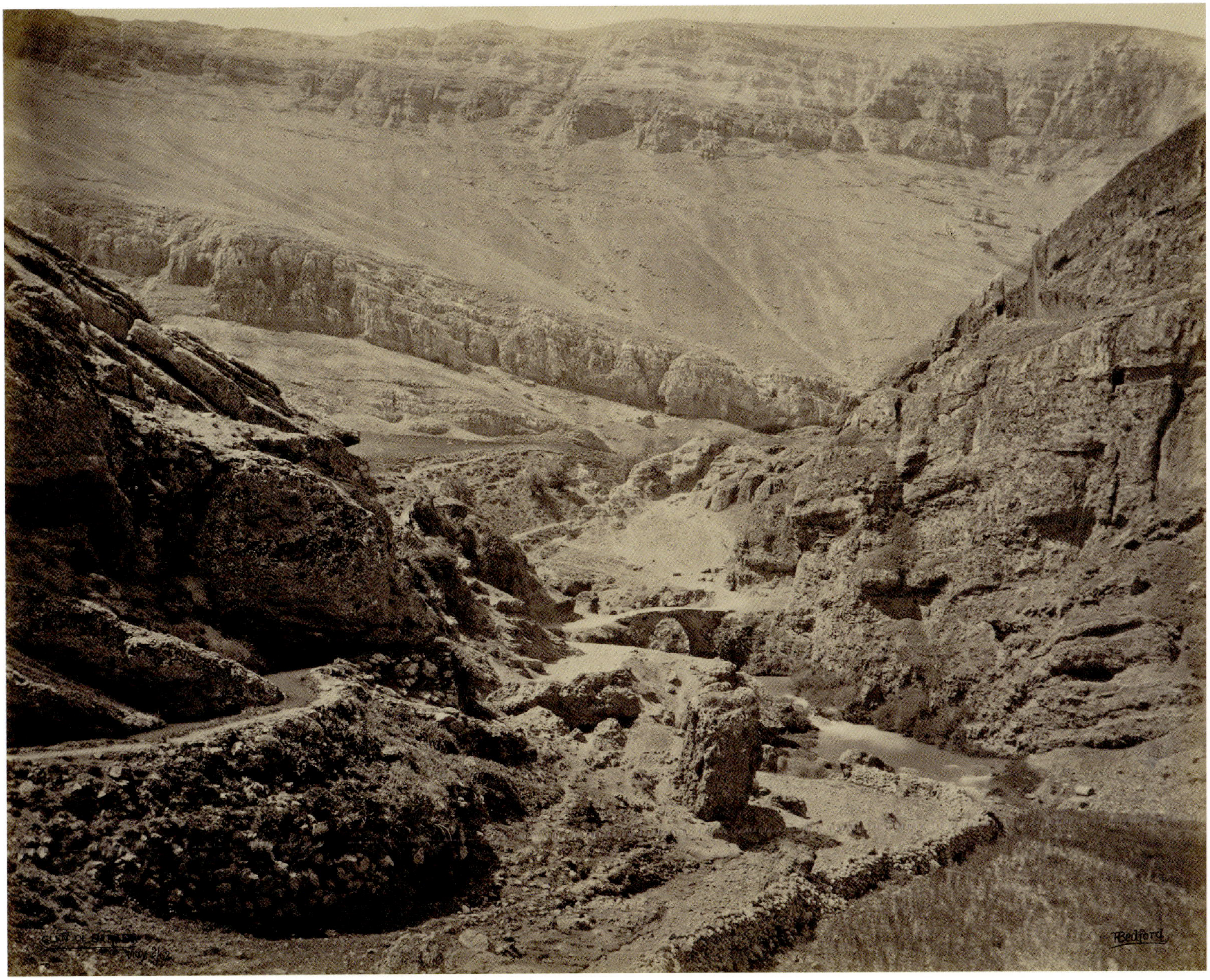

The Barada River, Syria, 2 May 1862

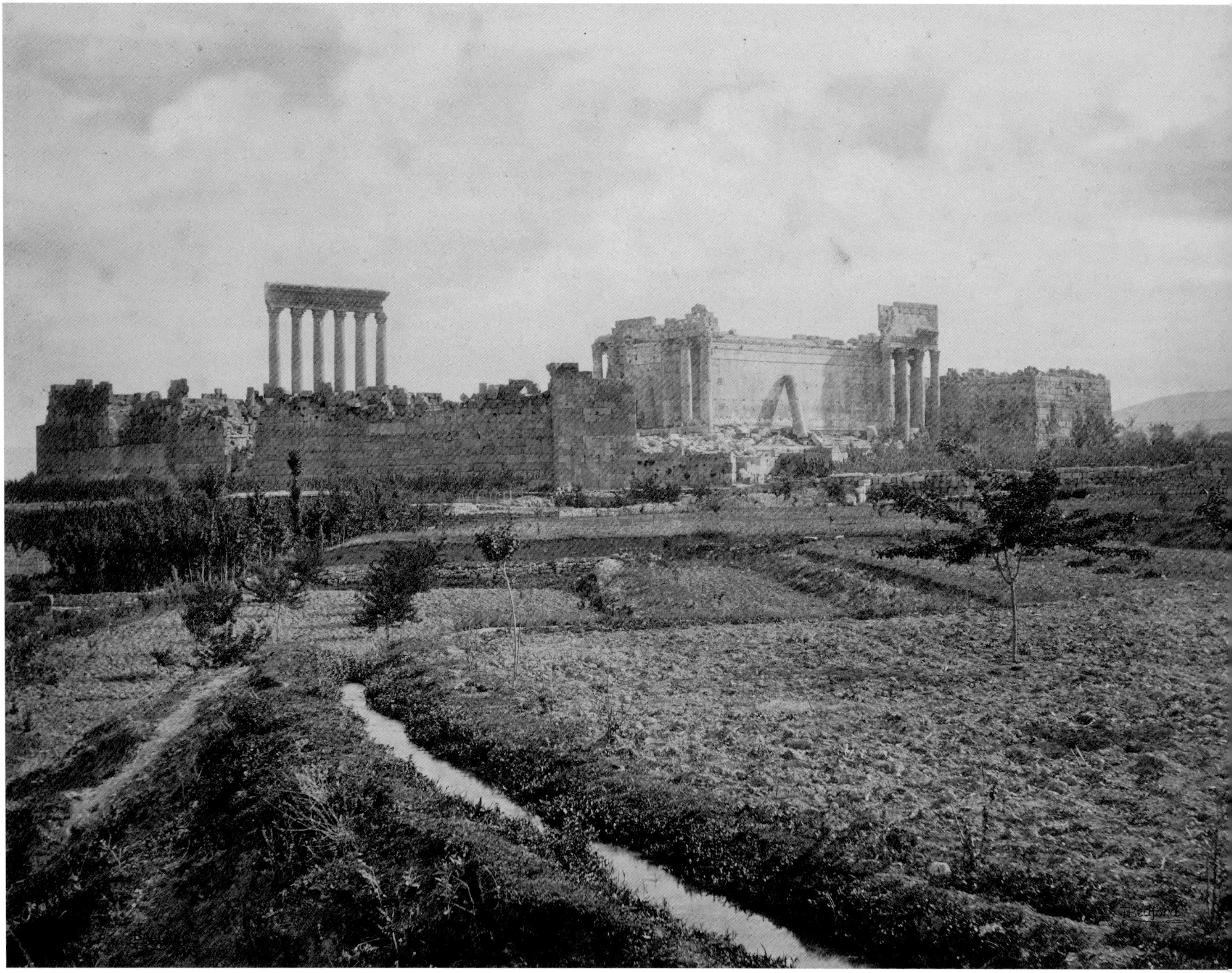

The Temple of Jupiter, Baalbek, Lebanon, 3 May 1862

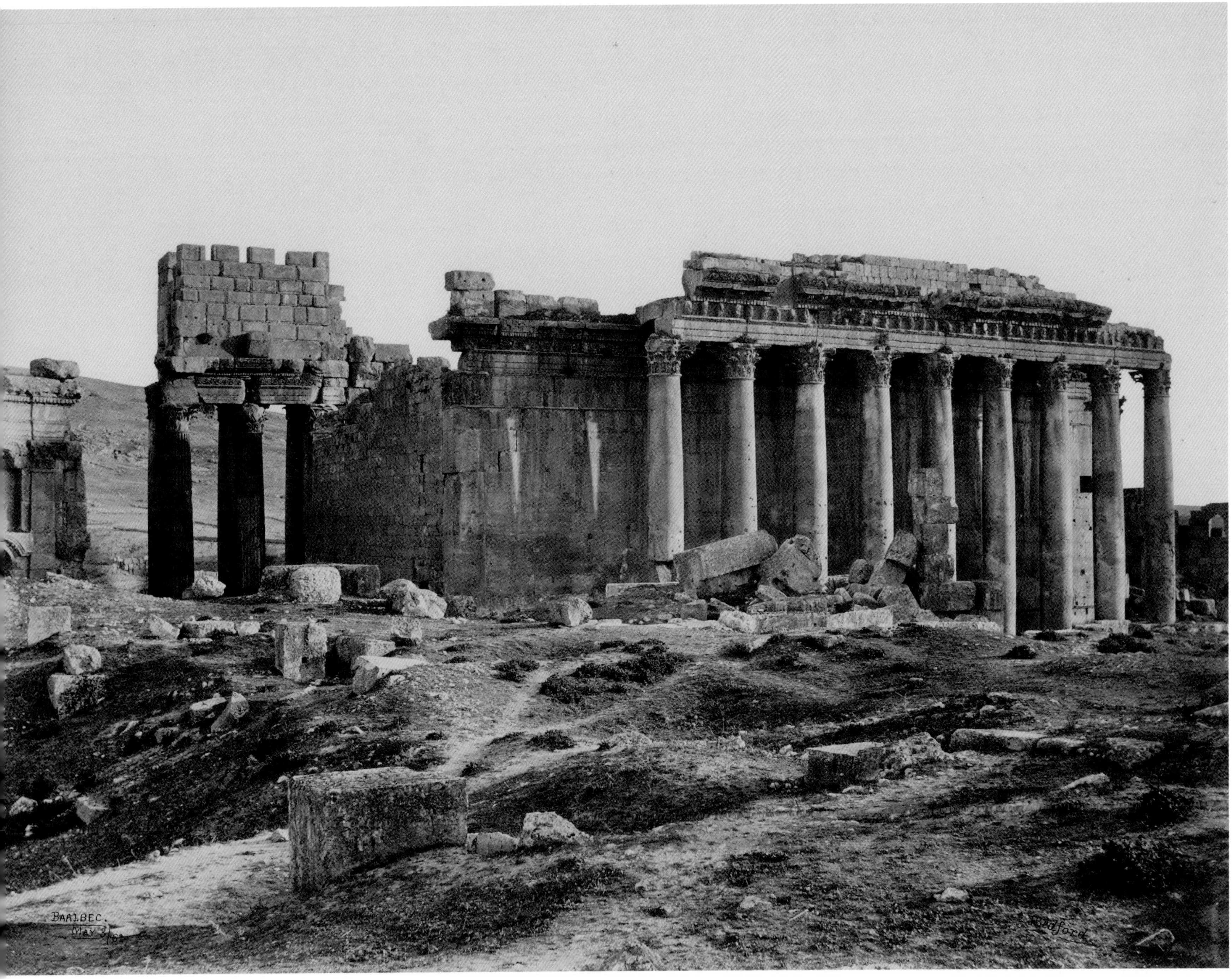

The Temple of Jupiter, Baalbek, Lebanon, 3 May 1862

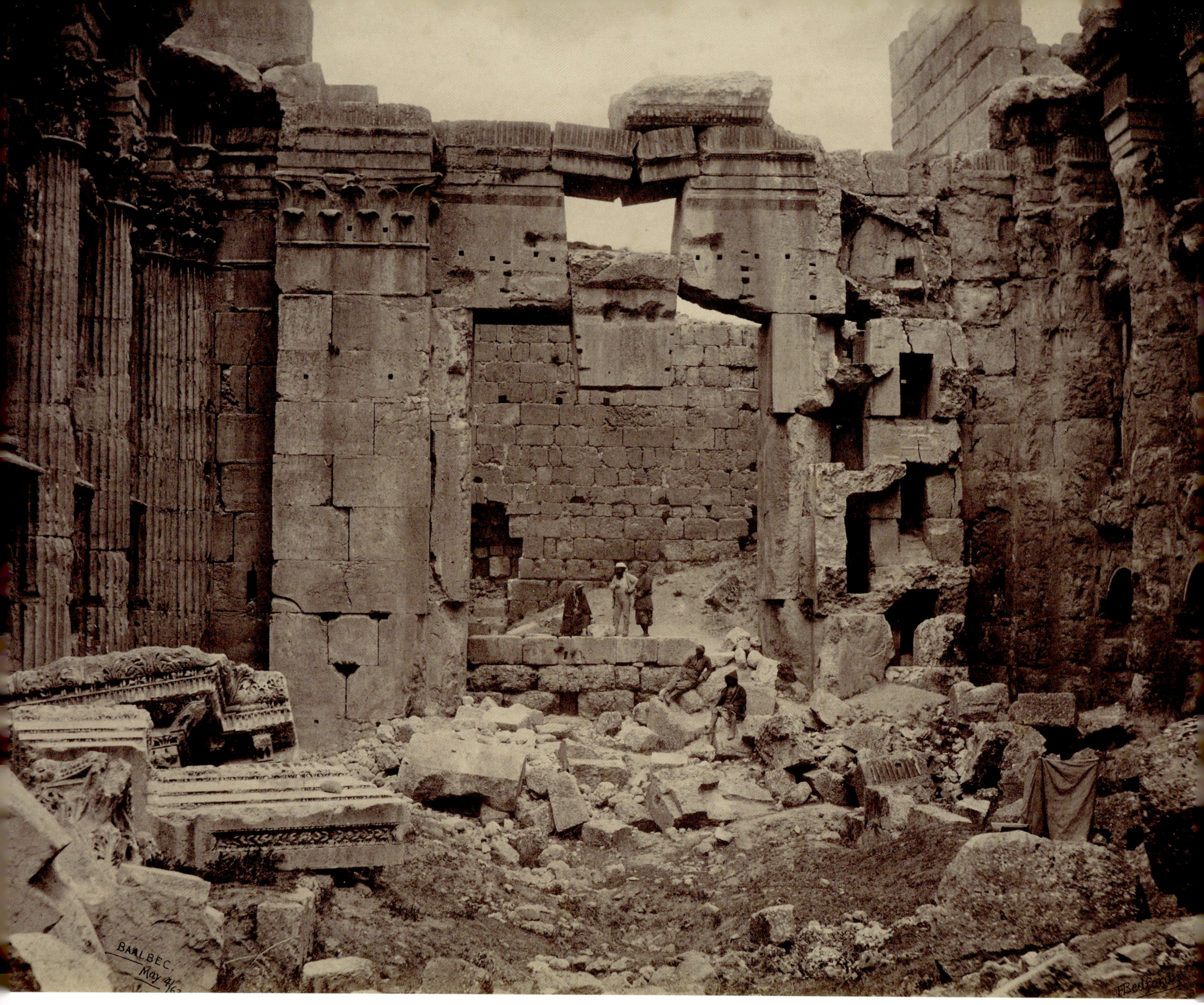

The Temple of Jupiter, Baalbek, Lebanon, 4 May 1862

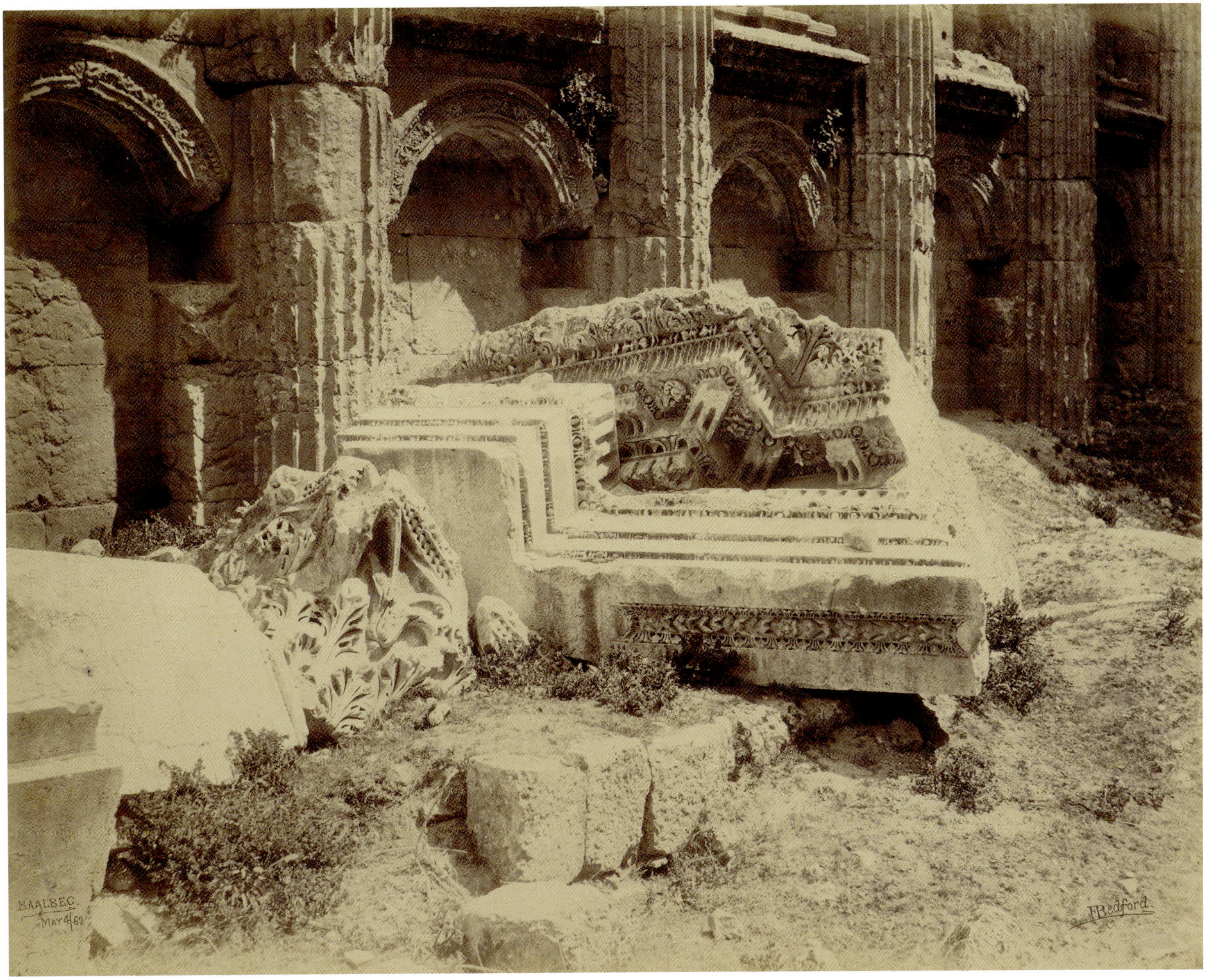

The Temple of Jupiter, Baalbek, Lebanon, 4 May 1862

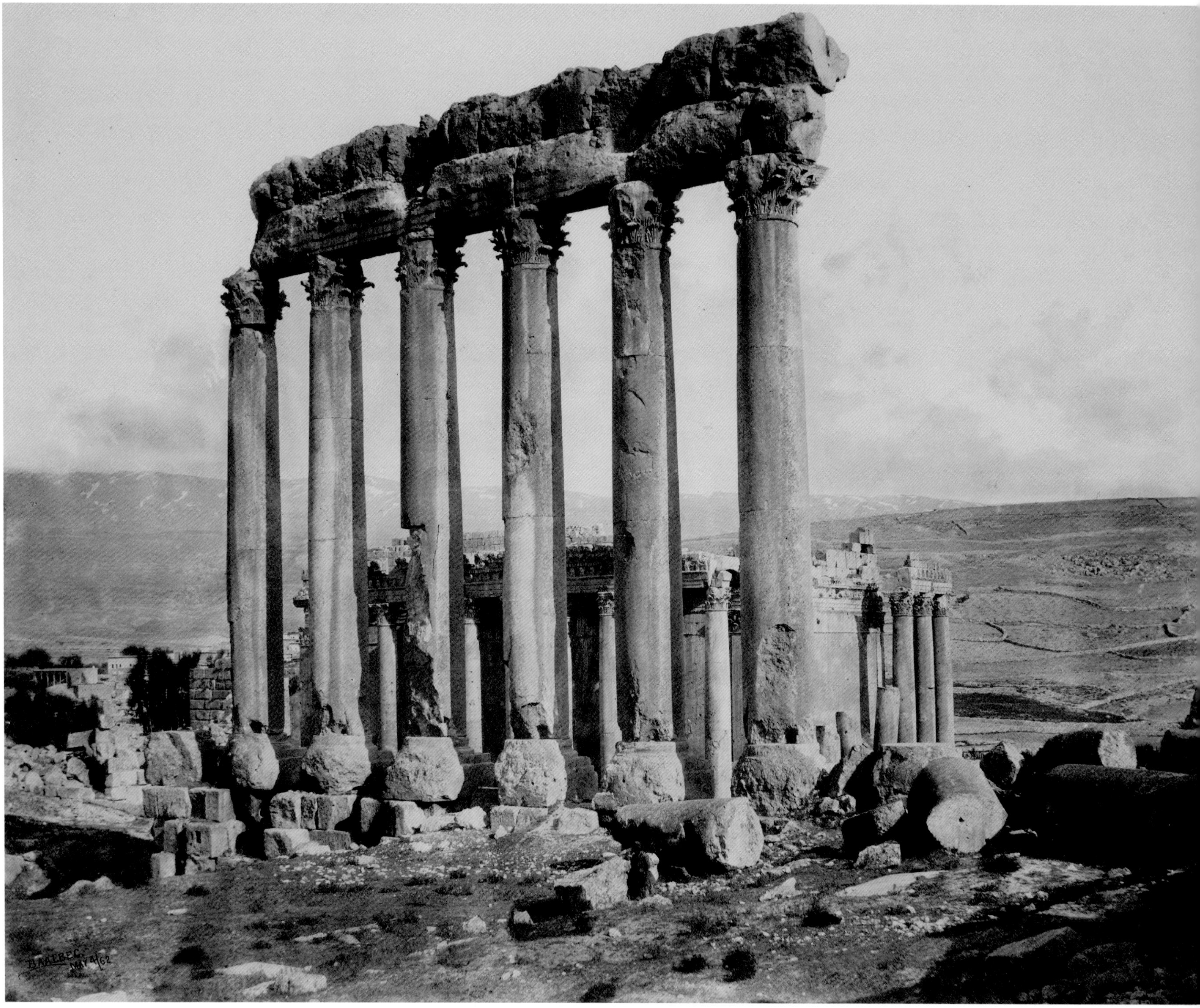

The Temple of Jupiter, Baalbek, Lebanon, 4 May 1862

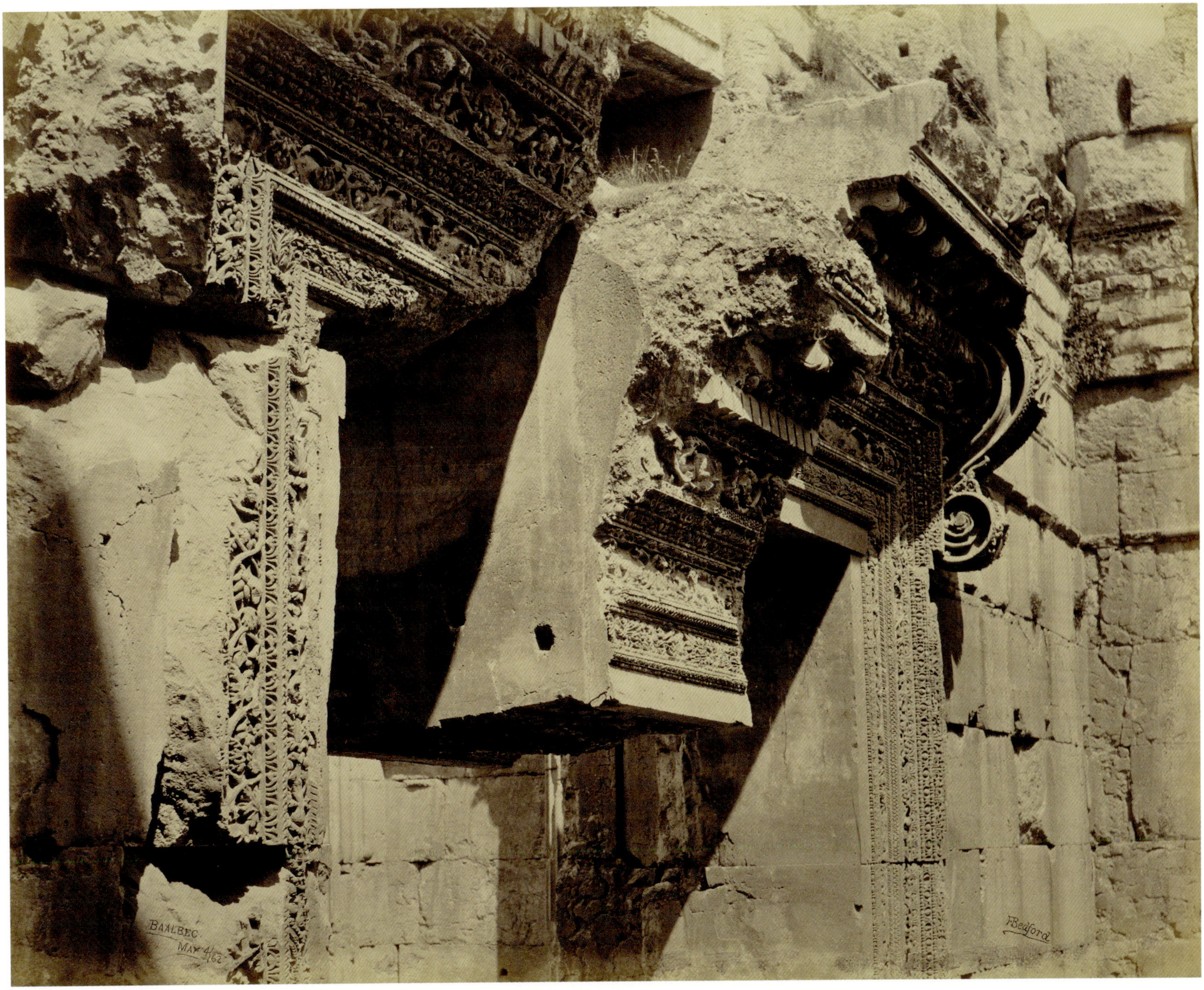

The Great Doorway, Baalbek, Lebanon, 4 May 1862

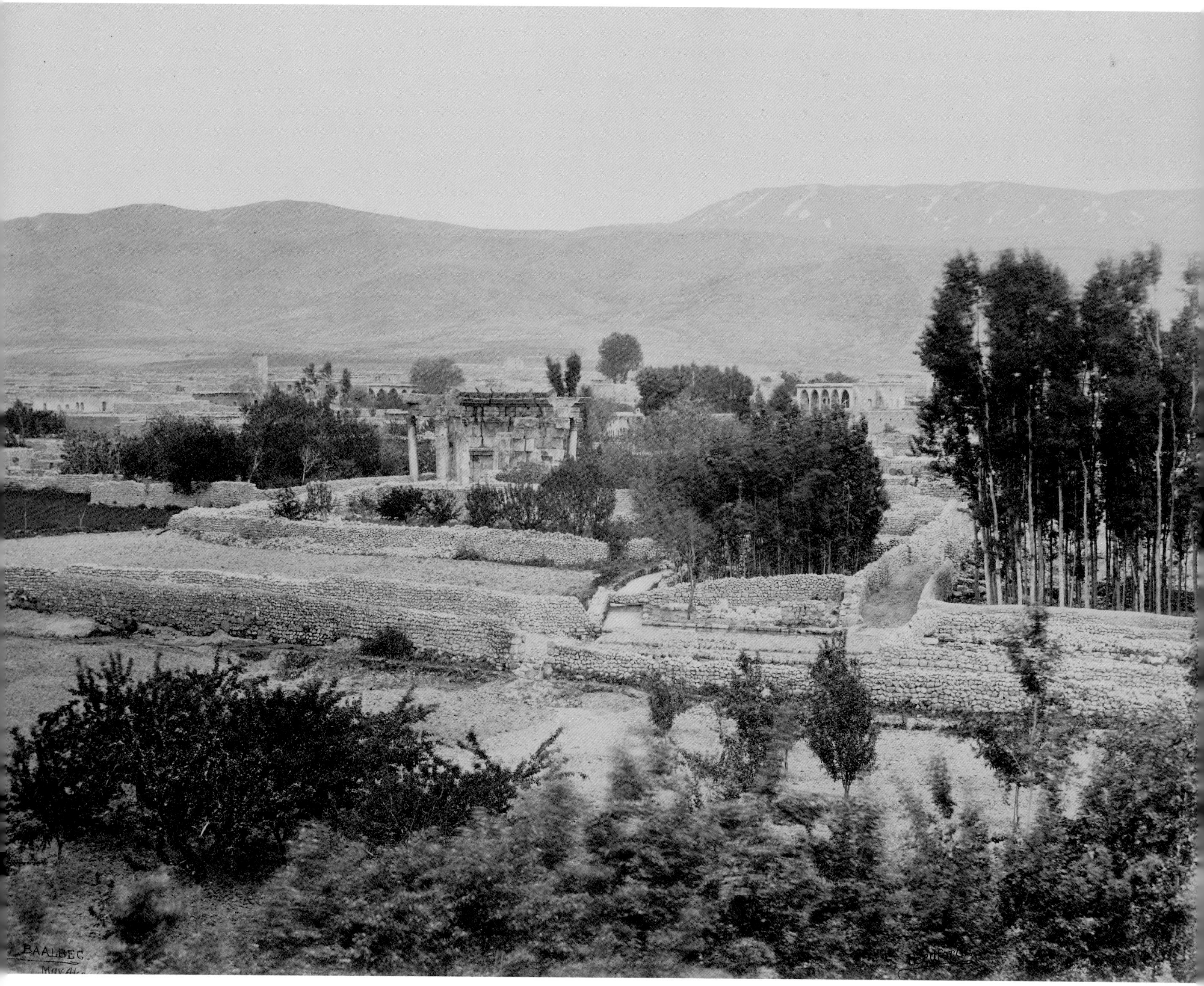

Baalbek, Lebanon, 4 May 1862

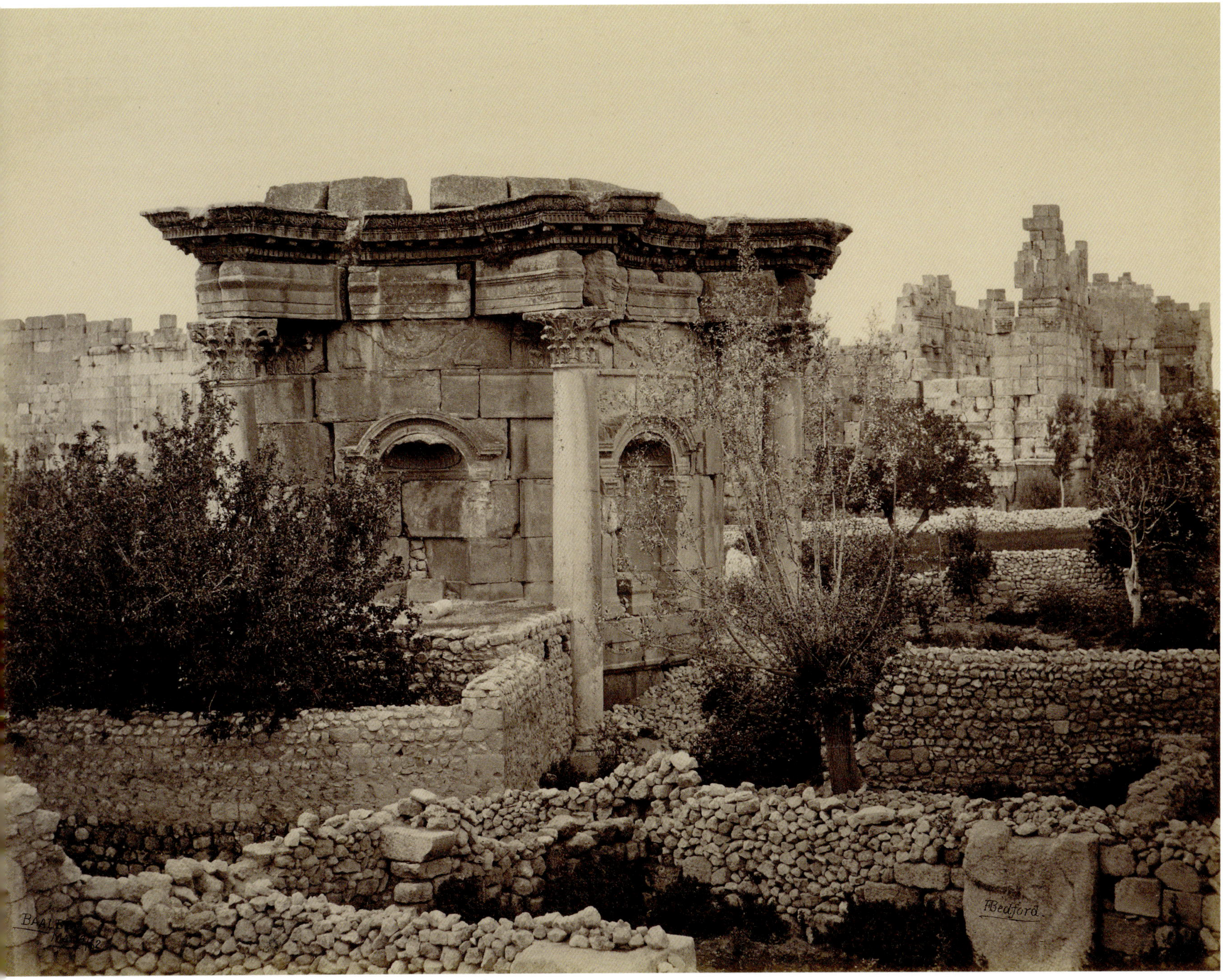

The Circular Temple, Baalbek, Lebanon, 4 May 1862

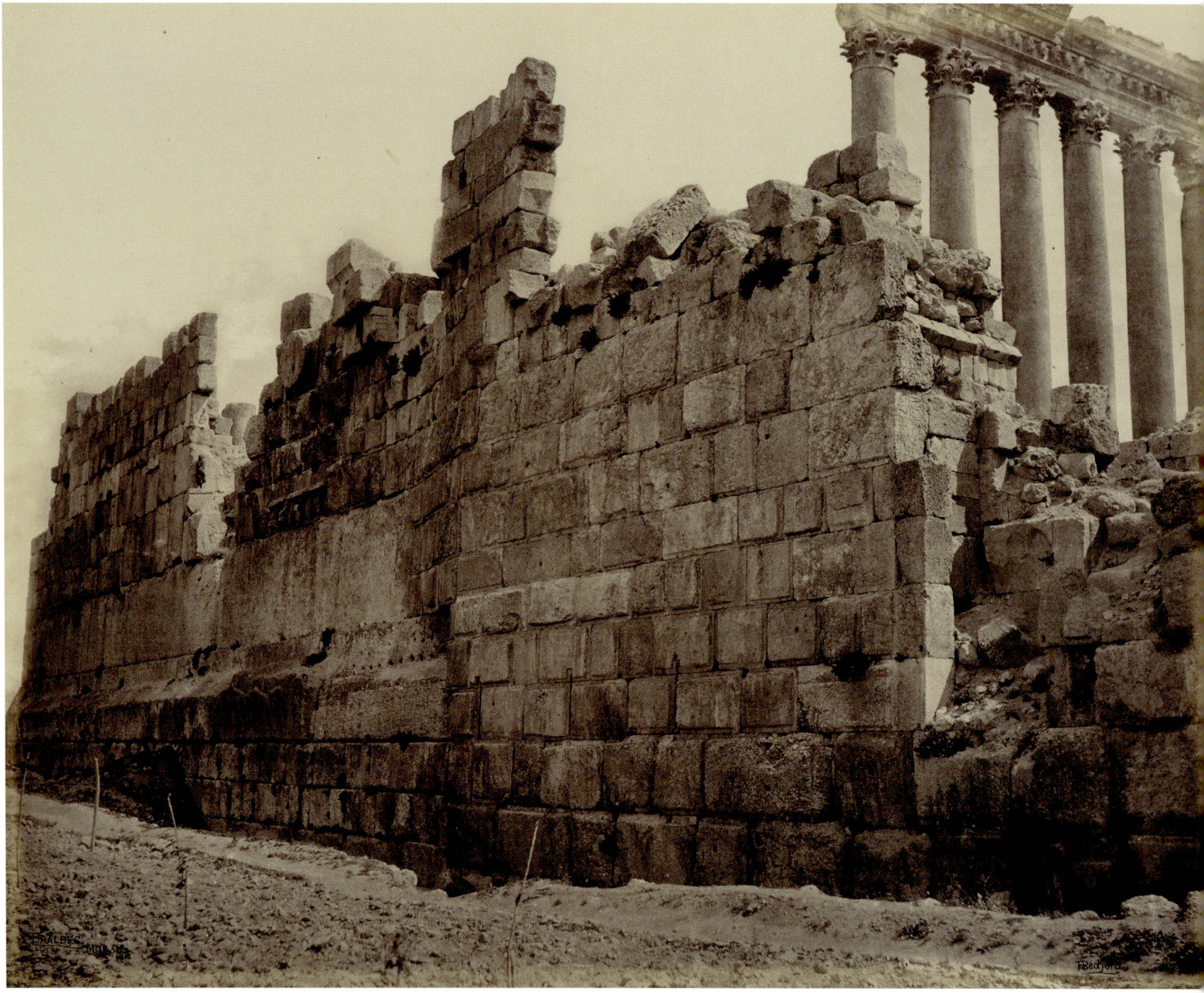

Baalbek, Lebanon, 5 May 1862

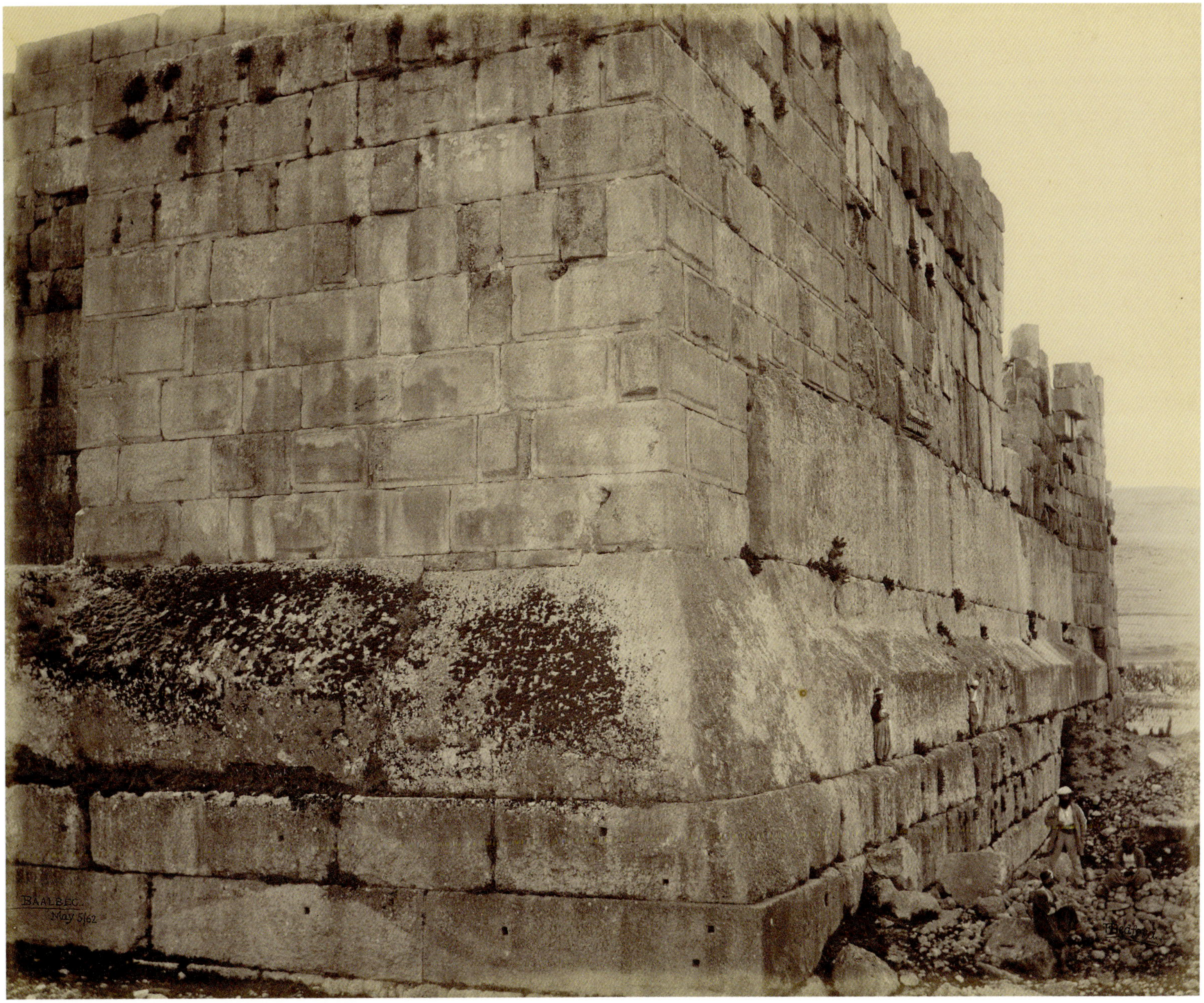

Baalbek, Lebanon, 5 May 1862

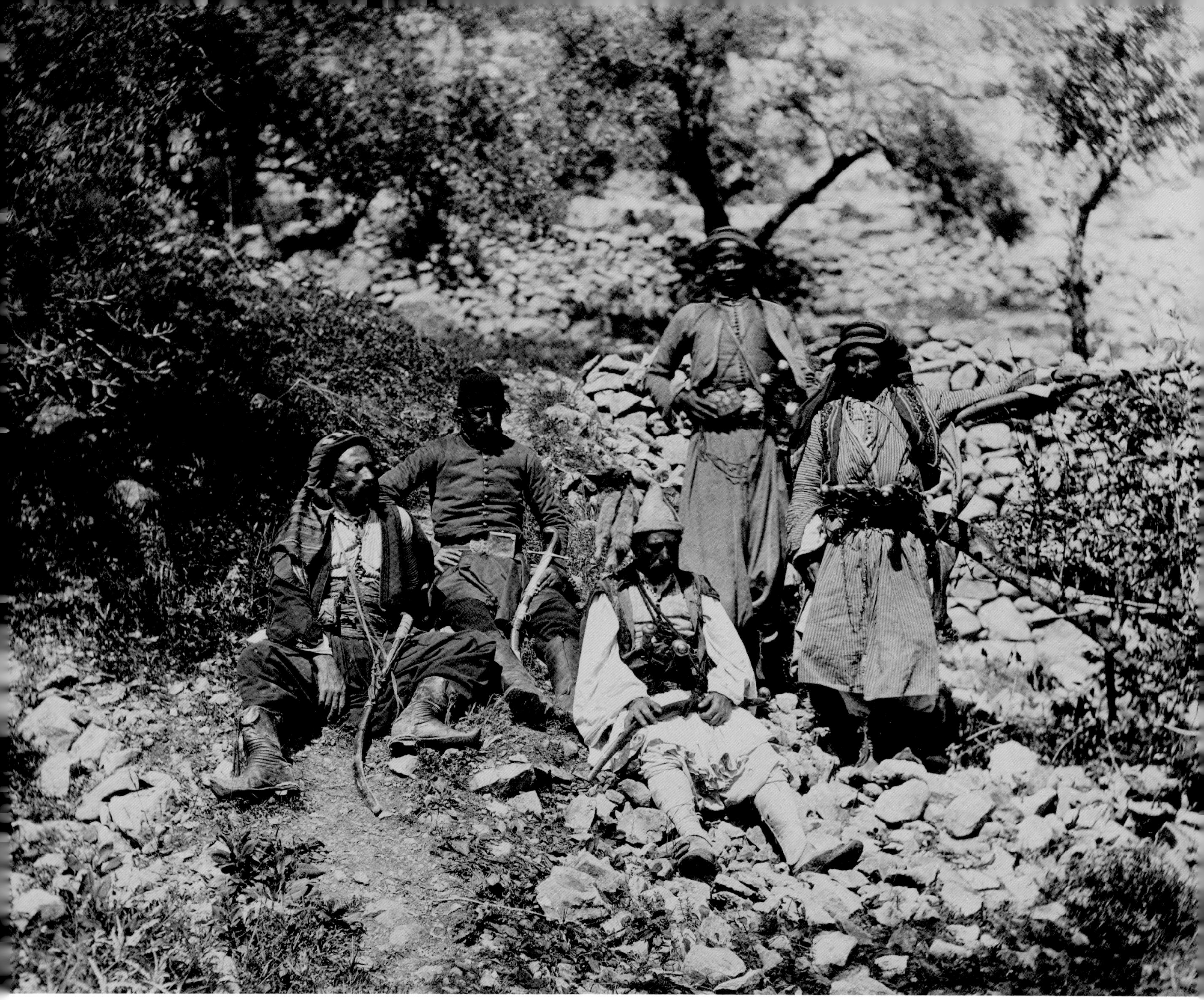

Bashi-bazouks, Beirut, 6 May 1862

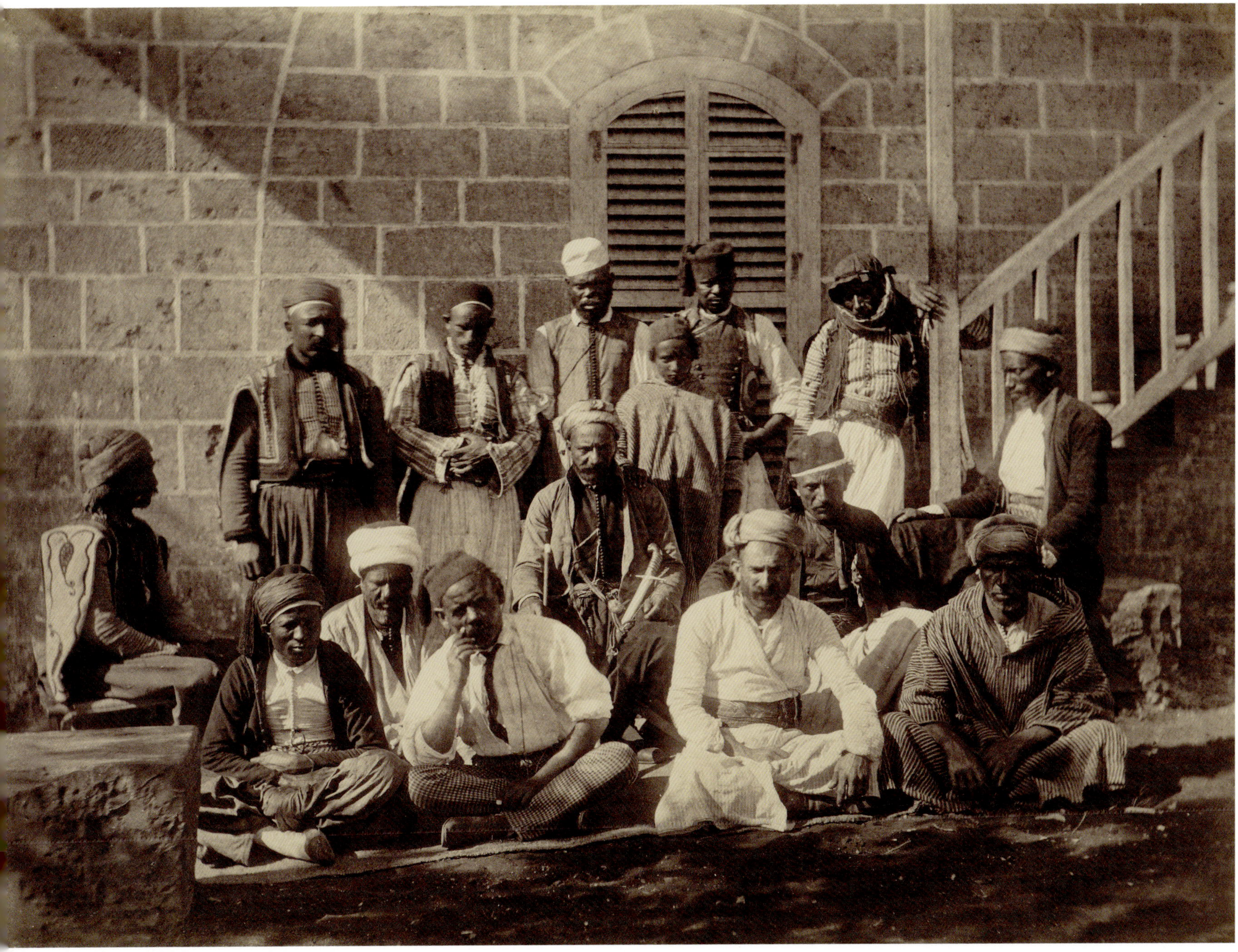

Camp attendants, Beirut, 6 May 1862

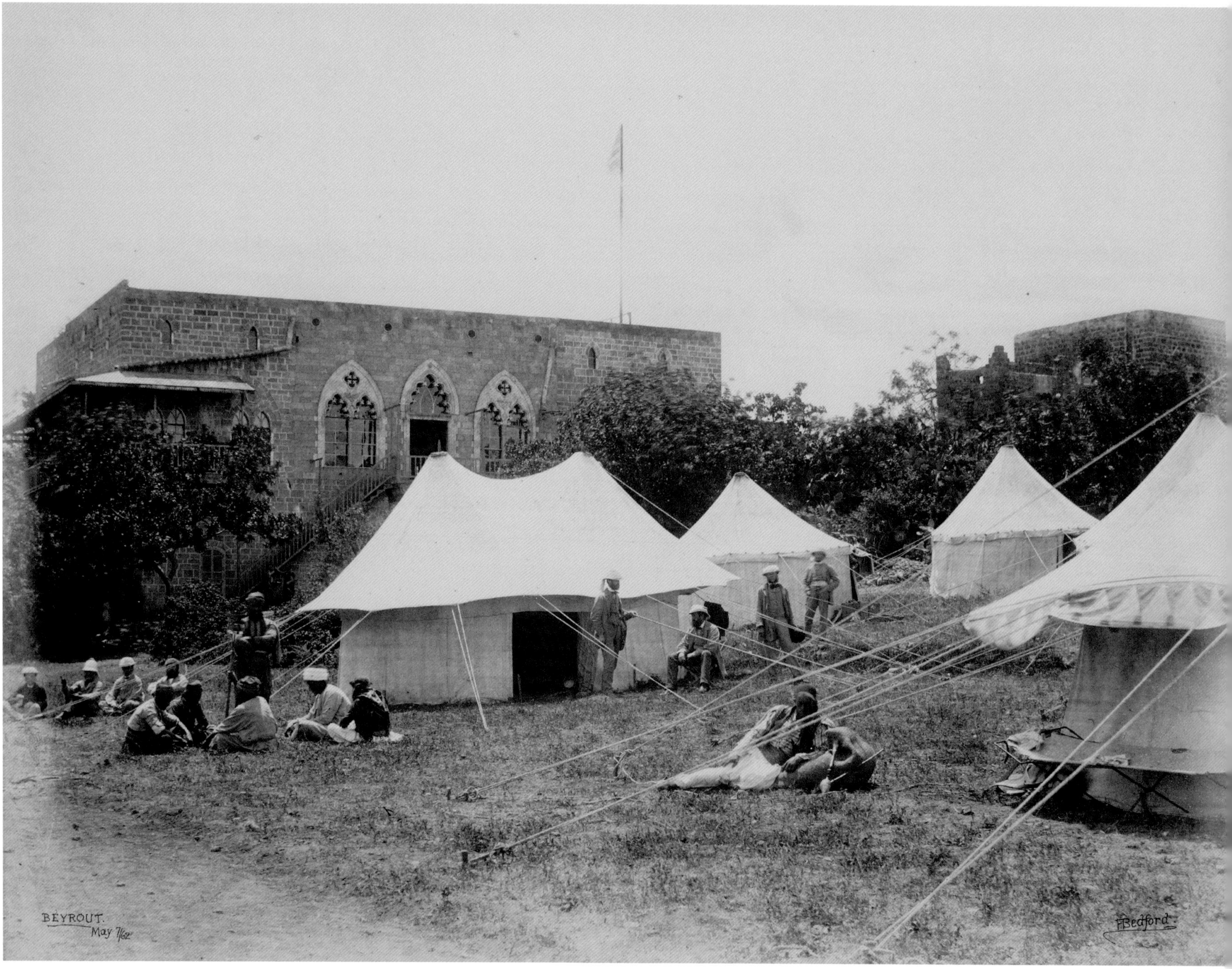

The British Consulate, Beirut, with the prince's camp, 7 May 1862

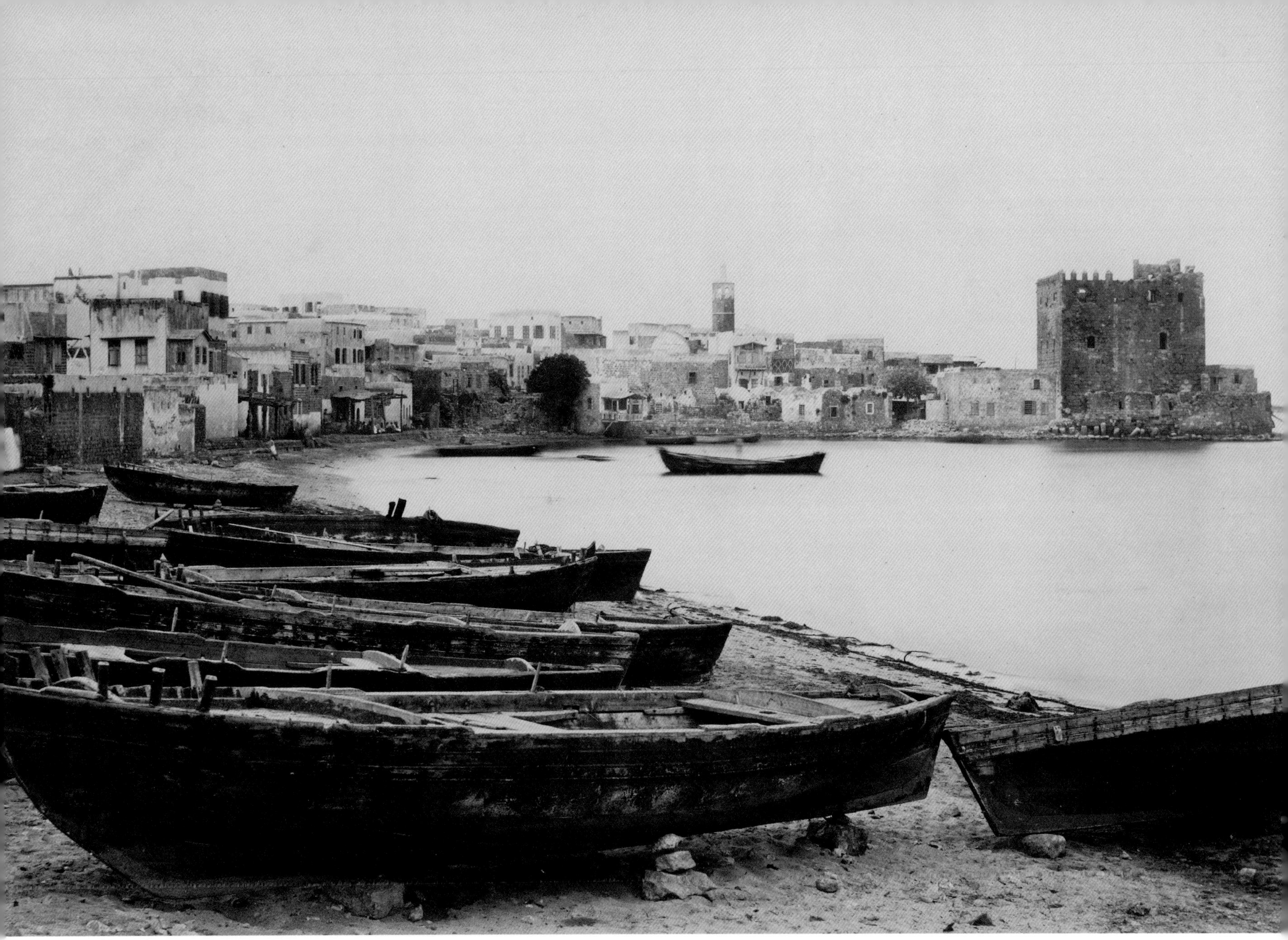

Tripoli, Lebanon, 10 May 1862

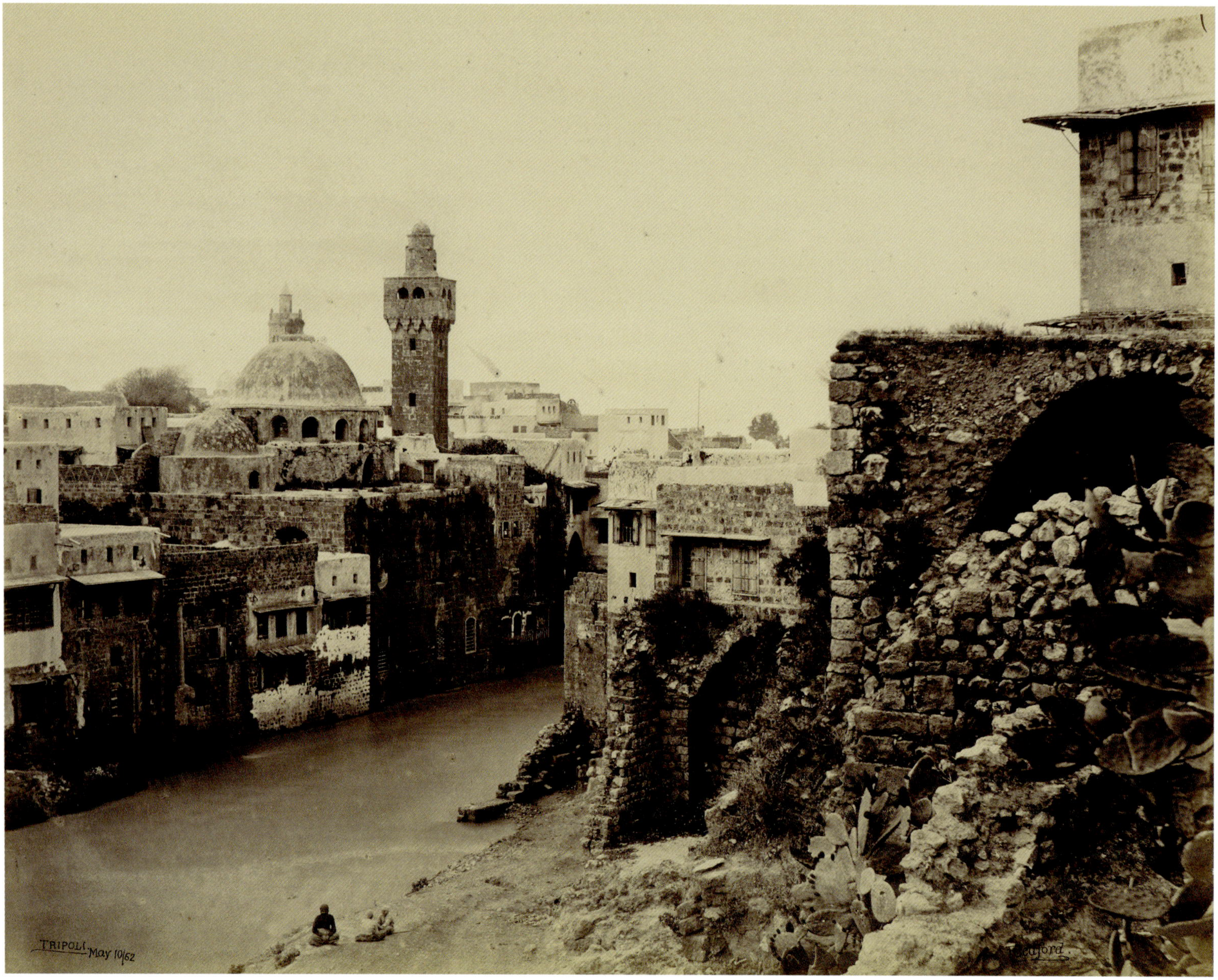

Tripoli, Lebanon, 10 May 1862

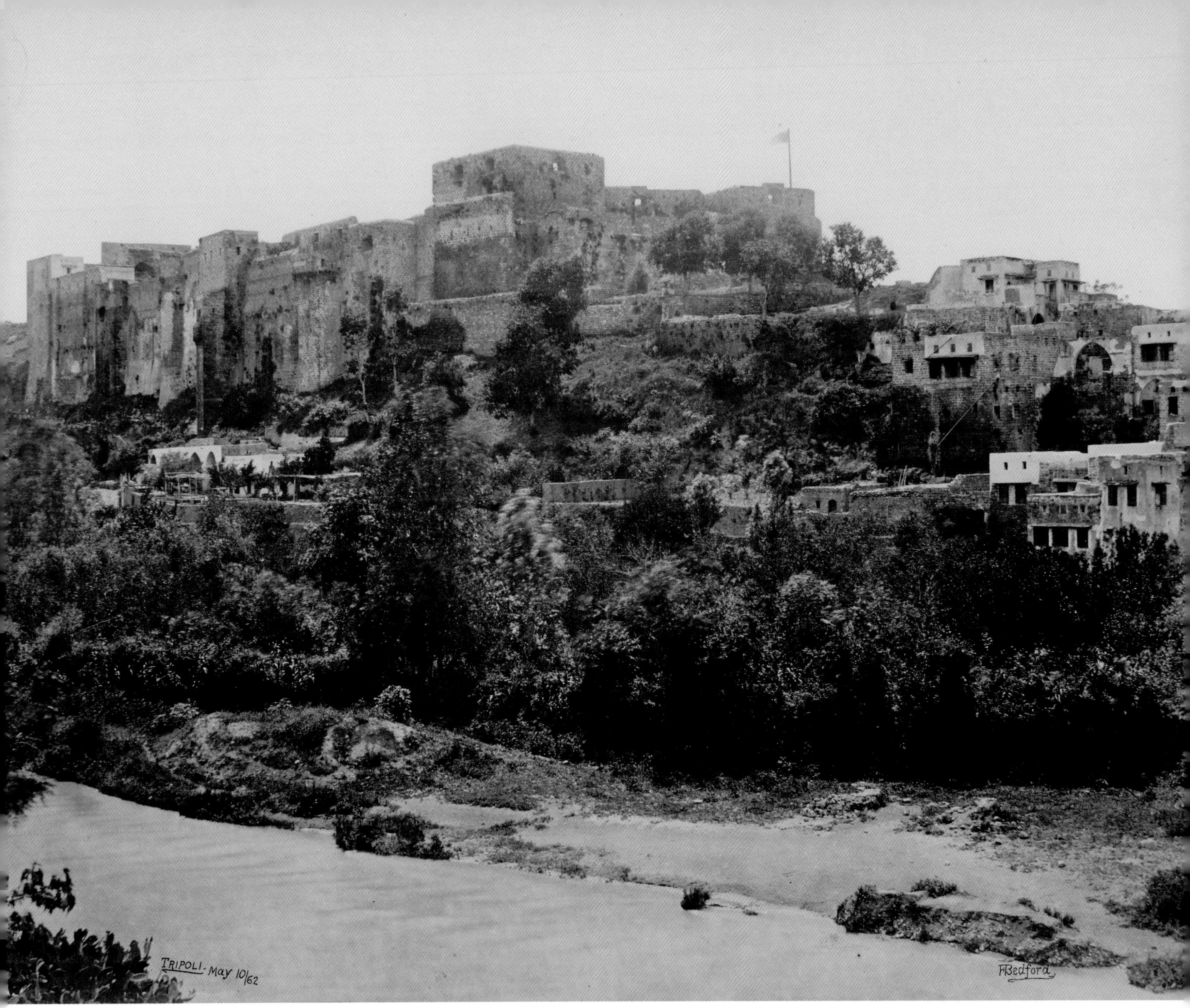

The castle at Tripoli, Lebanon, 10 May 1862

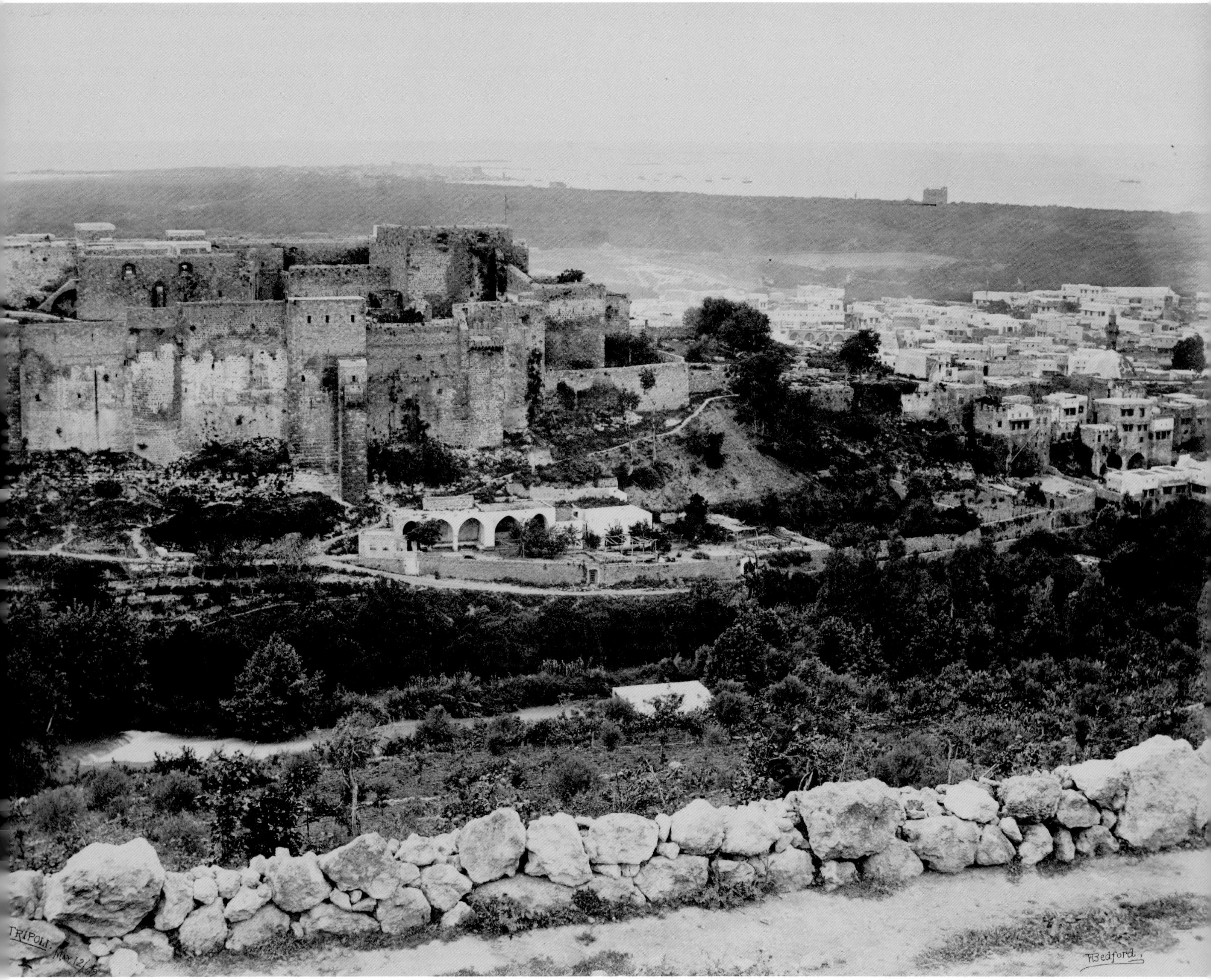

The castle and town of Tripoli, Lebanon, 12 May 1862

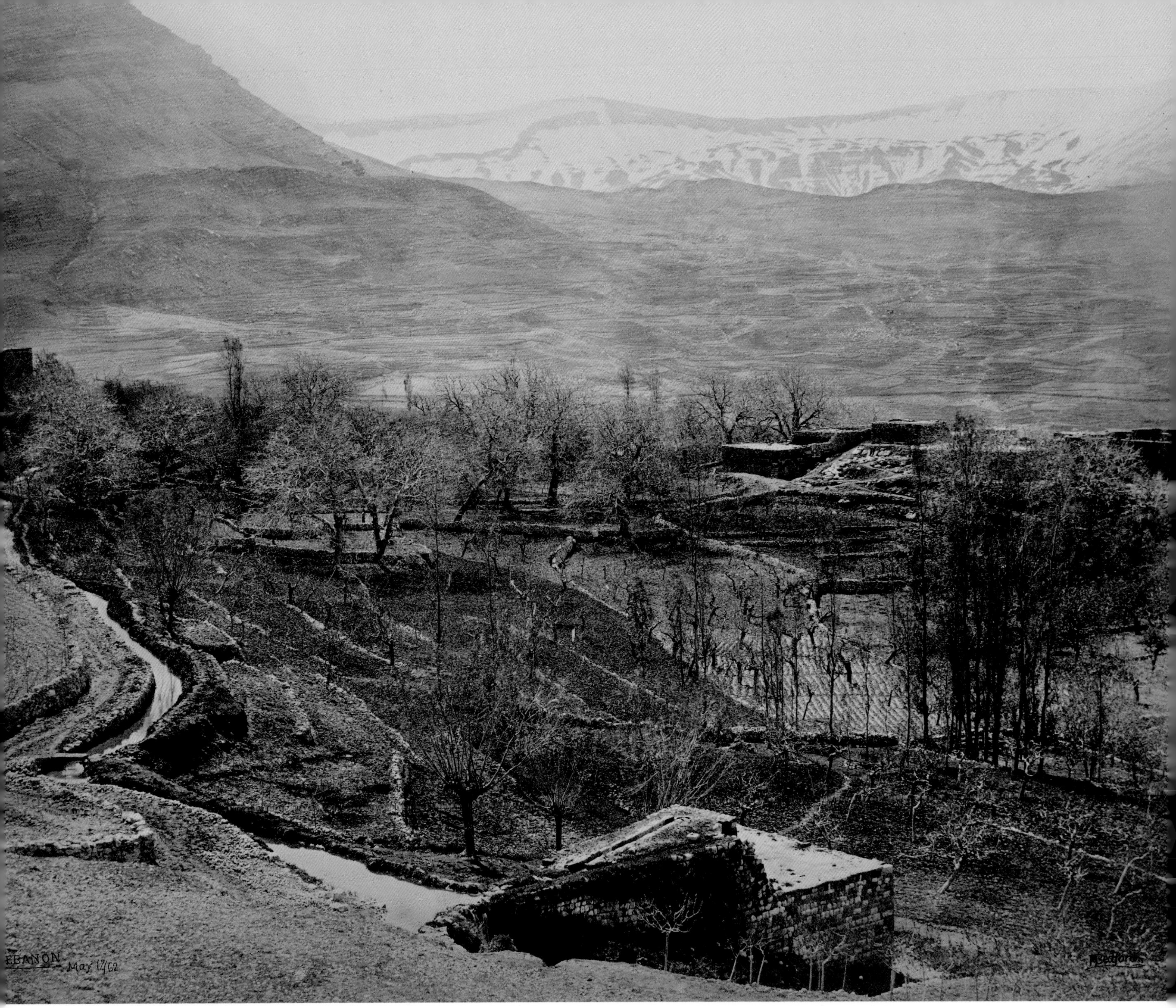

Lebanon from above the village of Ehden, 12 May 1862

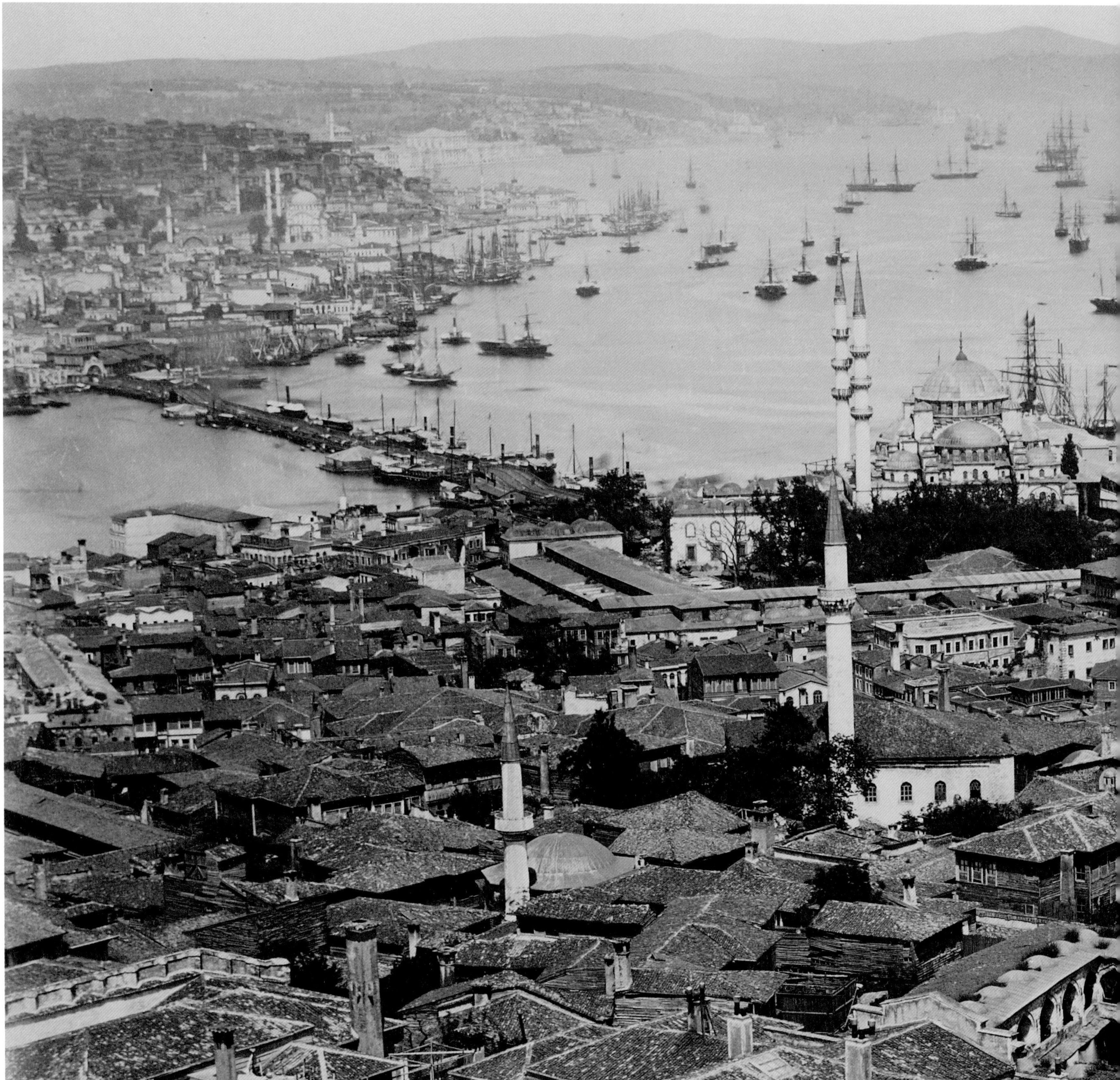

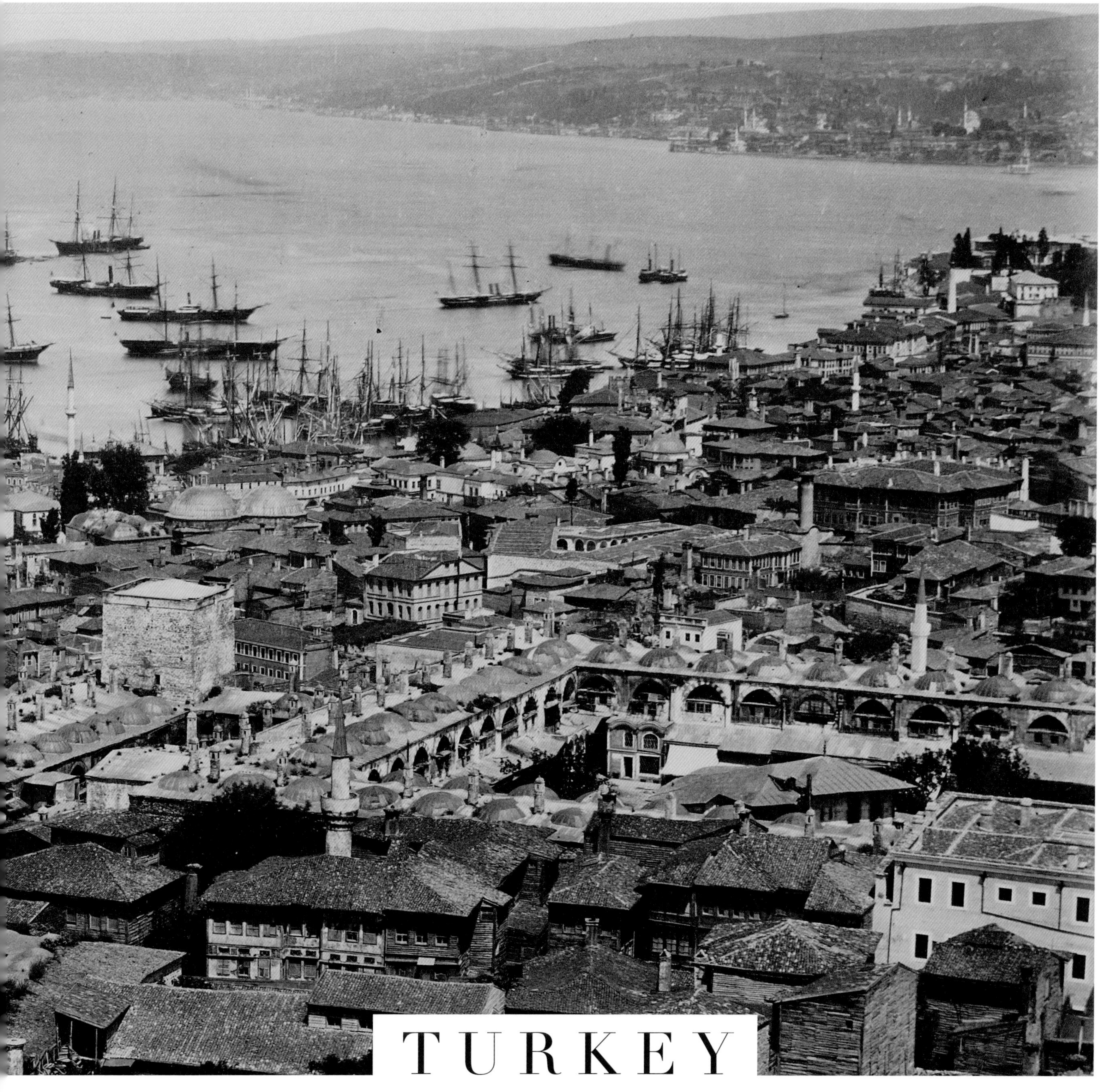

TURKEY

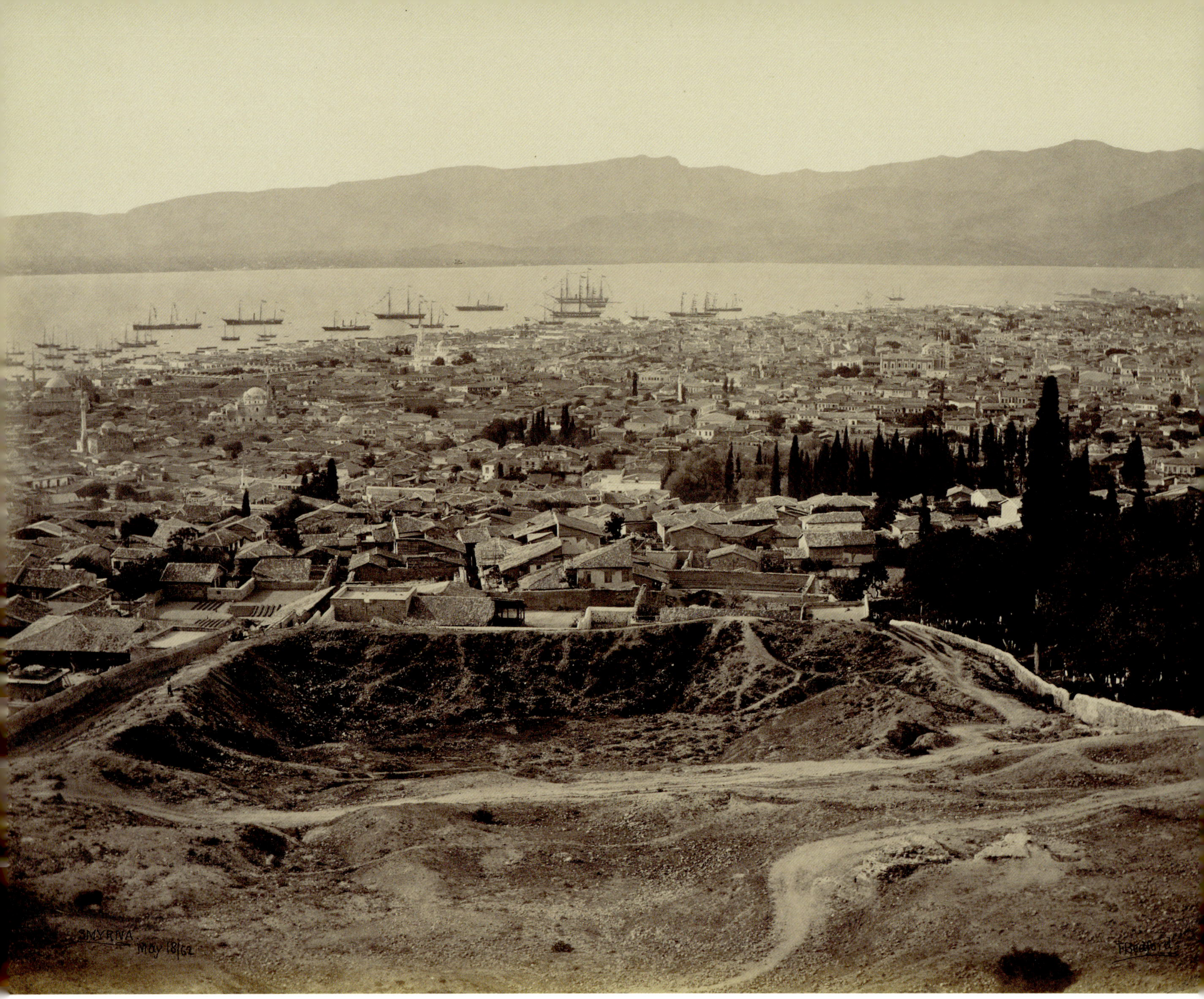

Smyrna (Izmir), 18 May 1862

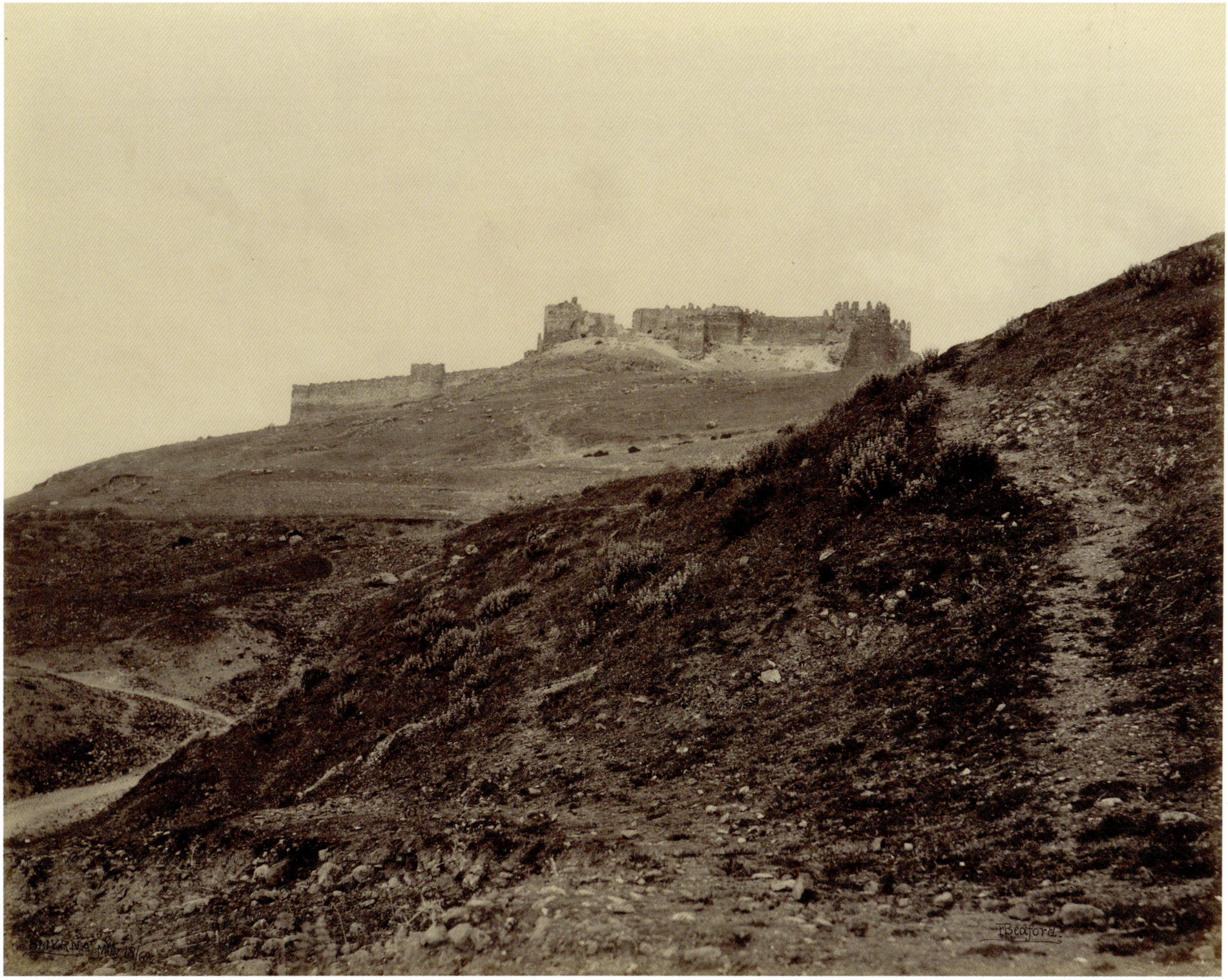

The castle at Smyrna (Izmir), 18 May 1862

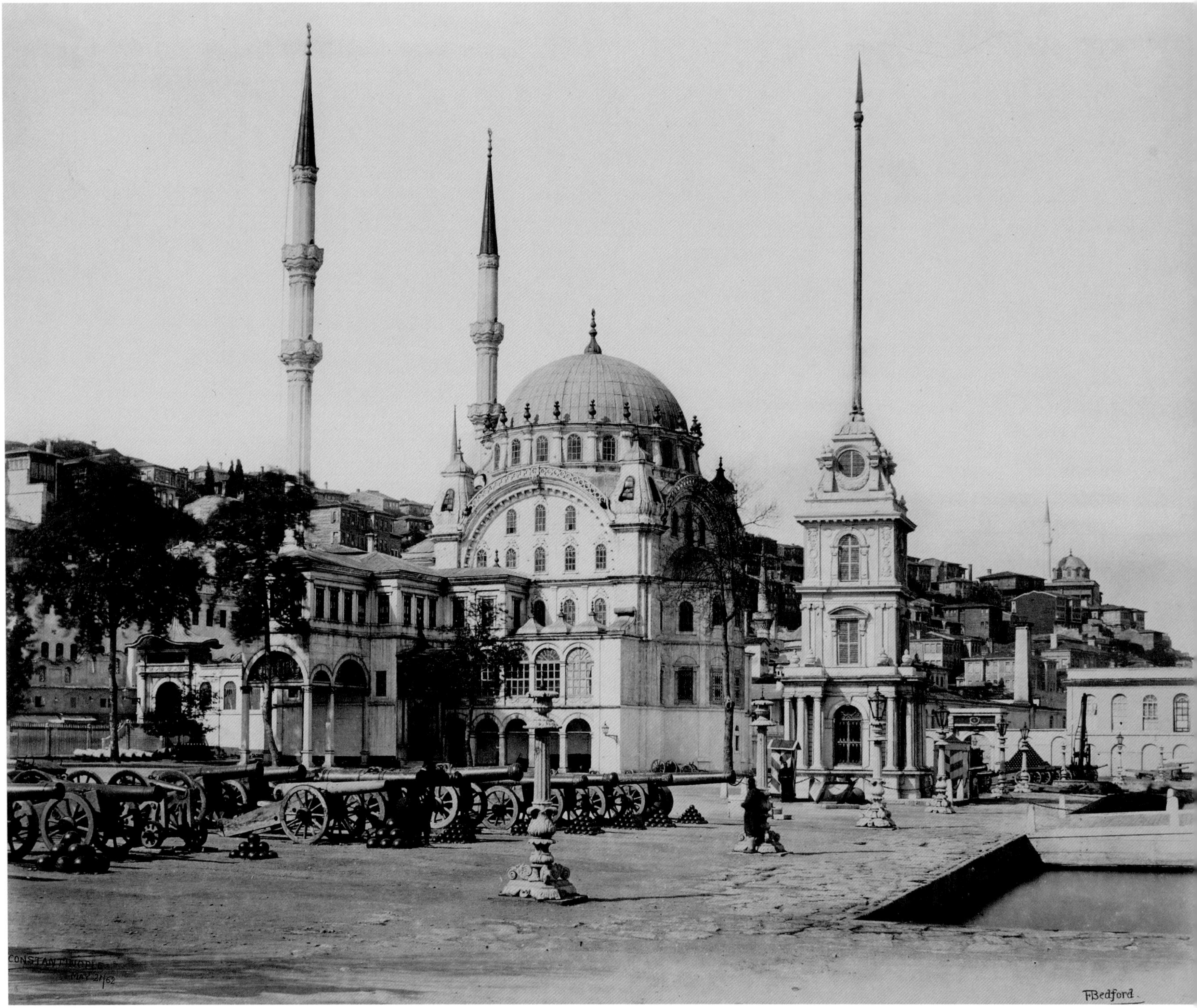

Nusretiye Mosque, Tophane, Constantinople (Istanbul), 21 May 1862

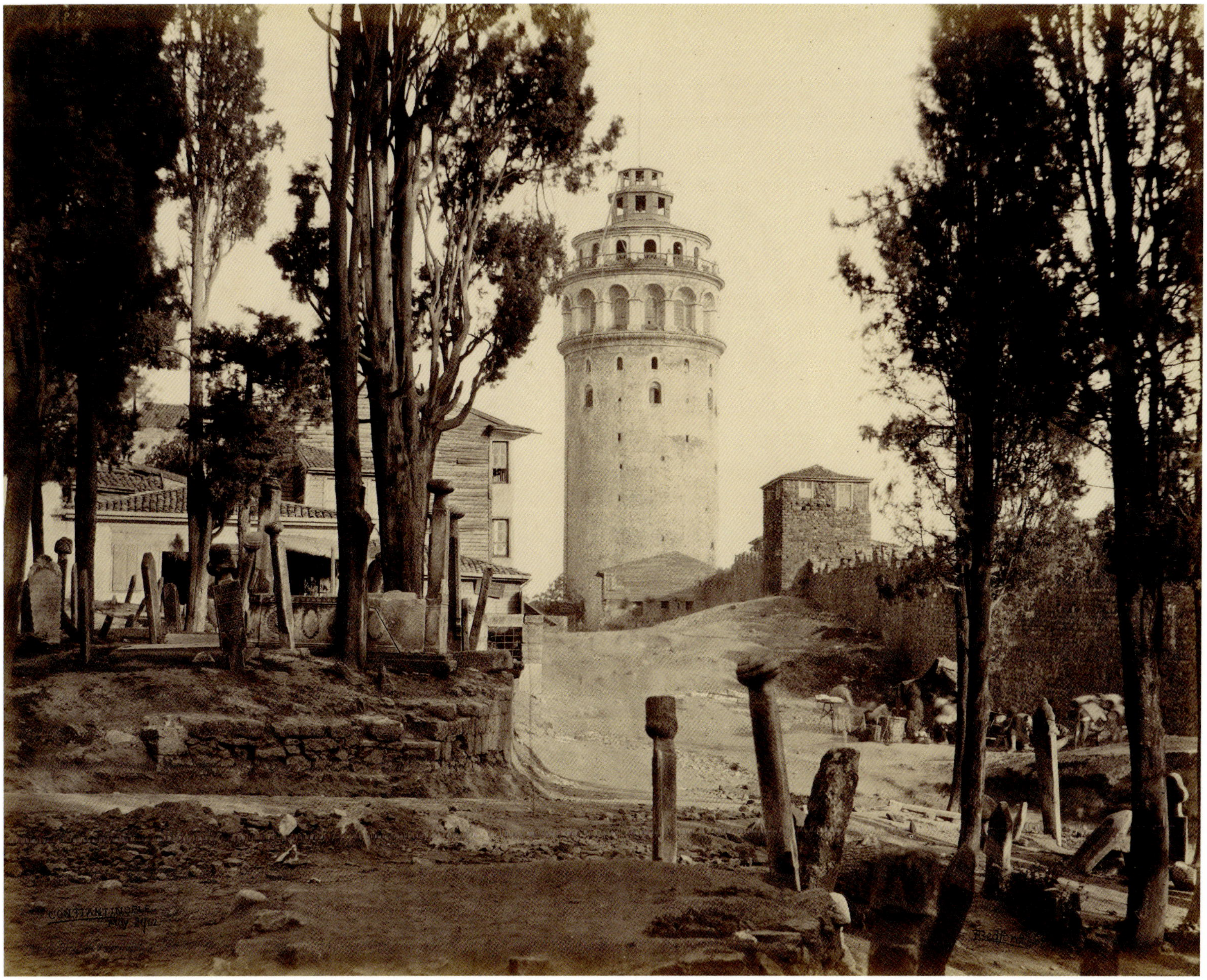

The Galata Tower, Constantinople (Istanbul), 21 May 1862

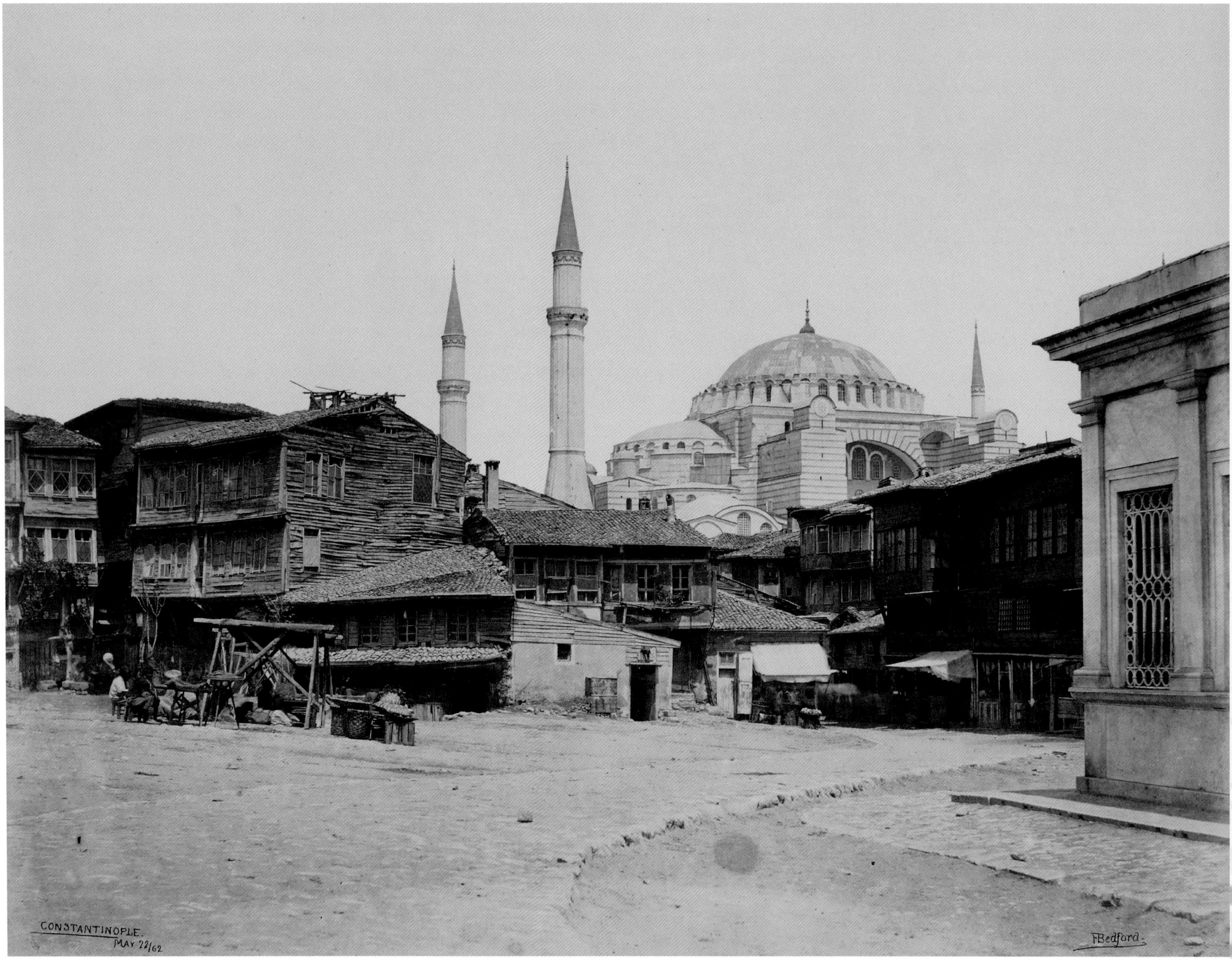

Hagia Sophia, Constantinople (Istanbul), 22 May 1862

"[T]he finest I have seen in the East. It was formerly a Xtian church."
Prince of Wales's Journal, 22 May 1862

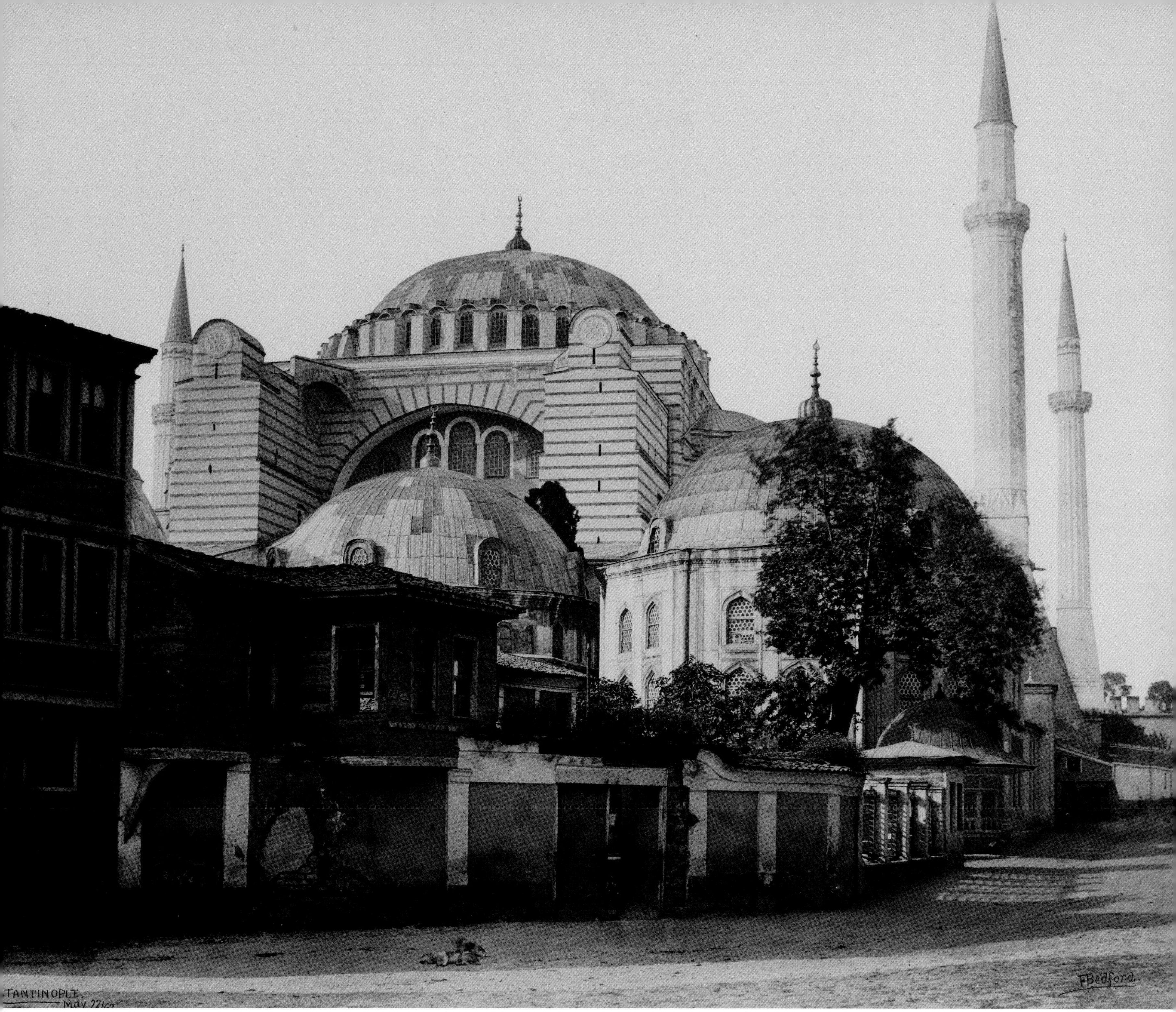

Hagia Sophia, Constantinople (Istanbul), 22 May 1862

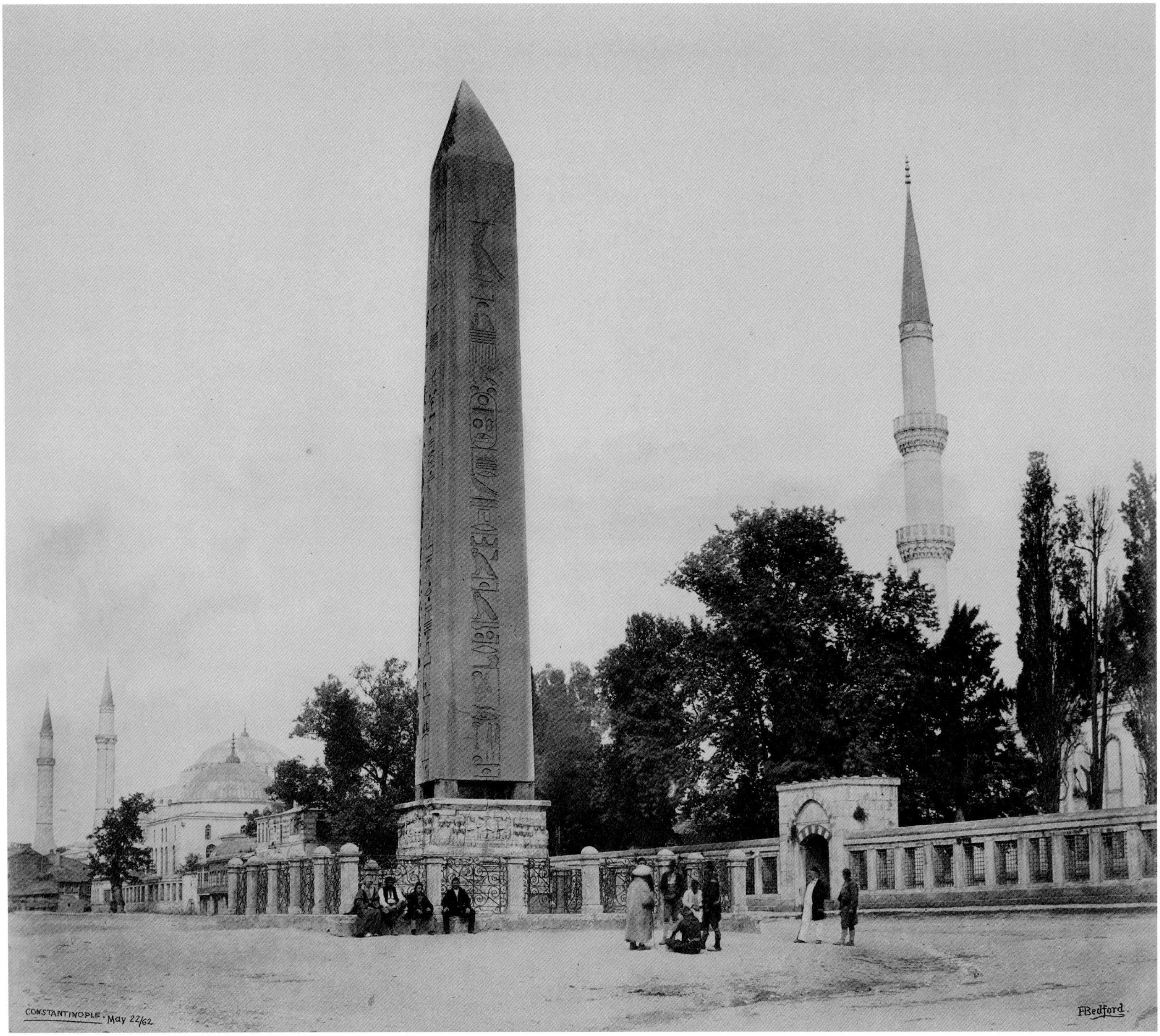

The Obelisk in the Hippodrome, Constantinople (Istanbul), 22 May 1862

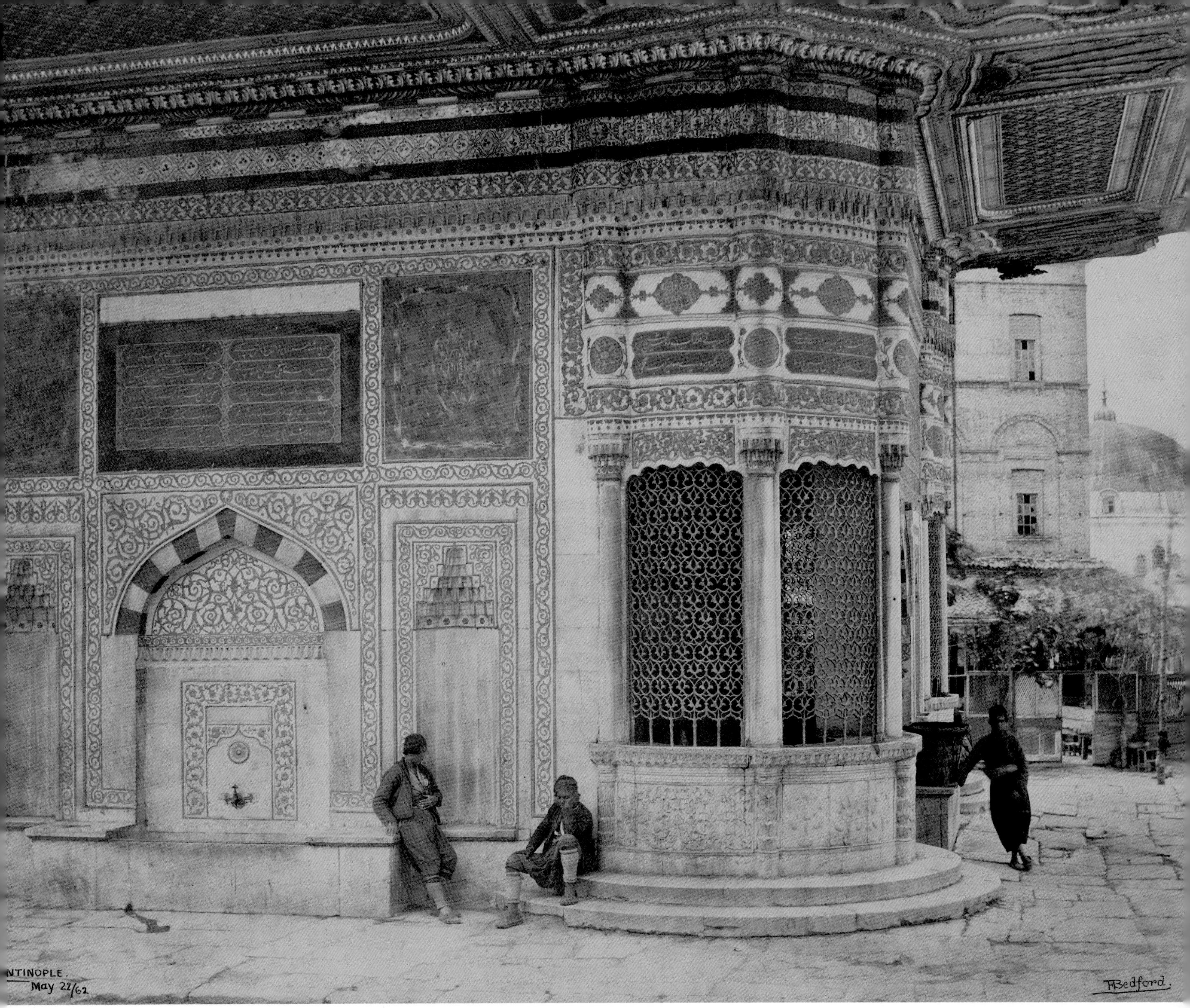

The Fountain of Ahmed III, Constantinople (Istanbul), 22 May 1862

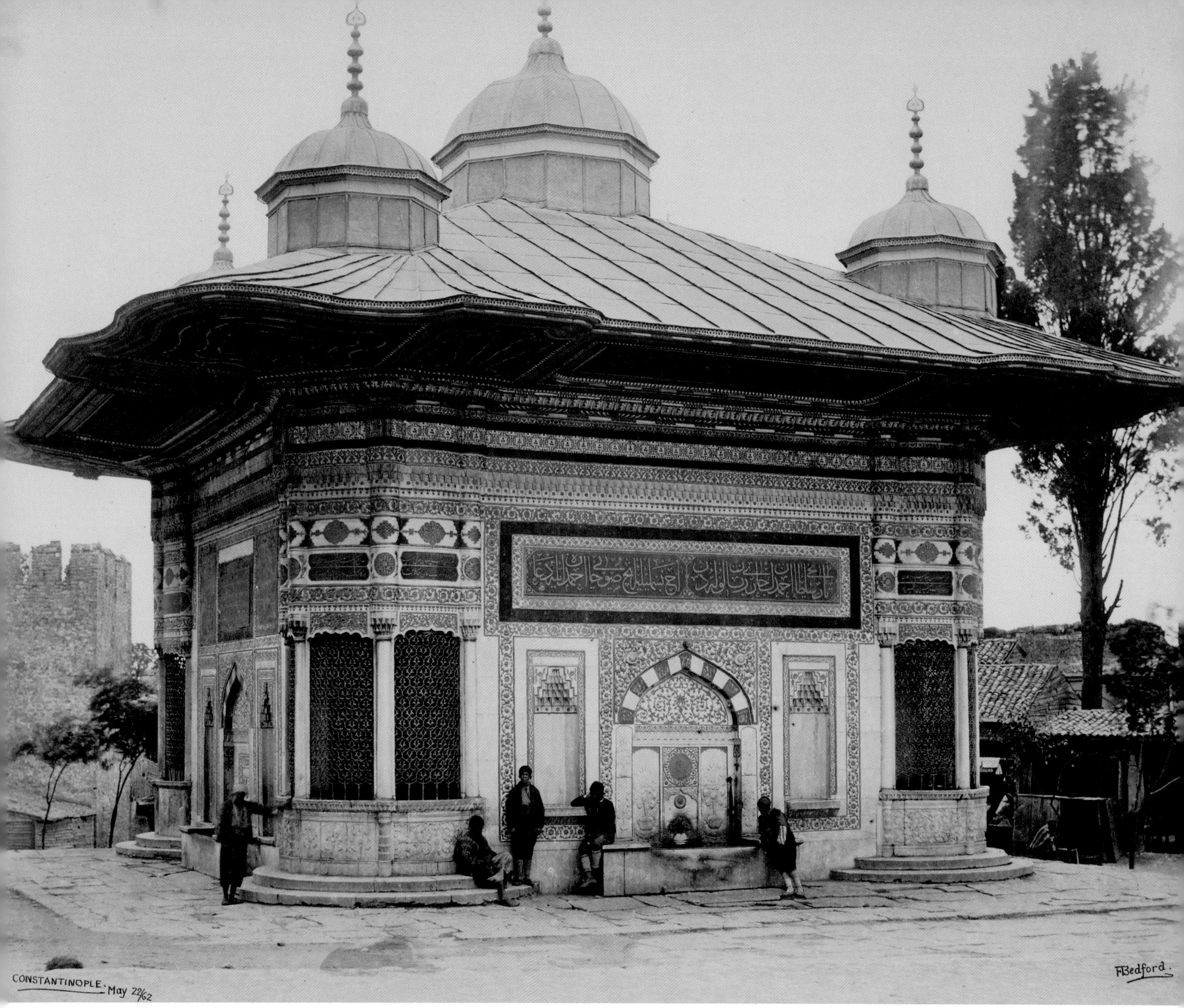

The Fountain of Ahmed III, Constantinople (Istanbul), 22 May 1862

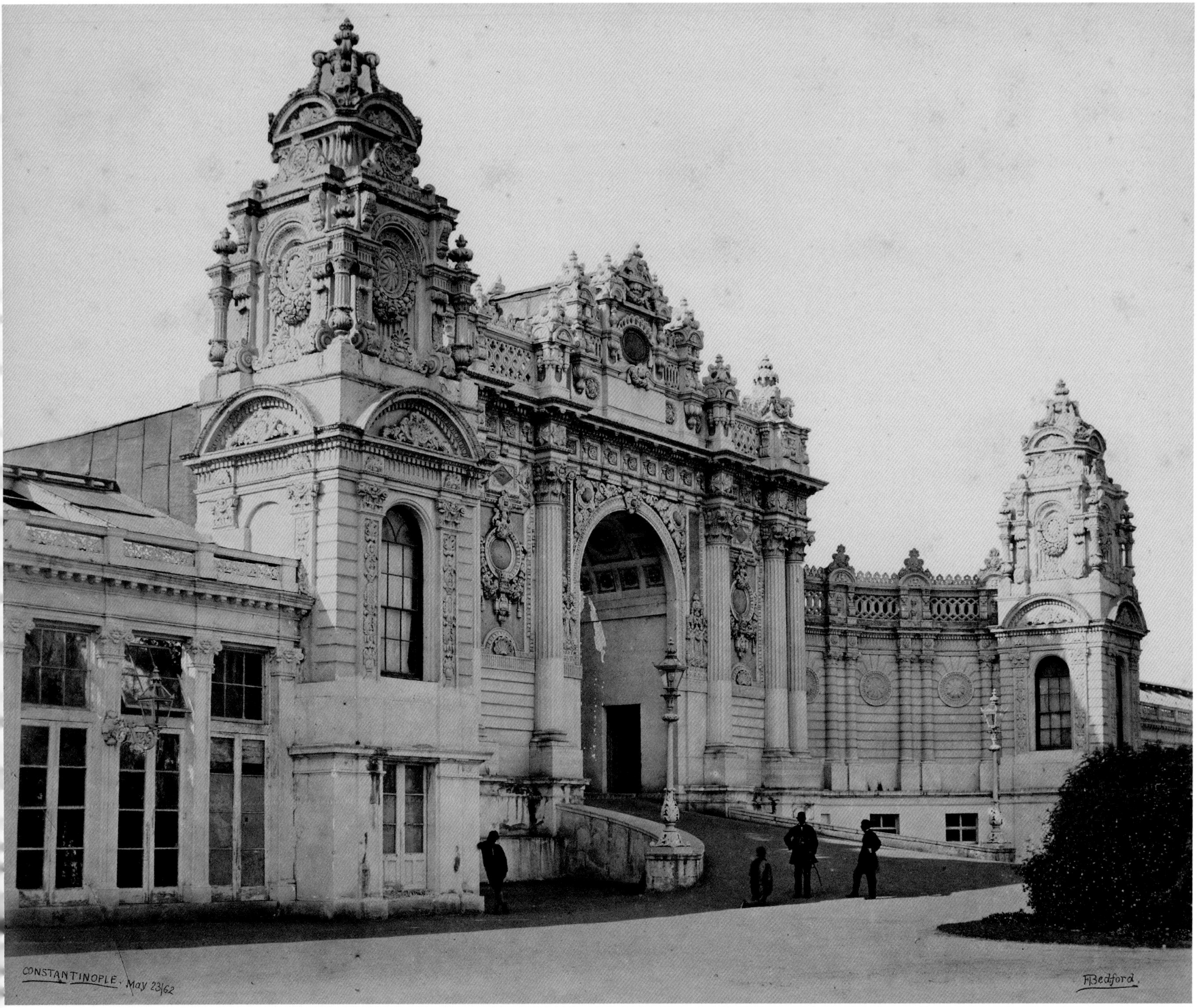

The Dolmabahçe Palace, Constantinople (Istanbul), 23 May 1862

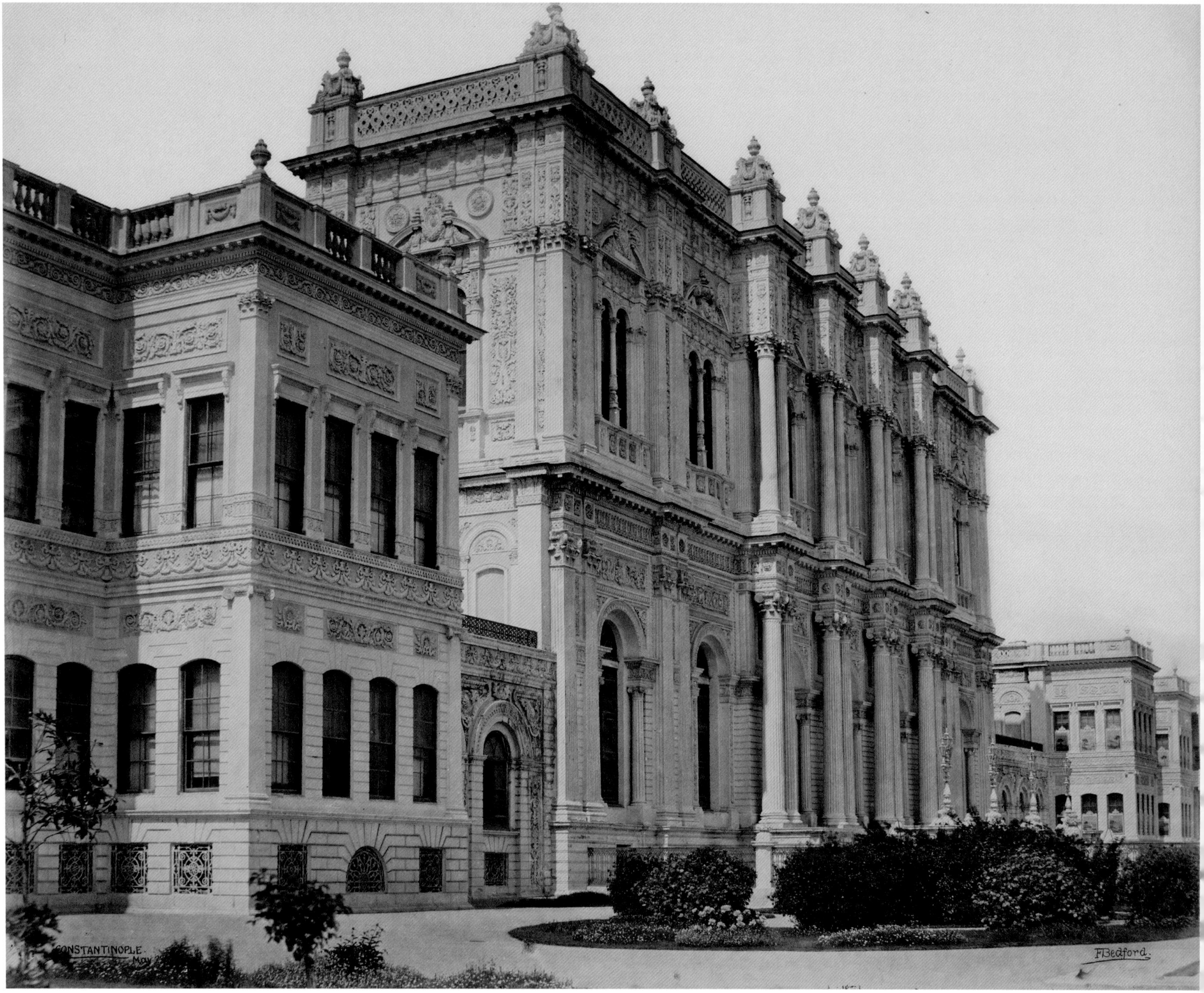

The Dolmabahçe Palace, Constantinople (Istanbul), 23 May 1862

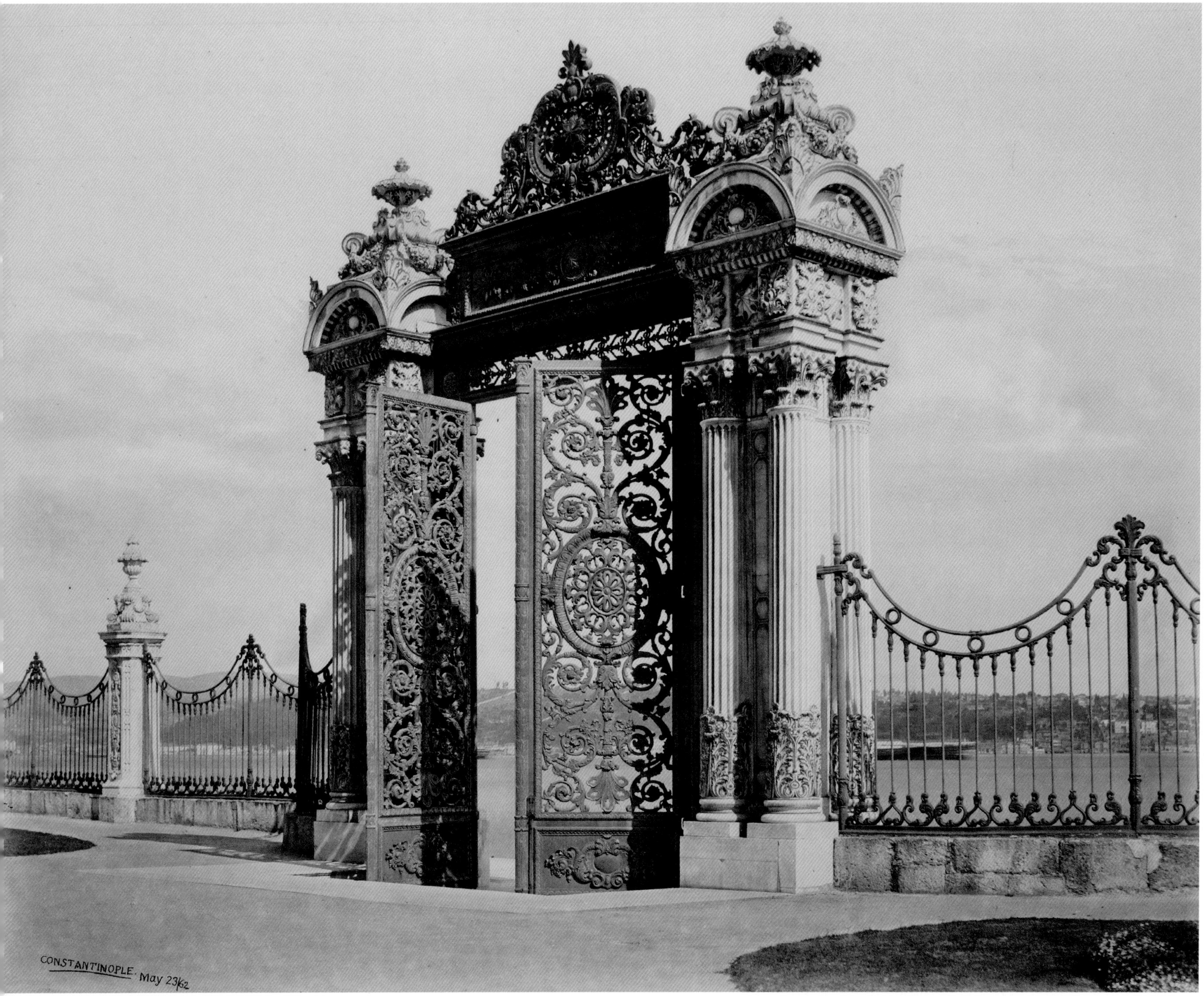

The Dolmabahçe Palace, Constantinople (Istanbul), 23 May 1862

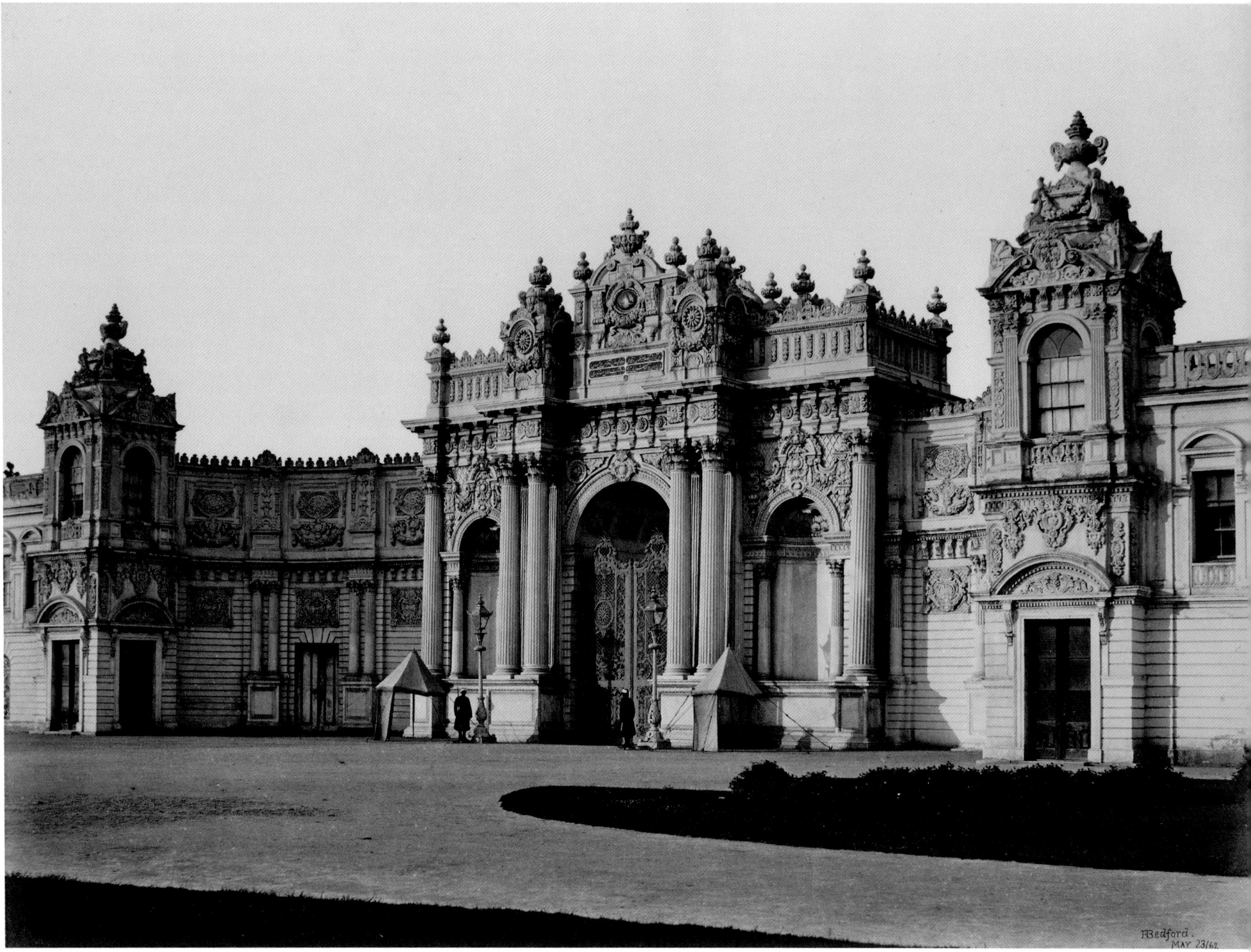

The Dolmabahçe Palace, Constantinople (Istanbul), 23 May 1862

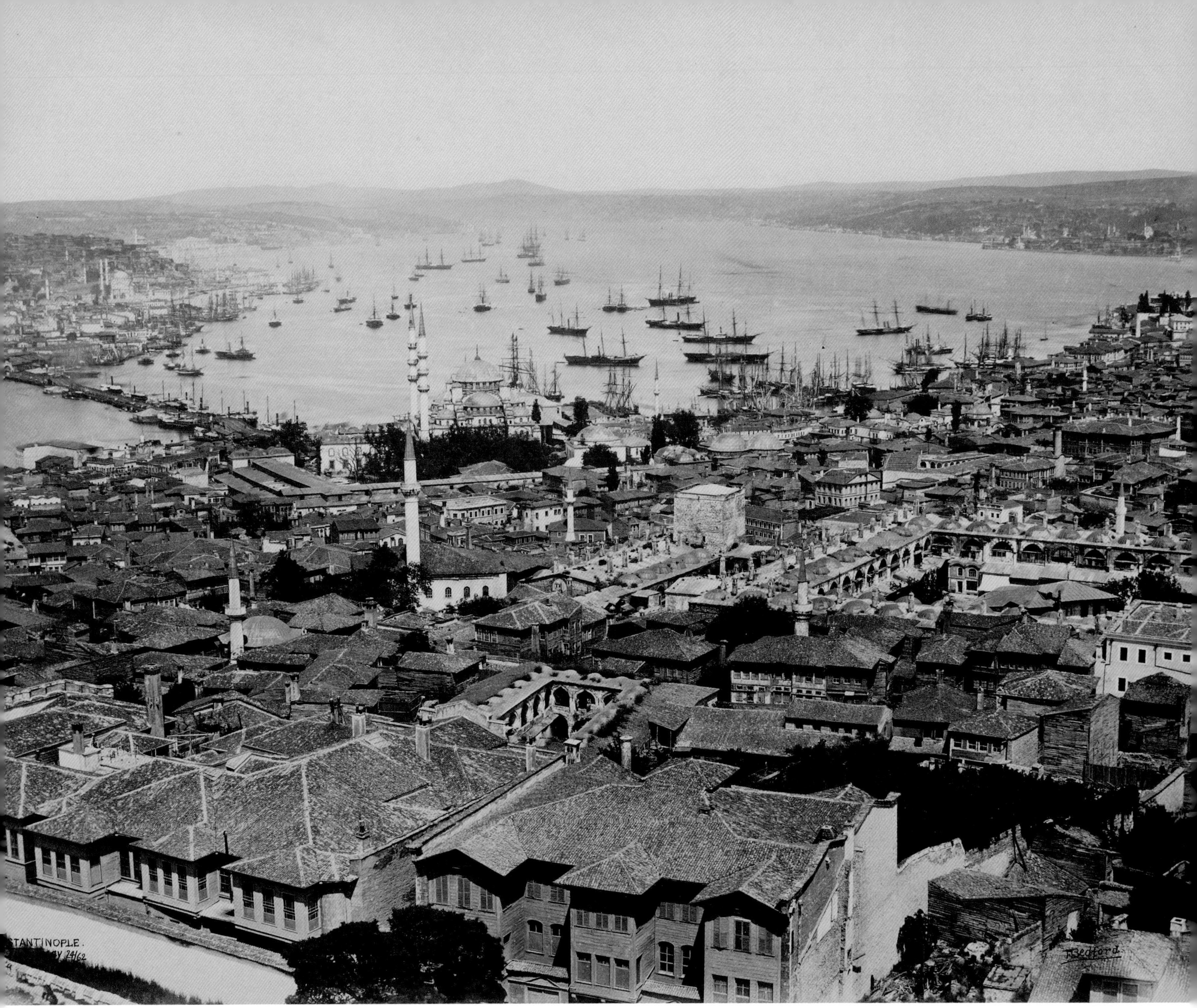

The Golden Horn, Constantinople (Istanbul), 24 May 1862

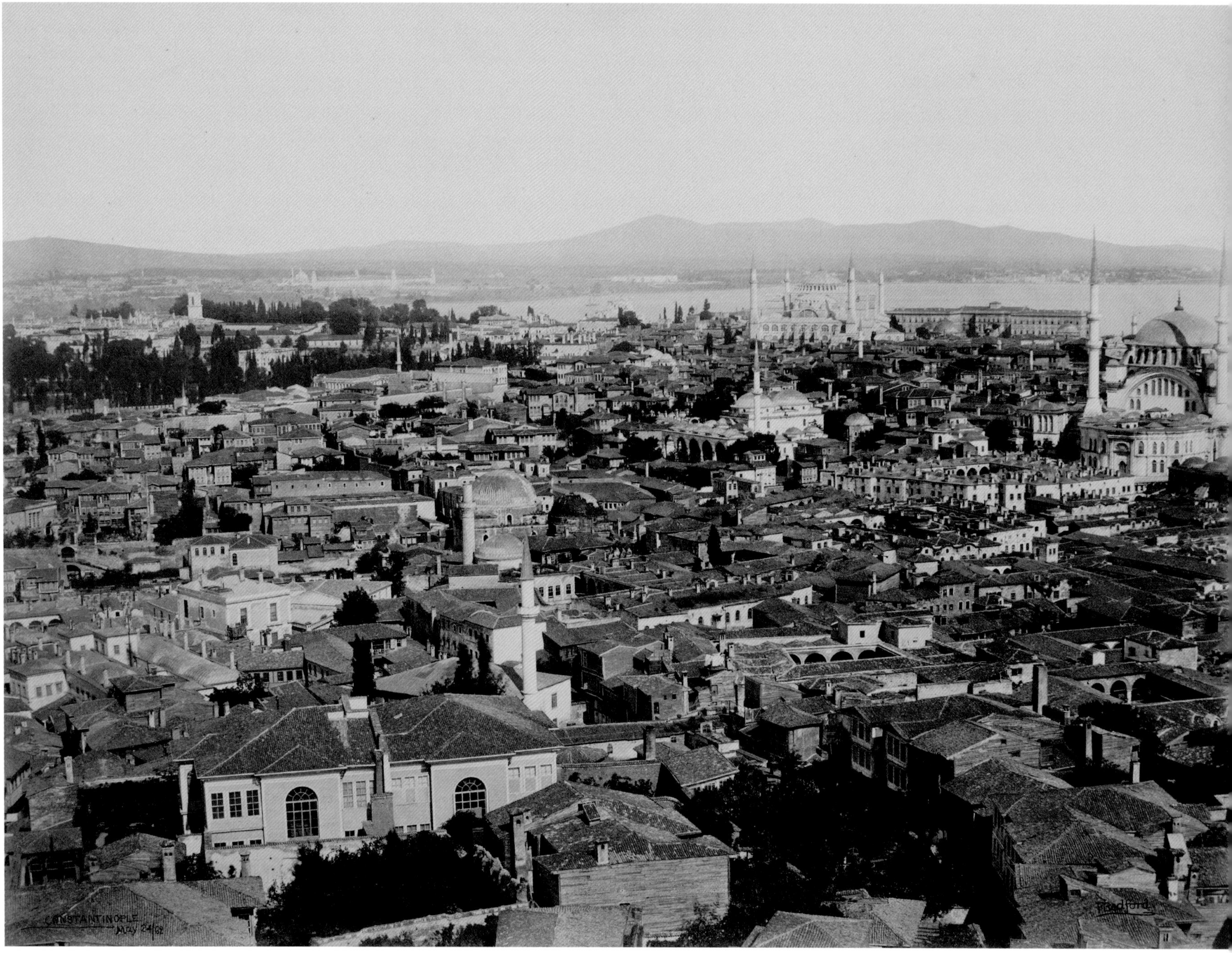

Sultanahmet quarter, Constantinople (Istanbul), 24 May 1862

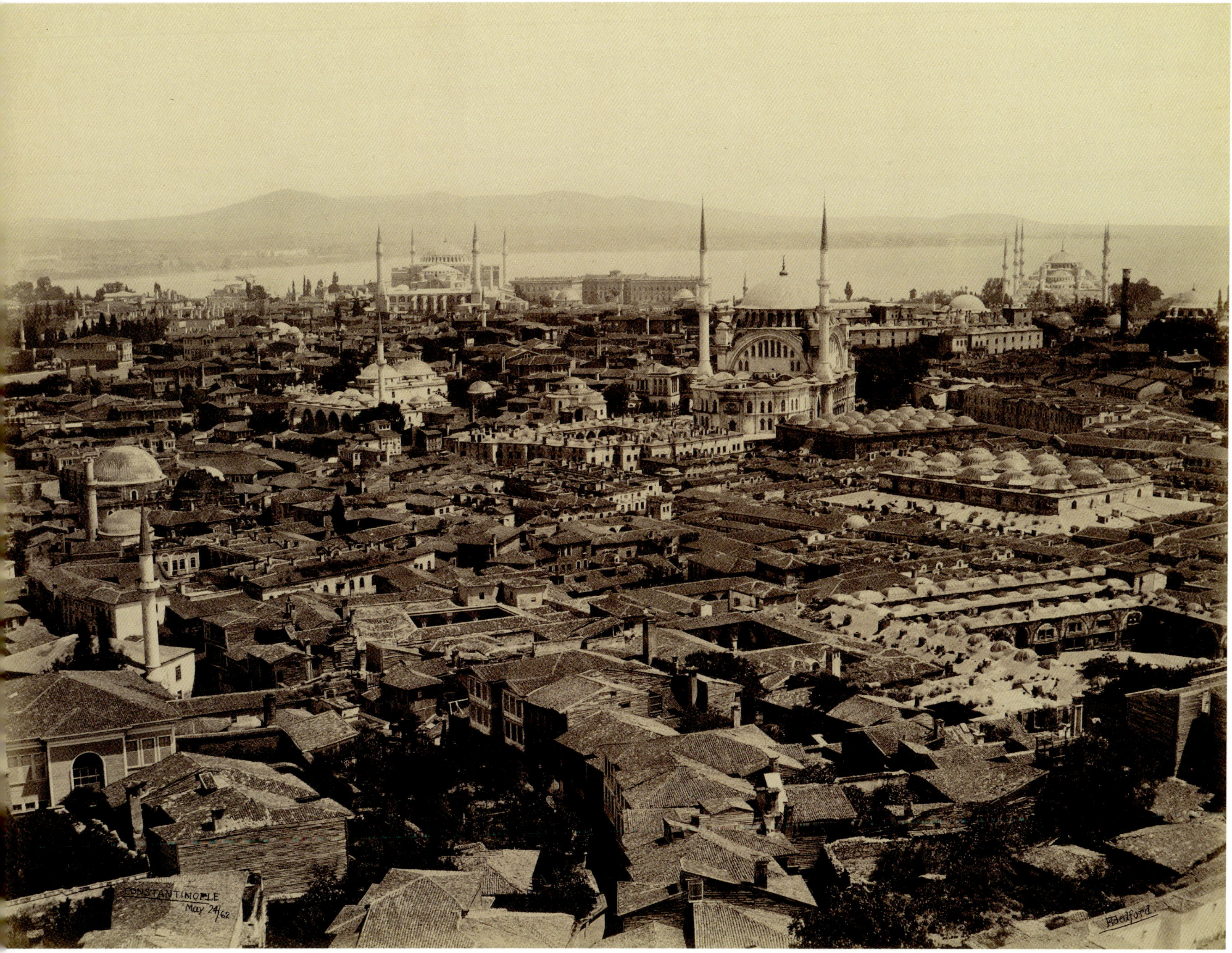

Sultanahmet quarter, Constantinople (Istanbul), 24 May 1862

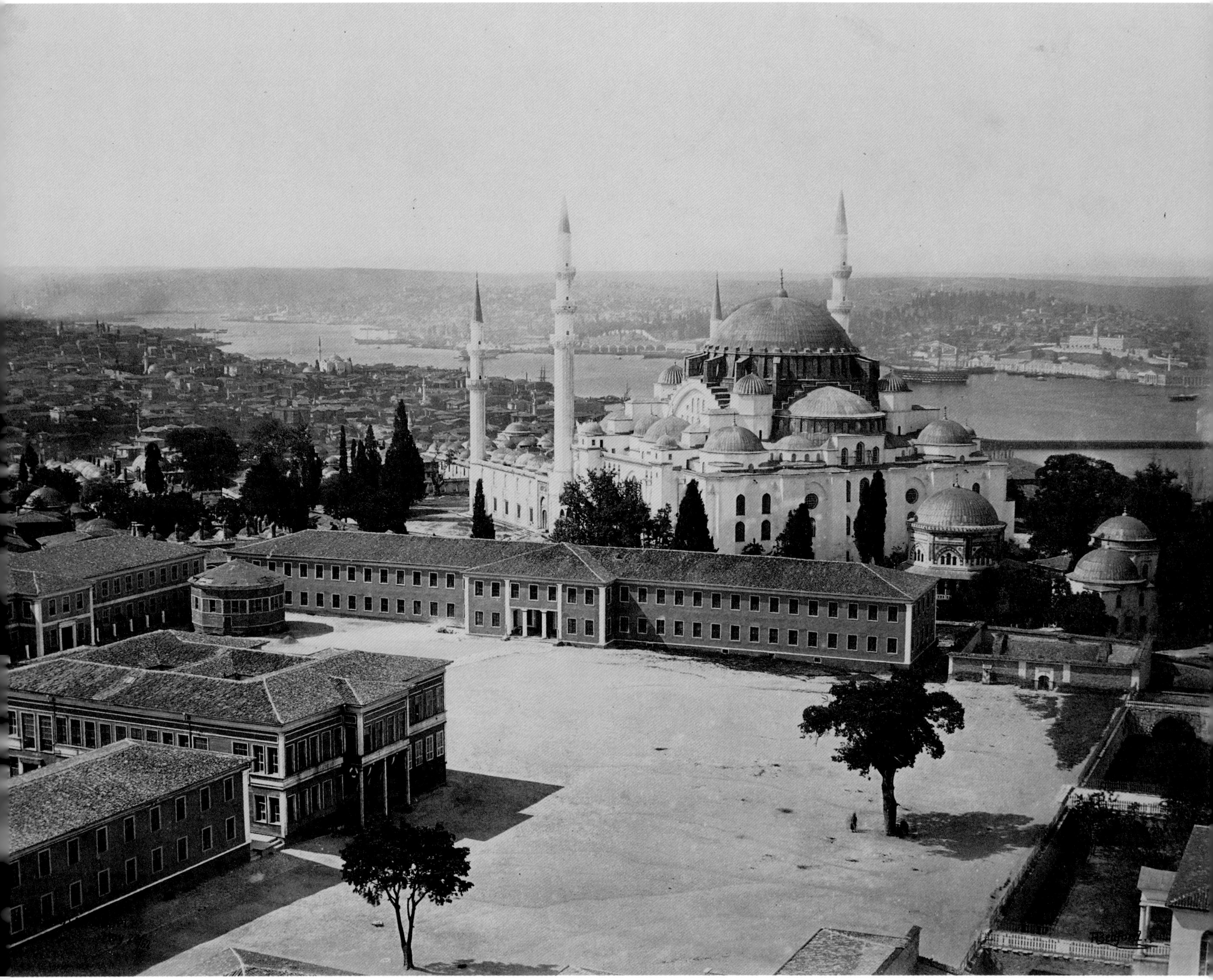

Süleymaniye Mosque, Constantinople (Istanbul), 24 May 1862

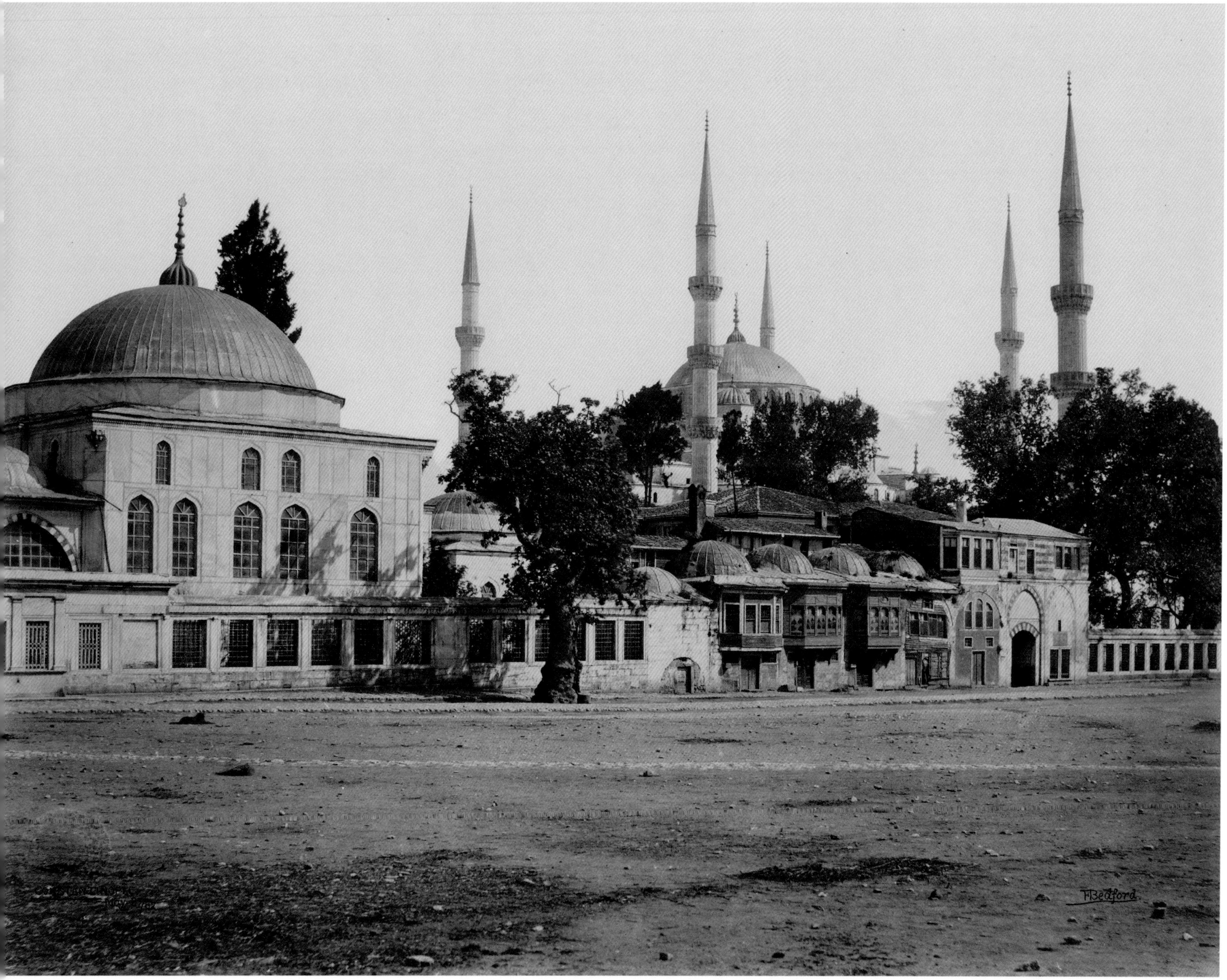

The Blue Mosque, Constantinople (Istanbul), 27 May 1862

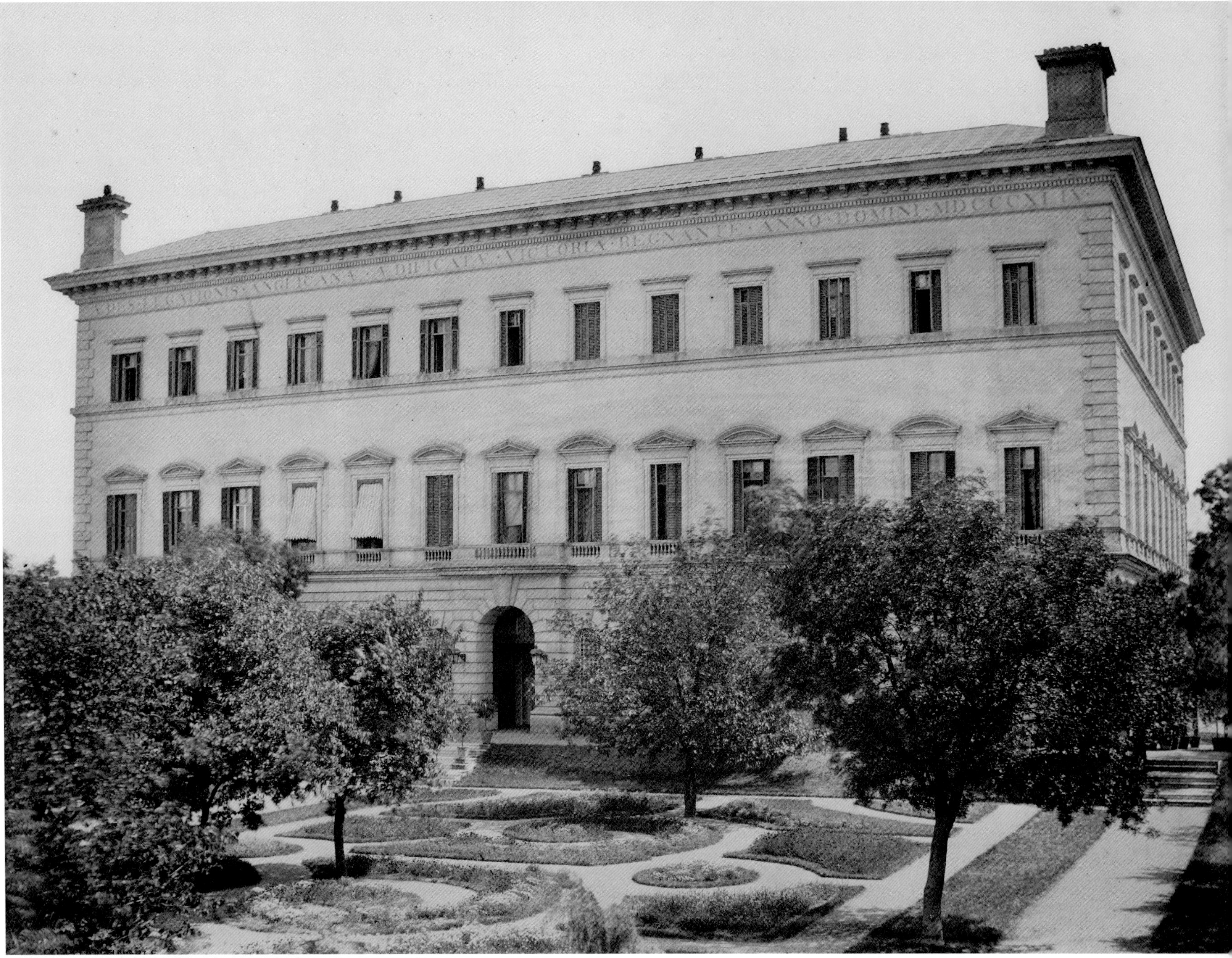

The British Embassy, Constantinople (Istanbul), 27 May 1862

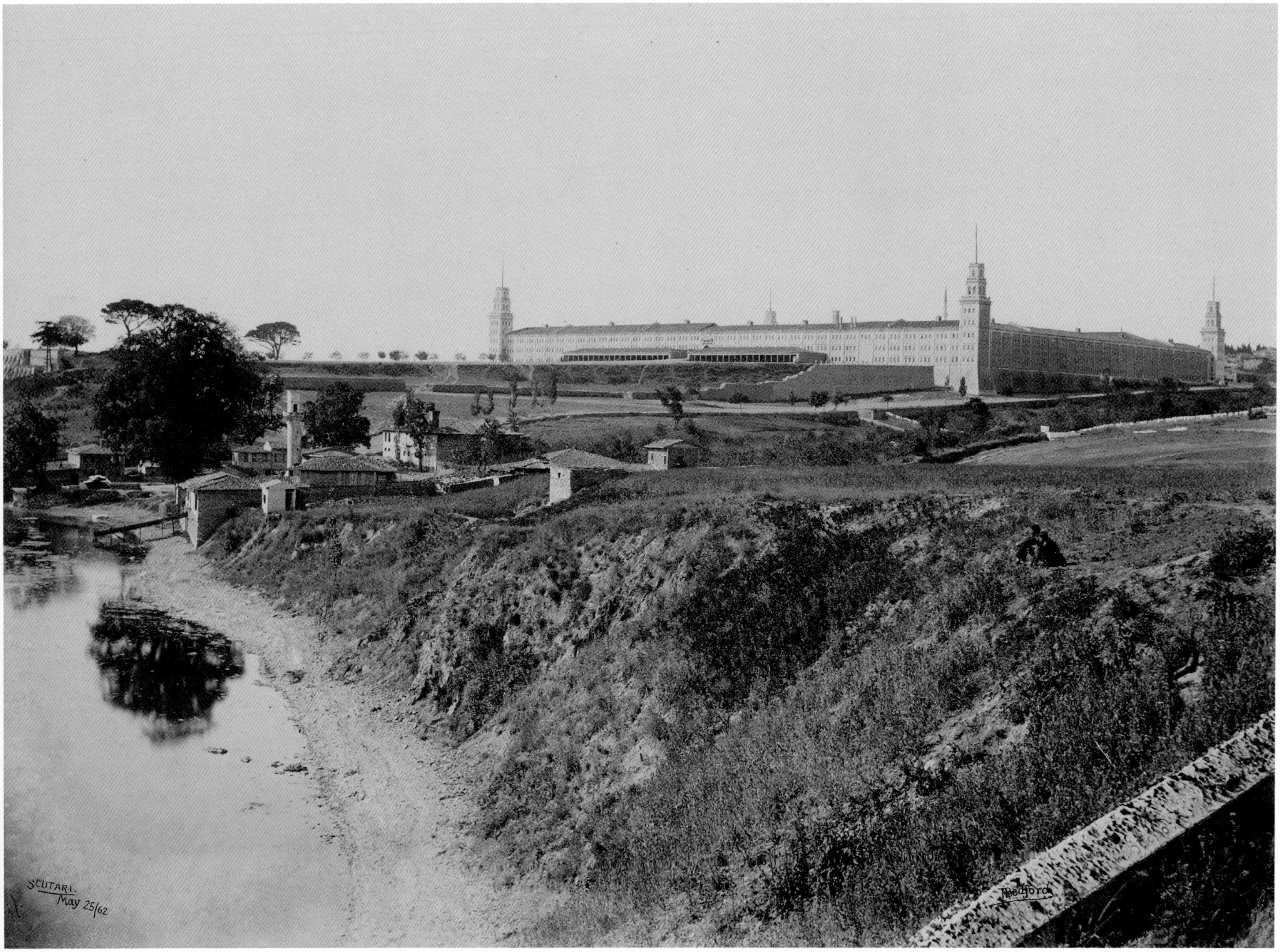

The Selimiye Barracks, Üsküdar, Istanbul, 25 May 1862

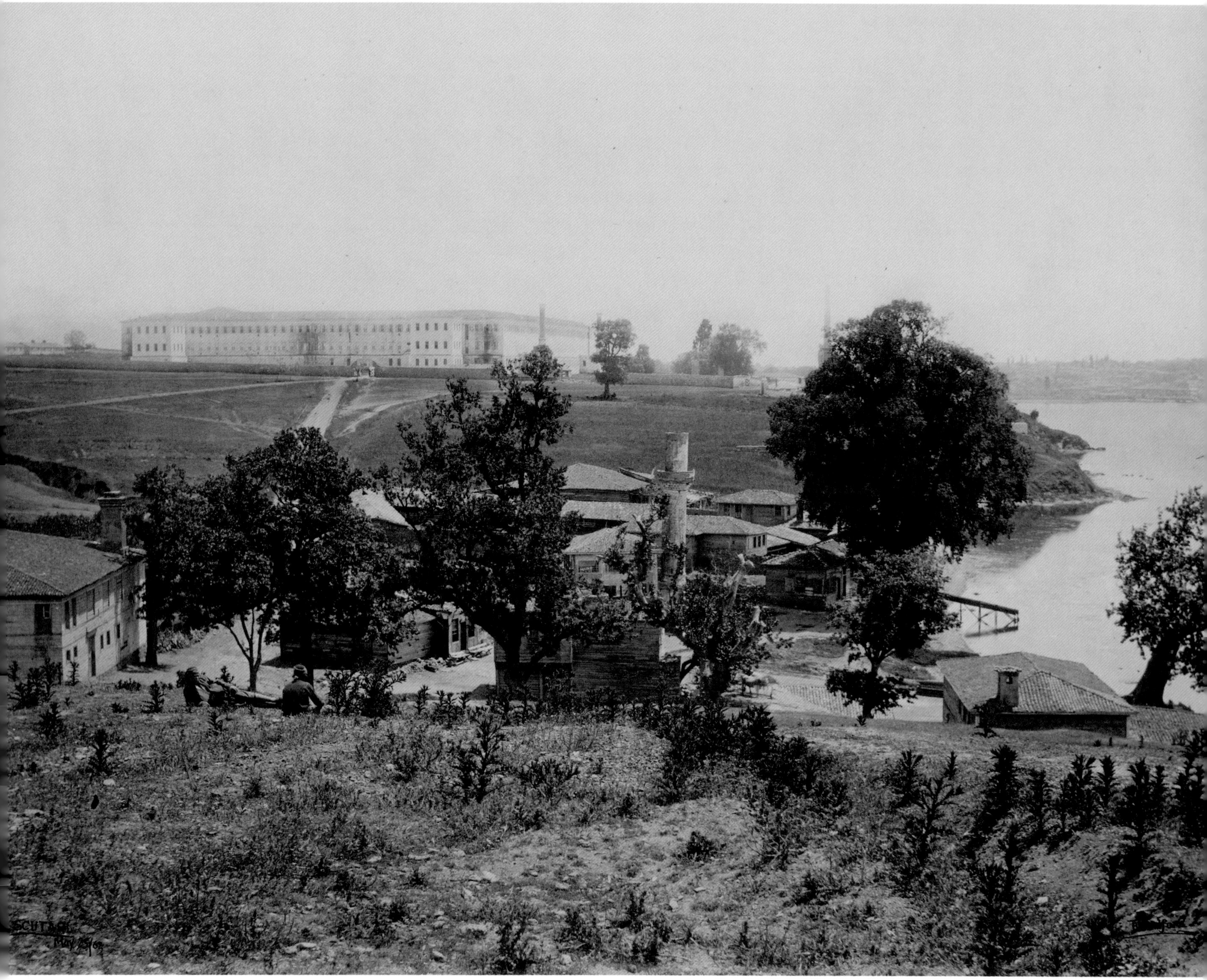

The Selimiye Barracks, Üsküdar, Istanbul, 25 May 1862

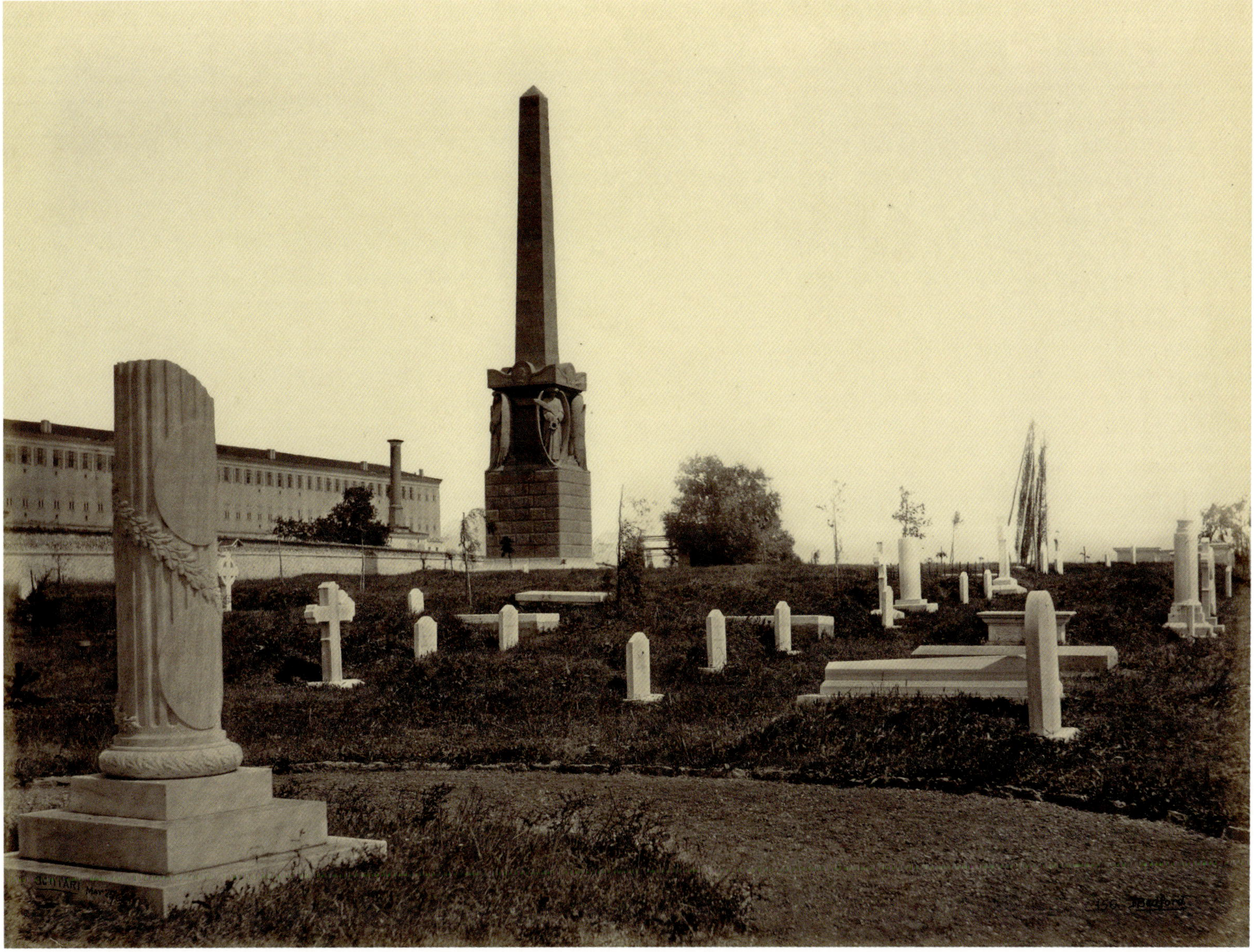

The English Cemetery, Üsküdar, Istanbul, 25 May 1862

Notes

1 The prince's name was included among the list of subscribers for the photographs, as were his parents. A complete set of Roger Fenton's Crimean photographs survives in the Royal Collection (RCINs 2500229–2500578).

2 RA VIC/ADDA5/523/145, letter from Lord Dufferin to Col. Charles Phipps, 7 November 1861.

3 RA VIC/MAIN/QVJ, 18 January 1862: "Saw Gen. Bruce. Dr Stanley will go with Bertie. They are to start on the 5th of next month."

4 Stanley 1856. The Prince of Wales owned a copy of this work (RCIN1133175).

5 For example, *Photographic Journal*, vol. 7, no. 118 (15 February 1862), p. 368. Despite a later suggestion, Bedford does not seem to have been summoned to Osborne to meet the queen (Pritchard 1882, p. 9). The journey was reported as it progressed in the *Illustrated London News* and summary accounts were also featured in the Court Circular.

6 RA VIC/MAIN/QVJ, 6 February 1862.

7 For the duration of the tour, the Prince of Wales kept a journal (RA VIX/MAIN/EVID/1862). The first entry is 6 February; the last is 14 June. The journal, although ostensibly private, was evidently written with a view to others seeing it, particularly Queen Victoria.

8 *Journal of the Photographic Society*, no. 13 (21 January 1854), p. 153. See also VIC/MAIN/QVJ, 3 January 1854.

9 "Specimens from Marlborough House, 1854" contains 84 albumen prints (RCINs 2800159–2800242), the majority probably dating to 1853. Most are signed in the negative, "F. Bedford, Phot." On some of the photographs, the date 1854 has been added by hand in black ink, but it is not clear whose hand this is. There is no archival evidence to support the claim that this was a separate commission from the royal family (see Jay 1974 and other sources). Most of the objects photographed by Bedford were not from the Queen's Collection, but were part of the Government School of Design's collection at Marlborough House. That collection subsequently moved to the South Kensington Museum and is today part of the Victoria and Albert Museum. See also London 2010, pp. 47–49 on the Marlborough House museum.

10 This date of birth differs from the more commonly cited date of 1816. Bedford's baptism record clearly gives his date of birth as 13 August 1815; he was baptized on 31 January 1816 (London Metropolitan Archives, St George, Bloomsbury, Register of Baptisms, P82/GE01, item 004, entry no. 979).

11 See Colvin 1995, pp. 116–17 for further information on his architectural career. Examples of his work, including the drawings from the 1811–13 tour, are in the collection of the Royal Institute of British Architects, London.

12 London Metropolitan Archives, St Giles, Camberwell, Register of Marriages, P73/GIS, item 015, p. 67.

13 Clara, b. 1819; John, b. 1823; Edwin, 1826–84; Louisa, b. 1829; and Sophia, b. 1831. Edwin Bedford married Caroline Donkin; the illustrator Francis Donkin Bedford was one of their eight children. Clara and Sophia were both still alive in 1851, as they are recorded on the census returns for 1851, living with their father in Kennington, south London, aged 32 and 20 respectively.

14 Graves 1905, p. 157.

15 Also published at this time, but both undated, were *The Churches of York* with text by J. Fawcett (York, R. Smith, containing 24 lithographs and 23 ground plans) and *Views of Castle Howard* (York, Robert Sunter "Bookseller in Ordinary to Her Majesty," 10 plates based on drawings by William Richardson). *The Churches of York* was reviewed in the *Gentleman's Magazine* under "new publications" in 1843, vol. XX, p. 624. Bedford also worked with Richardson on *The Monastic Ruins of Yorkshire* (York, R. Sunter, 1843–56). See also Bloore 1991, particularly the list on p. 399.

16 The register states that Francis Bedford, aged 28, of 40 Ely Place, married Mary Graham, aged 32, daughter of William and Emma Graham, at St Andrew's Church, Holborn (London Metropolitan Archives, Guildhall, St Andrew Holborn, Register of Marriages, 1843–4, P69/AND2/A/01/Ms6672/12).

17 Census Returns of England and Wales, 1851 (TNA, HO107/1498, fol. 316, p. 15).

18 William Day began working as a printer in the 1820s. In 1833, he was styled "lithographer to the King" (i.e., King William IV) and, after the accession of Queen Victoria, as "lithographer to the Queen and the Queen Dowager." Louis Haghe began working with William Day in the 1820s, although the firm "Day & Haghe" was not recorded in the directories until 1834. Haghe worked with the firm until 1851, continuing after William Day's death in 1845 to work with Day's sons, William, John, and Joseph. The company continued until 1867, when it was wound up (RA PPTO/PP/QV/PP1/65/6, letter dated 28 August 1867). See also Millar 1995, p. 398.

19 It has been suggested that Bedford became a shareholder in Day & Son. Kathy D. Kajander, "Colour Lithography during the Nineteenth

Century," unpublished PhD thesis, University of Reading, 1981, p. 279, cited in Bloore 1991.

20 "Illustrations of metalwork etc.," in Royal Commission on the Great Exhibition 1851, vol. II, p. 825.

21 Bedford also designed the invitations to a ceremony witnessing the construction of the first column of the Crystal Palace.

22 NAL, Cole Collection, 55.AA.16, diary for 1853. On 2 May, Cole noted the appointment "Mr Bedford lithographer." In 1852, Delamotte had photographed works of art at the museum; examples survive in the Royal Collection. In August 1853, Cole decided that Bedford was to be the museum's photographer rather than Delamotte (TNA, ED 28/1, no. 227).

23 Minutes of the Department of Science and Art, July 1852 – Dec. 1853 (TNA, ED 28/1, no. 227).

24 This publication is undated, although the British Library catalogue dates it to 1858. However, the text mentions the "forthcoming gathering of art treasures at Manchester," a reference to the Art Treasures Exhibition that opened in June 1857. The text would therefore date to between March 1856, when the exhibition began to be discussed widely, and June 1857. The copy of this work in the British Library has an accession stamp date of 29 January 1858.

25 Robinson n.d. [*c.*1857], introduction [unpaginated].

26 Bedford's obituarists agree that it was while working for Day & Haghe in the early 1850s that he took up photography: Anon. 1894a, p. 475 and Anon. 1894b, p. 191.

27 See London 2010, p. 387. At least one of Bedford's drawings for *Industrial Arts* is in the Victoria and Albert Museum, Prints and Drawings, E.738–1950.

28 Albert Edward, Prince of Wales, visited the London premises of Day & Son in 1856, as part of an educational program of visiting various "factories." In a report (RA VIC/ADDA5/82/6, no. 6), he described the lithographic process that he saw and ended with the comment, "We also saw some letters lithographed and designs by Owen Jones, called 'The Grammar of Ornament,' lithographed by Chromo-Lithography."

29 The source for this and subsequent information on early photographic exhibitions is the online catalogue of "Photographic Exhibitions in Britain, 1839–1865" by Roger Taylor (http://peib.dmu.ac.uk), published in book form as *Photographs Exhibited in Britain*, Ottawa, National Gallery of Canada, 2002.

30 See London, Bradford, and Florence 1987–89, pp. 50–55.

31 See "Royal Gifts" in London 2010, pp. 456–62.

32 "Photographs of Coburg, 1857" (RCINs 2102815–2102876). From 23 Rochester Road, Bedford issued an invoice dated 19 August 1857 to Dr. Becker for the expedition: for "taking sixty photographic pictures . . . including one proof of each" £126 and for "travelling & other expenses £34," making a total of £160 (RA PPTO/PP/QV/PP2/25/8124).

33 "Exhibition of the Photographic Society," *Photographic News*, I:20 (21 January 1859), p. 231.

34 "The Photographic Exhibition at the Crystal Palace," *Photographic News*, I:5 (8 October 1858), p. 53.

35 "North Wales Illustrated" contained 205 views; "Chester Illustrated" had 55 views.

36 Fourteen titles are known to exist. See Gernsheim 1984, pp. 74–75 and Johnson 1990, pp. 45–48.

37 The servants occasionally appear in the expenses when given money to go sight-seeing: "Servants Excursion to Pyramides £1 10s" on 25 February (RA VIC/ADDA5/523/153: 25 February 1862). Stanley was accompanied by his own servant, Waters, "whose talent for bird-stuffing made him a valuable addition to the party" (Prothero 1894, p. 66).

38 RA VIC/ADDA5/523/153: 6 February 1862. Tour account books [date], travelling expenses ledger, p. 7.

39 *Photographic News*, VI:201 (11 July 1862), p. 336.

40 *Photographic Journal*, vol. 13, no. 200 (15 December 1868), p. 188. This was Bedford's recollection some years after the tour. In 1862, the average exposure for his Eastern work was said to be "about thirty seconds," which seems to be quite a long time. *Photographic News*, VI:203 (25 July 1862), p. 352.

41 RA VIC/ADDA5/523/153: 26 May 1862. Tour account books (26 May 1862).

42 RA VIC/MAIN/QVJ, 19 July 1862.

43 RA VIC/ADDA5/501/1431, 2 October 1862, check book stub. This sum presumably covered the time spent on tour as well as the photographs themselves. Bedford had also received a payment of £100 while on the tour (RA VIC/ADDA5/ 523/100). A total sum of £494 9s would be worth, very roughly, £21,500 today.

44 Roberts returned to England in July 1839 with 272 drawings as well as his sketchbooks (Mancoff 1999, p. 107).

45 See in particular Nickel 2004.

46 *Photographic Journal*, vol. 8, no. 124 (15 August 1862), p. 103.

47 Russell 1869, 2 vols.

48 RA VIC/ADD/C07/1/0009, letter dated 1 February 1863 to General William Knollys.

49 Arthur Bedford attended several meetings of the South London Photographic Society. In 1867, reports in the *British Journal of Photography* mention him addressing various technical points. The *Photographic News* also noted: "A brief but instructive communication was made to the members of the South London Photographic Society, at the last meeting, by Mr. Arthur Bedford, in whose charge the printing department of Mr. Francis Bedford is placed," cited in *Photographic Mosaics. An Annual Record of Photographic Progress*, Philadelphia, Benerman & Wilson, 1867, p. 88. William is reported as exhibiting work in Coventry, for example, and at the London Photographic Society exhibition in 1867. *British Journal of Photography*, no. 392, vol. XIV (8 November 1867), p. 531.

50 *British Journal of Photography*, no. 394, vol. XIV (22 November 1867), p. 536.

51 The forthcoming work was announced in August 1863. The sculptures had been recently excavated and were significant as "the only known specimens of the art of Cyrene, a city renowned in ancient history. Photographs, by Mr. F. Bedford, will accompany the text." *British Journal of Photography*, no. 196, vol. X (15 August 1863), p. 324.

52 For Alexandra Park, see Day & Son 1866, p. 30 and for Warwick Castle, see *Art Journal*, vol. 9, no.1 (January 1870), p. 29.

53 See Cardiff 1981.

54 Bedford's retirement as vice-president is reported in the *British Journal of Photography*, no. 397, vol. XIV (13 December 1867), p. 590.

55 See Bibliography for full references. Two of the lectures are reproduced in St Louis 1992.

56 The marriage of William and Wilhelmina took place on 9 June 1874 at St. Mary Magdalene Church in Camden. The profession for both Francis and William is given as "gentleman" (London Metropolitan Archives, St. Mary Magdalene, St. Pancras, Register of Marriages, P90/MMG, item 006). Francis Perch was born on 16 March 1875. The census returns for 1881 show all three generations living at 326 Camden Road, with three servants.

57 Photographs of Chester taken by William Bedford were registered for copyright purposes on 24 June 1887. The copyright was held by T. Catherall (TNA, COPY/1/380/524).

58 William Bedford died of typhoid on 13 January 1893. *Photographic Times*, vol. 23, no. 596 (17 February 1893), p. 88.

59 Probate Registry, *Calendar of the Grants of Probate*, London, HMSO, 1894, p. 150. "BEDFORD, Francis of 326 Camden-road Middlesex esquire died 15 May 1894. Probate London 28 June to Wilhelmina Bedford widow and Monier Faithfull Monier-Williams esquire. Effects £18298 7s 3d resworn September 1894 £17902 6s 5d."

60 "The Francis Perch Bedford" prize was founded at University College London under the will of Mrs. Wilhelmina Bedford in memory of her son. At Cambridge, a fund for new purchases was established at the University Library.

61 For example, see the opening pages of "Mr Francis Bedford at Camden Road" in Pritchard 1882, pp. 9–14.

62 Both guidebooks were used by the prince during the tour and are referred to in his journal. See Wilkinson 1858 and Porter 1858.

63 Some of the photographers who opened studios included Wilhelm Hammerschmidt (Cairo); James Graham (Jerusalem); Félix Bonfils, Tancrède Dumas, and Jean-Baptiste Charlier (Beirut); Henri Rambeau (Damascus), and the German chemist Rabach (Istanbul).

64 *Photographic News*, VI:179 (7 February 1862), p. 72.

65 This, and subsequent entries, are from the Prince's journal (RA VIC/MAIN/EVIID/1862, 2 March).

66 RA VIC/MAIN/EVIID/1862, 4 March.

67 RA VIC/MAINE/EVID/1862, 5 March.

68 RA VIC/MAINE/EVID/1862, 13 March.

69 RA VIC/MAINE/EVID/1862, 14 March.

70 RA VIC/MAINE/EVID/1862, 26 March.

71 See Paris and Los Angeles 2002, particularly pp. 175–205.

72 The decision to seek permission had already been made back in London. According to Dr. Stanley, "From the moment that the expedition was definitely arranged in January 1862, it was determined by His Royal Highness and his advisors that the attempt should be made to visit the mosques of Jerusalem and Hebron (al-Khalil)." See Stanley 1863, p. 147.

73 *Illustrated London News*, XL:1142 (3 May 1862), p. 448.

74 RCINs 2700916–2700919, 2861579 and 2861584.

75 Quoted from a letter written by Dr. Stanley and published in *The Times*, 26 April 1862, and reproduced in London 1862, p. 27. Stanley also writes about the visit in Stanley 1863. Very few non-Muslims managed to visit the mosque in the nineteenth century, but the small number that did included the architectural historian James Fergusson in 1864; the Crown Prince of Prussia (Queen Victoria's son-in-law) in 1868; and the Prince of Wales's two sons, Prince Albert Victor and Prince George, in 1882. See Merrill 1890, pp. 327–35.

76 Stanley also describes the concerns raised by Suraya Pasha, who considered that the responsibility was too grave and that he could not undertake to guarantee the prince's safety. Although permission was given, when the prince eventually entered the mosque, "it was in fact, a complete military occupation of the town" (Stanley 1863, p. 170).

77 Pritchard 1882, p. 10.

78 Rosen went on to publish *Das Haram von Jerusalem und der Tempelplatz des Moria*, Gotha, Rud. Besser, 1866.

79 RA VIC/MAIN/EVIID/1862, 21 April.

80 RA VIC/MAIN/EVIID/1862, 4 May.

81 Thompson 1866, p. 85.

82 Three Armenian brothers, Hovsep, Kevork and Vichen, were together known as the Abdullah Frères, and were photographers to the sultan. RA VIC/MAIN/EVIID/1862, 27 May.

83 RA VIC/MAIN/EVIID/1862, 14 June.

84 *Illustrated London News*, XLI:1175 (25 November 1862), p. 550. The photographer Maxime Du Camp toured Egypt and the Middle East with Gustave Flaubert in 1849–51.

85 See Day & Son n.d. [1863] and London 1862.

86 *Illustrated London News*, XLI:1156 (26 July 1862), p. 99.

87 *Illustrated London News*, XLI:1175 (22 November 1862), p. 550.

88 *Illustrated London News*, XLI:1156 (26 July 1862), p. 99.

89 *British Journal of Photography*, no. 171, vol. IX (1 August 1862), p. 288.

90 *The Times*, no. 24441 (29 December 1862), p. 12.

91 Thompson 1866, pp. 2–3.

92 *Photographic News*, VI:202 (18 July 1862), p. 336.

93 *British Journal of Photography*, no. 381, vol. XIV (23 August 1867), p. 399.

Bibliography

Archival Sources

The National Archives (TNA)

COPY 1/380/524 Copyright registration records, 1887, for William Bedford

ED 28/1 no. 227 Minutes of the Department of Science and Art, 1852–53

National Art Library, Victoria and Albert Museum (NAL)

Cole Collection 55.AA.16

Royal Archives (RA)

VIC/MAIN/QVJ Queen Victoria's Journal

VIC/MAIN/EVIID/1862 6 February – 14 June 1862 Prince of Wales's Journal

VIC/ADDA5/82/6 Prince of Wales visits the firm of Day & Son, 15 April 1856

VIC/ADDA5/501/1431 Check issued on behalf of the Prince of Wales, 2 October 1862

VIC/ADDA5/523 Papers relating to the Prince's 'Eastern Tour' of 1862 including accounts

VIC/ADDC07/1 Letter from the Prince of Wales to William Knollys RA

PPTO/PP/QV/PP1/65/6 Letter dated 28 August 1867 regarding the liquidation of Day & Son

PPTO/PP/QV/PP2/25/8124 Royal Archives: Privy Purse Records

Published Sources

Anon. 1894a, "Death of a veteran lithographic artist," *British Lithographer*, vol. 3, no. 18 (August–September), p. 191

Anon. 1894b, [Obituary], *The Bookseller* (6 June), p. 475

Bedford, Francis n.d., *A Chart Illustrating the Architecture of Westminster Abbey by F. Bedford Jnr.*, London, W.W. Robinson

_____ n.d. [1841], *Sketches in York by F. Bedford Jnr.*, York, H. Smith [J. Smith]

_____ 1843, *A Chart of Anglican Church Architecture*, London, John Weale

_____ 1845, *The Architecture of York Cathedral, arranged chronologically, shewing all the different styles of architecture in that edifice, with examples of each*, York, W. Hargrove

_____ 1867, "Landscape photography and its trials," *Yearbook of Photography and Photographic News Almanac*, p. 23

_____ 1868, "Landscape negatives and some hints for their improvements," *Yearbook of Photography and Photographic News Almanac*, pp. 23–25

_____ 1871, "Some hints on landscape photography," *Yearbook of Photography and Photographic News Almanac*, pp. 24–26

_____ 1873, "Photography applied to architecture," *Yearbook of Photography and Photographic News Almanac*, p. 21

Bedford, Francis and W. Monkhouse, with J. Fawcett n.d. [1843], *The Churches of York by W. Monkhouse and F. Bedford, Jnr.*, York, J. Smith

Bedford, Francis (lithographs) and William Richardson (drawings) n.d., *Views of Castle Howard*, York, R. Sunter Benson 2008

Bloore, Carolyn 1991, "Photography and Printmaking 1840–1860," unpublished PhD thesis, University of Reading, Department of Typography

Colvin, Howard 1995, *A Biographical Dictionary of British Architects, 1600–1840*, New Haven and London, Yale University Press, 4th edn.

Day & Son n.d. [1863] *Photographic Pictures of Egypt, The Holy Land and Syria, Constantinople, The Mediterranean, Athens . . . taken during the Tour in the East*, London, Day & Son, 3-page handlist

Day & Son 1866 *Monthly circular of forthcoming or lately issued illustrated and illuminated works*, London, Day & Son, 32-page handlist

Gernsheim, Helmut 1984, *Incunabula of British Photographic Literature 1839–1875*, London and Berkeley, Scolar Press

Graves, Algernon 1905, *The Royal Academy of Arts. A complete dictionary of contributors and their work from its foundation in 1769 to 1904. Vol. 1: Abbayne to Carrington*, London, Henry Graves & Co.

Jay, Bill 1974, "Francis Bedford, 1816–1894. English Landscape Photographer of the Wet-Plate Period," unpublished MFA thesis, University of New Mexico, Albuquerque

Johnson, William S. 1990, *Nineteenth-Century Photography. An Annotated Bibliography 1839–1879*. Boston, G.K. Hall & Co.

Mancoff, Debra N. 1999, *David Roberts. Travels in Egypt and the Holy Land*, San Francisco, Pomegranate Communications

Merrill, Selah 1890, "The Cave of Machpelah," *Old and New Testament Student*, vol. 11, no. 6 (December), pp. 327–35

Millar, Delia 1995, *The Victorian Watercolours and Drawings in the Collection of Her Majesty The Queen*, London, Philip Wilson Publishers, 2 vols

Nickel, Douglas R. 2004, *Francis Frith in Egypt and Palestine. A Victorian Photographer Abroad*, Princeton, Princeton University Press

Porter, Josias Leslie 1858, *A Handbook for Travellers in Syria and Palestine*, London, John Murray

Pritchard, H. Baden 1882, *The Photographic Studios of Europe*, London, Piper & Carter, 1882 [the section on Bedford is a reprint of an article from *Photographic News*, no. 24 (23 April 1880), p. 195]

Prothero, R.E. 1894, *The Life and Correspondence of Arthur Penrhyn Stanley, D.D.*, London, John Murray
Robinson, John Charles and Francis Bedford (lithographs), n.d. [*c.*1857] *The Treasury of Ornamental Art. Illustrations of Objects of Art and Vertu*, London, Day & Son
Royal Commission on the Great Exhibition 1851, *Official Descriptive and Illustrated Catalogue of the Great Exhibition of the Works of Industry of All Nations*, London, Spicer Brothers
Russell, William Howard 1869, *A Diary in the East, during the tour of the Prince and Princess of Wales*, London, George Routledge and Sons, 2 vols
Stanley Arthur Penrhyn 1856, *Sinai and Palestine in Connection with their History*, London, John Murray
______ 1863, *Sermons Preached before His Royal Highness the Prince of Wales during his Tour in the East in the Spring of 1862*, London, John Murray
Thompson, William M. 1866, *The Holy Land, Egypt, Constantinople, Athens... A series of forty-eight photographs taken by Francis Bedford, for HRH the Prince of Wales during the tour in the East, in which, by command, he accompanied his Royal Highness*, London, Day & Son
Wilkinson, John Gardner 1858, *A Handbook for Travellers in Egypt*, London, John Murray (originally published 1847)

Exhibition Catalogues

Cardiff 1981 *The Strange Genius of William Burges 'Art-Architect', 1827–1881*, National Museum of Wales, Cardiff
London 1862 *Mr. F. Bedford's Photographic Pictures taken during the Tour in the East*, German Gallery, London
London, Bradford and Florence 1987–89 *Crown and Camera. The Royal Family and Photography 1842–1910*, Queen's Gallery, London, National Museum of Film, Photography and TV, Bradford, and Museo Alinari, Florence
London 2010 *Victoria and Albert. Art and Love*, Queen's Gallery, London
Paris and Los Angeles 2002 *Gustave Le Gray 1820–1884*, Bibliothèque Nationale, Paris and J. Paul Getty Museum, Los Angeles
St Louis 1992 *Commercial Aesthetics. Nineteenth Century British Photographs by Francis Bedford, Francis Frith, James Valentine and George Washington Wilson*, St Louis Community College, St Louis, MO

Photograph Numbers

The Royal Collection inventory numbers of the photographs in this book are as follows:

Page	
24	2700861
25	2700862
26	2700860
27	2700864
28	2700863
29	2700866
30	2700867
31	2700868
32	2700869
33	2700870
34	2700871
35	2700872
36	2700874
37	2700875
38	2700876
39	2700878
40	2700879
41	2700880
42	2700881
43	2700883
44	2700885
45	2700887
46	2700888
47	2700892
48	2700891
49	2700889
50	2700893
51	2700898
52	2700899
53	2700900
54	2700901
55	2700902
56	2700903
57	2700904
58	2700905
59	2700906
60	2700907
61	2700908
62	2700909
63	2700911
66	2700912
67	2700914
68	2700915
69	2700916
70	2861579
71	2700919
72	2700920
73	2700921
74	2700922
75	2700923
76	2700926
77	2700927
78	2700928
79	2700931
80	2700932
81	2700933
82	2700934
83	2700937
84	2700938
85	2700939
86	2700943
87	2700945
88	2700947
89	2700949
90	2700951
91	2700952
94	2700953
95	2700954
96	2861619
97	2700955
98	2700956
99	2700957
100	2700958
101	2700959
102	2700961
103	2700962
104	2700963
105	2700964
106	2700965
107	2700966
108	2700967
109	2700969
110	2700971
111	2700973
112	2700974
113	2700975
114	2700976
115	2700977
116	2861637
117	2861638
118	2700979
119	2700980
120	2861649
121	2700981
122	2700982
123	2700983
124	2700984
125	2700985
128	2700993
129	2861676
130	2700994
131	2700995
132	2700996
133	2700997
134	2700998
135	2700999
136	2701000
137	2701001
138	2701002
139	2701003
140	2701004
141	2701005
142	2701007
143	2701006
144	2701008
145	2701011
146	2701009
147	2701010
148	2861696
149	2861694